Delirious Milton

Delirious Milton

THE FATE OF THE POET IN MODERNITY

Gordon Teskey

HARVARD UNIVERSITY PRESS

Cambridge, Massachusetts
London, England   2006

For Beth

Library of Congress Cataloging-in-Publication Data

Tesky, Gordon, 1953–
    Delirious Milton : the fate of the poet in modernity / Gordon Teskey.
      p. cm.
    Includes bibliographical references and index.
    ISBN 0-674-01069-8 (alk. paper)
      1. Milton, John, 1608–1674—Aesthetics.
  2. Milton, John, 1608–1674—Criticism and interpretation.
  3. Creation (Literary, artistic, etc.)—History—17th century.
  4. Poetry—Authorship—History—17th century.
  5. Poetry—Authorship—Psychological aspects.
  6. Hallucinations and illusions in literature.   7. Delirium in Literature.
  8. Aesthetics, British,   I. Title.
PR3592.A34.T47 2005
821′.4—dc22   2005052542

Acknowledgments

*O*NE IS NEVER MORE ALONE and more in company than when writing an academic book. I have many people to thank for assistance with this one. First, Helen Vendler coaxed it out of me and read it as it came. Sean Kane and Angus Fletcher provided invaluable criticism. For the occasions on which I was invited to present for discussion the ideas in this book, I thank Regina Schwartz, Michael Lieb, David Loewenstein, and Helen Marlborough of the Newberry Library Milton seminar; Lawrence Buell and Stephen Greenblatt of Harvard University; Stuart Curran of the University of Pennsylvania; Marshall Grossman of the University of Maryland; Jennifer Lewin of the University of Kentucky; John Mulryan of Saint Bonaventure University; and Charles Mahoney of the University of Connecticut. I am grateful for discussions with Joseph Campana, Elise Cavaney, William Flesch, Kenneth Gross, Janel Mueller, Trevor Muñoz, Reeve Parker, Laura Quinny, Yulia Ryzhik, and Ramie Targoff. Stanley Fish generously permitted me to read *How Milton Works* when it was still in manuscript, an invaluable experience. Thanks are due as well to William Sisler, Lindsay Waters, Thomas Wheatland, Maria Ascher, and the staff of Harvard University Press, and to the press's anonymous readers. I wish particularly to thank my very fine editor, Amanda Heller, who also edited *Allegory and Violence* (Cornell University Press, 1996). That great Miltonist, "who sails between worlds and worlds with steady wing,"

Mary Ann Radzinowicz, has given me friendship and high example for twenty-five years. The journals *Diacritics*, *English Literary History*, and *University of Toronto Quarterly* and their editors kindly granted permission to redeploy in this book material first published there. Despite my large debts to the scholars named here, and a greater debt still to the long tradition and wide community of Miltonists, I am of course responsible for the errors and shortcomings—there will be many, I fear, in such a speculative book—that remain.

～ Quotations from *Paradise Lost* are from the new Norton Critical Edition, ed. Gordon Teskey (New York: W. W. Norton, 2005), abbreviated in references in the text as *PL*. Quotations from Milton's other poems are from *Complete Shorter Poems*, 2nd ed., ed. John Carey (Harlow, Essex: Longman, 1997). References to *Paradise Regained* and to *Samson Agonistes* are abbreviated in the text as *PR* and *SA*, respectively. References to Milton's prose works are from *The Yale Edition of the Prose Works of John Milton*, 7 vols., ed. Don M. Wolfe et al. (New Haven: Yale University Press, 1953–1980), abbreviated as *YP*, and occasionally from *The Works of John Milton*, 20 vols., ed. Frank Allen Patterson et al. (New York: Columbia University Press, 1923–1940), abbreviated as Col. I have also occasionally referred to the first and fourth variorum editions of *The Poetical Works of John Milton*, ed. Henry John Todd, the first in 6 vols. (London, 1826), the second in 4 vols. (London, 1842); to *The Poetical Works of John Milton*, 3 vols., ed. David Masson (London, 1874); and to *Paradise Lost*, ed. Alastair Fowler, 2nd. ed. (London: Longman, 1998).

Contents

Milton flottait entre mille systèmes. . . . La création particulière de l'univers n'est à ses yeux qu'un petit coin du chaos arrangé, et toujours prêt à retourner dans le désordre.

Milton floated among a thousand systems. . . . In his eyes, the created universe is nothing more than a little corner of chaos that happened to be arranged and is ready at any moment to fall back into disorder.

      Lamartine

Introduction

ℳILTON IS ONE of four English poets—the other three are Chaucer, Spenser, and Shakespeare—who have been subject to continuous scholarly study for three hundred years. The project of Milton studies is therefore old, comparatively speaking. But it is also a deep project, by which I mean that it cuts deeper into our persistent theological, metaphysical, moral, and political questions than do studies in any other major English poet. That sequence of qualifying adjectives indicates something else about Milton studies and about Milton: they are at base a theoretical project because Milton is a theoretical poet. His poetics is very much of a piece with his revolutionary politics, his libertarian conception of human nature, his spectacular conception of the physical world, and his sublime notions of ultimate reality and God.

꙳ THERE IS ONE sense in which a *poetic* approach to these things —to the theory of the state, the theory of liberty, the theory of nature, and the theory of God—must differ from theory itself. "Theory," which means "visualizing, abstractly and synchronically, that which already exists," is turned toward a past from which it remains quite distinct. Claiming no primary existence for itself, theory is the detached representation of what already is, rather than a part of what already is. In contrast, "poetry," which means "production" or, as we would now say, "creation," is turned toward the future, a future in which it will it-self be a presence and a power, whence the nearness of poetry to prophecy. To be a *theoretical poet*, therefore, is to look in both directions at once, like Janus, the double-faced Roman god of thresholds. For a Christian poet such as Milton, it is to look back into the past, into the totality of what has already been made by man within the frame of the larger totality of divine Creation—"Creation," as I shall put it when the word is used in this sense, with a capital *C*. But it is also to look for-ward in time, into the temporal scene of the emergence of everything human that has yet to be made, including the poem that the poet is working on now.

The underlying claim of this book is that because of this double per-spective—on divine Creation in the past and human creativity in the future—Milton represents a watershed in the seventeenth century, and therefore in the history of art in the West, in which the artist begins to play a new and unfamiliar role, as one who mediates spiritual power, like a shaman. As far as I can tell, this thought came to me while I was visiting an exhibition of the work of the modern German artist Joseph Beuys, at the Barbican gallery in London. I had been interested in Beuys for some time, more as a cultural phenomenon than an artist: he was a fired professor, a founder of the Green Party, a creator of fantas-tic performances or, as he called them, "actions," a deliverer of lectures which were regarded as themselves works of art—the written black-boards from such lectures are in major museums throughout the world —and by his own account he was rescued, in World War II, from the burning wreckage of his Luftwaffe aircraft by nomads in the Caucasus who swathed him in honey and wrapped him in felt, and from whom he received training as a shaman. Then he went to art school.

While I had long been absorbed by Beuys's drawings and small works on paper, which are mostly on shamanistic themes, I had made little effort to come to terms with the elaborate symbolism of sub-stances, such as fat, felt, and honey, which he deployed in a vast allegor-ical system, one in which human communication and warmth are fos-tered on a cosmic scale by spiritual power mediated through works of art, or rather through artists. No longer was the artist to be separated from other people by the mastery of a technique and the possession of unusual talent. Every person is an artist, Beuys said—"jeder Mensch ist ein Künstler"—or at least potentially so. For every person, aided by magical substances deployed in the spiritual practice of art, may become a means of communicating cosmic energy. There should be no obstacles to becoming an artist (obstacles such as formal instruction in a technique), for the more of us who are artists, the better it will be for the planet.

The effect of such an ideology on the actual works, or, rather, on the concept of what a work of art is, was striking. A work of art could be a jar of honey, or a lump of congealed fat, or flashlights and rolls of felt on sleighs emerging from a decrepit Volkswagen van, or a performance in which the artist arrives at the airport in New York in May 1974, having flown there from Germany, and, so as not to touch American soil during the Vietnam war, is wrapped in felt and carried by ambulance into the city, where for three days, hooded like a figure in Beckett, he shares a room with a coyote (an animal with strong shamanistic associations) before being returned to the airport in the same manner that he was brought thence.

When I saw the Beuys show at the Barbican, it occurred to me that the point was not so much to interpret the work, interesting as it can be to do so, but simply to ask, What has happed to artists that they should be doing such things? Most of them, and certainly Beuys, are serious people who have at some time acquired technical skill and made works that are aesthetically pleasing and emotionally intense. But avant-garde artists—the term itself bears reflecting on—have no interest now in producing finely worked objects for the stimulation and pleasure of those who can afford them. For that is what avant-garde artists regard more traditional works of art as being: luxury objects for the rich. Hence the movement of the artists to large works and their alliance with the increasingly populist institution of the museum. Interestingly, Beuys moved to small works—multiples—to obtain the widest possible dissemination of cosmic warmth and so remain, as he put it, in touch with people. Formerly, the artist had been fundamentally a technician, though with a spiritual motive, who delivered an experience to us without undergoing it himself, evoking a stable but hallucinatory world of mimesis. Now, the artist—and avant-garde artists are increasingly women—undergoes an experience on our behalf and does not so much represent as mediate that experience to us, so that we seem to participate in it. It is the difference between *representing* an experience and *communicating* an experience. What is communicated is, in the first instance, simply the excitement of creating, which is performed by the artist in the work itself and entered into vicariously by us. But it is also, especially for poets such as Jorie Graham in her recent book, *Overlord*, an experience of prophetic frenzy generated by a rapid sequence of hallucinatory events (in Graham they are attempts at prayer) in which one is continually departing from a standard that is nevertheless felt to be present. Milton called that standard "reason," and Graham, I think, would call it "justice."

That archetypal poet of modernity, Arthur Rimbaud, wrote of this experience in his poetic letters as producible by means of a *dérèglement*, "a disordering, a maladjustment, an excess," by which the poet continually breaks through the frontiers of rational structure and common sense in order to discover what he called, simply, "the new." But this breaking through is always temporary and always implies a return, even if what is returned to is changed and enriched, as well as destabilized, by that departure. The full phrase Rimbaud used for this process is *dérèglement raisonné*, a "reasoned or methodical disordering," generating an experience I shall call (using another key word in Rimbaud) *delirium*. The Latin root of this word, *lira*, is the ridge of earth thrown up by the plow which serves as a guide to the plowman on the next pass across the field. To be *de-lirious* is to wander away from that guide. Rimbaud's great poem "Le Bateau ivre," "The Drunken Boat," is almost an *ars poetica* of delirium, in which the speaker is the boat itself, whose destruction—the boat is at last reduced to one sodden plank—is in proportion to the cosmic insight that the speaker attains. Like the prophet, or the suffering servant, the boat undergoes an intense, even annihilating experience on our behalf. Unlike *hallucination*, which is imaginatively stable, delirium works by a kind of oscillation, a flickering on and off of hallucinatory moments in rapid succession, driven by some underlying contradiction. In Rimbaud it is the contradiction between the desire to be given over to the annihilating power of the other, the chaos of the sea, and the more secret desire to recover the ancient parapets of Europe, the symbols of cultural order.

We see delirium everywhere now in the electronic media, from computer games to television advertising and rock music videos, in which images pass too quickly to be seen. But Rimbaud was its great, esoteric explorer in the early 1870s and has been a conscious influence not only on much modern poetry but also, if I may so term them, on the "deliriamentarians" of rock music spectacle from Jim Morrison to Patti Smith and Trent Reznor. Rimbaud's *Illuminations*, "Lightings," is a rapid series of hallucinatory moments in one of which, "Being Beauteous" (Rimbaud's title is in English), an "être de beauté," a "being of beauty," who seems to me an unintended avatar of Milton's Eve, shows us how hallucinatory beauty becomes deliriously changed. She, or rather it, is "sur le chantier," "on the worksite," and is already being transformed into something other, or into many things other, her body bursting with scarlet wounds and unspeakable exudations. Just as a kind of violence had once been necessary, in medieval and Renaissance allegory, to force universal abstractions to adhere to images—mostly of female bodies—drawn from the material world, so now violence is necessary, and more openly expressed, to compel hallucinatory, erotic fantasies (I imagine Rimbaud was thinking of Botticelli's Venus) to give way to a delirium that feels more artistically true.

In Milton this delirium arises from an inner conflict between the authority of God the Creator, the principle of absolute order and the ground of our being, and the poet's need to be a creator (not just a creature) in his own right. Composed mostly after the collapse of his political hopes, Milton's great poems, *Paradise Lost, Paradise Regained,* and *Samson Agonistes* (assuming that this last was the latest), are an effort to understand what it means to be a poet on the threshold of a post-theological world. Milton's creative power is drawn from a rift at the center of his consciousness over the question of creation itself, forcing him to oscillate between two incompatible perspectives, at once affirming and denying the presence of spirit in what he creates. From the theoretical perspective that Milton adopts to support his ideological vision, a vision that, quite apart from any question of its truth, has the structure of a hallucination, the act of creation is centered in God and the purpose of art is to imitate and praise this Creator. From the poetic perspective, which actually makes it possible to build the poem up, line by line, sentence by sentence, the act of creation is centered in the human, in the technological environment of the built, modern world, but is aided by a spirit-helper—Milton calls her Urania—that is only formally allied with the original Creator. For this spirit is actually something new, a resurgence into European culture, at the moment when the total authority of formal religion had begun its retreat before science, of very ancient, shamanistic practices mediated through art. Milton is the last major poet in the European literary tradition for whom the act of creation is centered in God and the first in whom the act of creation be-

gins to find its center in the human. Yet this human center resonates
with the world as a whole, communicating spirit from afar.

෨෨ SPENSER IS ALSO a theoretical poet, and an important one,
but his manner of thinking is so profoundly different from Milton's
that one could be forgiven for supposing that any comparison between
them as thinkers is doomed from the start. They can be contrasted,
however. Whereas Spenser is an *archaeological* thinker, that is, one who
thinks through the temporal layers of the accumulated remains of the
past—of what he calls *moniments*—Milton is a thinker of the *archē*, of
the origin and governing "principle." In this he is much more in harmony than Spenser is with the main tradition of philosophical and scientific thought in the West. Milton sees the cultural remains of the
past—and for him they are truly remains, dead things—not as reposito-
ries of secret wisdom but as evidence pointing back to an origin, which
he situates in the garden of Eden, the home of the truth about man. We
see this radical impulse everywhere in Milton, from the debates over
church government and the tenure of kings and magistrates to the
promise to restore "ancient liberty" to the heroic poem, freeing it, as
he says in the note on the verse of *Paradise Lost*, from "the troublesome
and modern bondage of rhyming." When he wanted to compose a
great poem that would seize human existence in its *archē*, Milton began
at the beginning, in the moment, in the garden of Eden, when perfect
human liberty was lost. This is why Milton's Adam and Eve are a theoretical representation not only of the first marriage but also, what is
more important, of the first state, the first human society.

The retrospective impulse to Milton's cast of mind has naturally influenced Milton scholars, including the present writer, who have been
inclined to see the poet in relation to the traditions of the Christian and
the classical past, or in relation to the political struggles of his day. Although Milton overleaped those traditions (and also those struggles) to
consider them in their origins, he was massively learned in them as well
and tended to reproduce them unconsciously in his art, quarrying the
language of the past for his present artistic purposes. The language in
Homer which Athene addresses to her father, Zeus, becomes the language of the Son in *Paradise Lost* when speaking to *his* father. Nor is this
true only of the classical tradition. Later episodes from the Bible are
folded back into *Paradise Lost* as similes and examples that intensify the

poet's account of the first, and the definitive, event in the Bible: the Fall of Man. It is hardly surprising, therefore, that Miltonists should excavate the historical materials Milton partly brings to light and should wish to explore the creative processes by which he aggressively appropriates, digests, and transforms those materials into the "proper substance" (*PL* 5.493) of his song.

It has been left to critics on the margins of Milton studies—the poets T. S. Eliot and William Empson are the most striking (though very different) examples—to consider Milton's relation to the future. Gestures are made in the direction of the relevance of Milton today, but these are mostly thematic. Thus, Milton is an example of principled adherence to liberty and reason in our private lives, in our political commitments, and even, if we have them, in our religious beliefs. Empson was perhaps right to say that if our sense of liberty and our moral conscience are revolted by the God Milton is compelled by the scriptures to portray in *Paradise Lost*, then Milton himself, given time, would have us reject such a God as "very wicked." (Empson was right to say this, even if the statement is not perhaps literally true.)

But except for T. S. Eliot, who argued that Milton had turned English poetry away from the clear, sharp, intellectually challenging images of Donne into the path of hollow eloquence, critics have not been much concerned with Milton's relation, as a poet, as an artist, to the future. The present book is an attempt at a beginning, for prior to anything he says in his poems, it is his heroic stature as a creative artist that has always fascinated me about Milton; and it is precisely the role of the creative artist—is the artist a technician or a shaman?—that modernity has called into question. Such questioning begins in Milton's reflection on his role as the composer and the inspired medium of *Paradise Lost*. We shall see how the questioning continues unconsciously in the revolutionary figure of Jesus in *Paradise Regained*, who hallucinates the kingdom of God, and in the delirious violence of the hero of *Samson Agonistes*, who cancels the Philistine hallucination of a unified and harmonious world.

I spoke earlier of how Milton, as a theoretical poet, is concerned with the past and with the future of making. The future of making, or *poiesis*, differs from the past in two respects. First, the future of making is a creation produced entirely by man, constituting what architectural theorists call a "built environment." We live not in nature but in what we have made. Second, the future of making is not a totality and is therefore not finished but forever emerging, continually canceling and replacing itself. The architectural theorist Rem Koolhaas, writing about the phantasmic and ephemeral yet monumental architecture of Manhattan, calls this "delirium." I do not know if Koolhaas was influenced by Rimbaud, which is in any case hardly the point, but his theory of the psychological consequences of modern architecture, of "Manhattanism," as he calls it, is a striking confirmation of what the French poet, a century before, set out to find. Not only do we live inside what we have made, but we also recognize that we can change it with exceptional rapidity. A technical process, building or making, is driven by an irrational desire for a succession of phantasmatic worlds.

This is the decisive departure in the art of modernity from the art of the past. It constitutes what I have called, perhaps with some drama, although not, I think, exaggeration, the "fate" of the artist in modernity. It is a fate in the precise sense of being something pronounced and inevitable. For the artists, unless they are amateurs or eccentrics, have little choice in the matter. But it is perhaps also a fate in the more common sense that it may not be altogether agreeable for artists to have to bear the responsibility for being the half-acknowledged mediators of an undefined spiritual power. This role is not, I think, one that Joseph Beuys freely decided to play. Whatever literal truth there is in his story about his fiery, symbolic death and rebirth, and his reemergence into life as a shaman, it is the fate that he had to explore. It is as much a fate as was Milton's blindness and the creative rebirth that it fostered in him.

By an *undefined* spiritual power I mean one that is not contained within, and distributed throughout, any comprehensive ideological order, such as Christian theology. Fragments of ideologies and ideological forms may be carried along in the current of spiritual power, but only as the unstable, continually altering content of something larger than themselves. At best, they are like Milton's diminutive islands of order, heaven, hell, and the universe, in the immense sea—or is it a river?—of chaos. In these circumstances, art seems to be given over to a pure expressiveness wherein what is being expressed comes not from any coherent ideological intention but rather from beyond, from spirit helpers such as Milton's muse.

What Milton's career predicts for the artist in modernity is not, therefore, a "loss of the aura," or halo, as in Baudelaire's poem of that name, and Walter Benjamin's one-sided reading of it, but a startling restoration of the aura, the fiery traces of a spiritual power that comes to the artist from beyond.

The modern artist mediates spirit in a way that makes no claims whatever on our belief and is only more intense for that refusal. This, it seems to me, is the direction of Milton's career through the great poems he wrote at the end of his life. Along that trajectory, Milton's ideological claims on us decrease even as his spiritual power over us grows.

To RETURN ONCE MORE to the distinction I made, perhaps too sharply, between retrospective theory and prophetic poetry, it is true that there is always a poetic element to theory and a theoretical element to poetry: each is, so to speak, a contrary moment in the other. But in a poet such as Milton, theoretical reflection and poetic production are so equally assertive, each dominating the other in turn, that the poet seems to be divided within by a sort of invisible rift. Let us, for the moment, imagine it as a mysterious veil suspended between contrary terms. When we read about the historical past in the final two books of *Paradise Lost* or in *Samson Agonistes*, the text itself seems to hang before us as a veil through which we dimly discern something else, a mystery that, if we could see it clearly, might bring before our eyes a scene of hectic production and shamanistic role-playing not unlike the art of our time. But just at the moment when the outlines of such a scene begin to appear, we find ourselves transported to the other side of the veil, in the very place of the modernity we had only begun dimly to perceive. But this modernity is no longer a mystery to us, for we are still looking into that veil, although from the other side, and what we see through it now is the past. I think it was some such experience as this, of moving from one side of the veil to the other and forever seeing mystery through it, on the other side, that was the driving force behind the creation of Milton's major poems.

ᖰ 1

Artificial Paradises

I BEGAN THIS BOOK thinking about the problem of creation and creativity in the poetry of Milton, in particular, of the relation between divine Creation and human creativity, especially, but not exclusively, artistic creativity. The subject has been treated in a learned and stimulating book by Regina Schwartz, in which the relation between divine Creation and human creativity is seen in a positive light: as a *harmonious* rather than a *discordant* relation, except when human creativity loses its capacity to remember the Creation and degenerates into compulsive repetition.[1] Such an argument is certainly in keeping with Milton's theology and poetics. For Milton, the beginning of wisdom and the foundation of morals, even the foundation of art, is in the recognition that everything, including oneself, has already been made by the Creator. This is the Creator Milton's Adam deduces, in his first moments of consciousness, and calls "some great Maker":

> Straight toward heav'n my wondering eyes I turned
> And gazed a while the ample sky, till raised
> By quick instinctive motion up I sprung . . .
>   "Thou Sun," said I, "fair light,
> And thou enlightened Earth so fresh and gay,
> Ye hills and dales, ye rivers, woods, and plains,
> And ye that live and move, fair creatures, tell,
> Tell, if ye saw, how came I thus, how here?

Not of myself: by some great Maker, then,
In goodness and in pow'r preëminent.
Tell me how may I know Him, how adore,
From whom I have that thus I move and live
And feel that I am happier than I know!"

᷒ *Paradise Lost 8.257–282*

The innate desire to *know* and to *adore*, Adam's first impulses upon deducing his creation, are the motives of the sciences and the arts. The sciences seek to know what God has made, and the arts strive to give God praise and thanks—in short, *adoration*—for having made the world and for having made us. Elsewhere in *Paradise Lost*, Milton composes the astonishingly beautiful prayers of Adam and Eve as examples of the highest human art, which is absolute praise. Such art does not *create* in our sense of the word, a sense we owe largely (but not exclusively) to Blake. The prayers of Adam and Eve reflect on what has already been made. But they do so only with respect to the source of this making. Rather than admiring all things that God has made as things wonderful in themselves, Adam and Eve enjoin all things to praise God. Even the waters in the atmosphere, the mists and the rains, are said to rise or fall "In honor to the world's Great Author" (*PL* 5.188). Adoration is the ground of their being and the action by which they authentically exist on that ground. That is why Adam puts a *question* to all created things: "Tell me how may I know Him, how adore?" Just by existing, they know.

But of course *this* Adam, not the Adam of Genesis but the Adam of *Paradise Lost*, is created by Milton, not God, and as a literary artifact has been added to the totality of what exists. Adam is a poetic creation, as is of course the entirety of *Paradise Lost* and the two great works that are an extension of the project of *Paradise Lost: Paradise Regained* and *Samson Agonistes*. Milton claims otherwise, of course. He says that his poems are mediated through him by the Spirit, the creative power of God, and are fashioned by an art that is the poet's own—his own talent, his own labor—only in a secondary way. For the things that are the poet's own were given him by his Creator, and the very poems he writes are extensions of the original Creation. That is the basis of Milton's poetic ideology, the conscious recognition that everything, including his poem, must be referred back to an original Creator.

Yet there is no escaping the obvious truth—so obvious that we are inclined to discount it—that the poetry of Milton is created, produced, brought forth, and added to the world not as something springing from the eternal fount but as something entirely new. This is all the more obvious to us because we have become increasingly aware in modernity of living in a world of our own making, an artificial, technological world, a built environment. But the awareness belongs essentially to modern poetry and modern art, which are no longer epiphenomena, representing something else, but spiritual gateways through which we pass in and out of such a world. When Rilke completed the *Duino Elegies,* one of the signal moments in modern consciousness, after ten years of labor, what he said, in exuberant letters written on February 11, 1922, to the princess Marie von Thurn und Taxis and to Lou Andreas Salomé, was that the completed work *is* and that the elegies *are:* "They are. They are."[2] That was to Rilke the deepest thing the elegies do: they stand in the world and change the world by their very presence. The same awareness of being a creator in one's own right sustains Milton's poetic production but cannot be acknowledged consciously by him without canceling, for a moment, the hallucination that everything has been created by God. This is what drives Milton's poetry and is its true inspiration: the repetitive canceling and restoring of the hallucination of universal *createdness.* I shall explain shortly why this oscillation between seemingly contrary terms is called "delirium." But it will be clearer if I first tell two stories on an old theme, that of nature and art.

⁓ TWENTY-FIVE YEARS ago I attended, in Toronto, the Larkin-Stuart lectures given by Northrop Frye, which were published in a small book, *Creation and Recreation.*[3] In Frye's account of this essentially biblical subject, God creates a world that is in harmony with human needs and with human desire. But with the Fall of Man this created world becomes alien and hostile, so much so that bare physical survival in it is impossible, a fact evident enough to Canadians, and not only in winter. (The pioneering study of Canadian literature by Margaret Atwood is titled, inevitably, as it now seems, *Survival.*) The hostility of the created world forces humans to invent means of survival, from the simplest clothing and shelter to the glass and steel towers of cities—of which more in a moment.

These means of survival include the cultural productions of artists, which, though spiritual, are understood to be continuous with the material productions—clothing, shelter, nourishment—that are necessary for survival. Culture is an envelope that protects us by transforming nature into imaginative forms that are reflections of human concern.

Frye compares this cultural envelope to the windows of a lit-up railway car at night.[4] The lights cause the windows to act as mirrors reflecting the interior of the railway car. But every so often the lights flicker and fail, leaving the interior of the car in darkness and revealing, through the windows, an alien nature in which it is impossible to survive without equipment, preparation, and skill. Our experience of the world is for the most part the experience in the railway car at night when the lights are on. If we try to look into nature, beyond our cultural envelope, what we see is mostly a reflection of ourselves. But at unexpected moments this hallucination fails and we glimpse the imponderable otherness of the wilderness in which we actually live.

The décor of the tale is revealing: the nineteenth-century mode of transport, the railway, which drives a narrow path through wilderness crowding it on either side, the rattling car, the faltering lights, the solitary student looking up from his book and staring through the window at a savage land. But in the 1930s, in rural New Brunswick, the wilderness that appeared, from a railway car, to be so indifferent to man had already been clear-cut for timber and mined. Its rivers had begun to be dammed for hydroelectric power, to be sold south to light Boston and New York. This is the irony of landscape, which is as powerful a force in the seventeenth-century landscape paintings of Jacob van Ruisdael as it is for modern-day canoe trippers, who see wilderness where it does not exist: on "wild rivers," for example, which have been narrowed and deepened by nineteenth-century loggers so that timber could be floated downstream. Frye said much the same thing about the Lake District and the Wordsworthian vision of nature: "When Wordsworth urges his reader to leave his books, go outdoors, and let nature be his teacher, his 'nature' is a north temperate zone nature which in nineteenth-century England had become, even in the Lake District, largely a human artefact."[5]

Here is another story about nature as an artifact. It is set in a rather different place and time: Fifth Avenue, New York City, at about 2:00 AM, sometime in the late 1970s. Huge tractor-trailer trucks were lined up on the avenue as forklift vehicles were removing something from them: fir trees. The trees decorating the esplanade at Rockefeller Center were being changed for the winter. The deciduous predecessors, their branches bound tightly about them, had already been removed, carried upright by the forklifts out onto the avenue, turned horizontally, inserted into trucks, and carried away. Now this procedure was going in reverse: new trucks had arrived and were being unloaded. Each tree was extracted horizontally, turned upright, and carried to the esplanade, its highest branches waving as if in distress, before being lowered into its prepared, fertilized place. The season had changed.

This is the irony of landscape as well, of urban landscape. One travels to what one supposes to be the capital of the artificial world, at the farthest distance possible from anything wild, to discover the wilderness itself extracted from machines by other machines, manipulated by machines, planted and even nurtured by machines, on a street that is itself a machine and in a city that is a gigantic experiment in re-creating nature—even wilderness—by means of the machine. It is a vision of what even the boreal forest, every inch of which has been photographed by cartographic satellites from space, has become in modernity: something given over to the purposes of human power, one of these being the pleasure of experiencing wilderness at Rockefeller Center.

Frye's vision of a protective envelope of culture inside nature is just as much a hallucination as was the image of the interior of his railway car reflected in its windows at night. But my own experience of an epiphany of modernity, one in which nature is now contained by technology as surely as the circumpolar forests are held in the jaws of machines in the middle of a city, is also, of course, a hallucination. Modernity appears to consist not in any stable vision of the world but rather in a succession of incompatible hallucinations such as these, an agitated movement like the flickering of lights in a train car or the shuddering of forest boughs beneath electric light. This change began, to speak approximately, as we must, in the seventeenth century and may be described as the transition in the art of the West from a poetics of hallucination typical of Spenser to a poetics of delirium, inaugurated by Milton. The change is anticipated in the satire of the 1590s and in the poetry of Jonson and Donne, especially in the Donne of the *Anniversaries* and the more outrageous love poems, in which the dependence of the imagery not on any objective, metaphysical order but on the subjective will of the speaker removes any need for consistency among the images and permits them to be rapidly changed. The effects of delirium are less obvious in Milton, whom we think of as the epitome of the classical, the rational, the stable, because he is not, as Donne is, foregrounding a speaker's subjective will, thus giving to delirium dramatic and psychological probability. But the effects of delirium are deeper in Milton because he subjects the very external order that Donne denies or negates (as in "The Sun Rising") to successiveness and transformation.

In Spenser, the poet of hallucination, the artist delivers an experience to us without, so to speak, taking any of the drug himself, attaching the hallucination to the actual world, like a tethered balloon, by means of allegory. In Milton, the poet of delirium, the artist no longer stands apart but undergoes the experience himself and, as I have said, mediates a portion of it to us. But the experience is no longer the pleasant one of hallucination, of imaginative participation in a heterocosmic, "golden" world, as Sidney called it. At its most extreme, it is an experience of shamanistic torment similar to that described by Rimbaud, in which the artist submits himself—and, increasingly, herself—to continual, even violent transformation.

For Rem Koolhaas, Manhattan—a vast, hallucinatory structure of buildings that are continually being raised and taken down—is the laboratory of a modernity in which the continual and theoretically infinite production of imaginary worlds (made possible by elevators, steel frames, electronic communications, etc.) produces a state of delirium, where *delirium* is not an experience without truth but rather the destabilizing of experience itself by succession: "The elevator establishes a direct relationship between repetition and architectural quality . . . [and] generates the first aesthetic based on the *absence* of articulation. In the early 1880s the elevator meets the steel frame, able to support the newly discovered territories without itself taking up space. Through the mutual reinforcement of these two breakthroughs, any given site can now be multiplied ad infinitum to produce the proliferation of floor space called Skyscraper."[6]

This statement by Koolhaas is accompanied by an illustration, dating from 1909, of a theoretical skyscraper, in which each floor is a paradisal home separated from those adjacent to it by the steel frame, seen in cross-section. Each paradise is strangely like every other, but at the same time sharply distinct from every other because each is so entirely discrete: we see no means of communication between them. The elevator has to be imagined. Koolhaas speaks of these successive worlds on successive floors of the skyscraper as "a utopian formula for the unlimited creation of virgin sites on a single, metropolitan location."[7] Yet what is striking about the stacked worlds in the illustration is how Edenic they are, evoking a return to the virgin site in which Adam and Eve lived alone, without children. (There are no children in the illustration, either.) The delirium works like a film being run slowly enough to discern the succession of frames, but also just fast enough to ignore them, creating an oscillation between belief in what one sees as real and recognition that each of these apparently real paradises is artificial.

That is how I think the paradise of Milton's *Paradise Lost* has to be seen: as a paradise that is already *lost* and yet *present* before us in the poem as a hallucination; and that hallucination is restored every time we open the poem again and start to read. Such a paradise is subtly changed with each reading, but the important thing is the absence of articulation between readings, even as we know they are different and reproducible to infinity in what the poet calls, in their first iteration, "a paradise within thee, happier far" (*PL* 12.587). The second iteration is announced in the title of *Paradise Regained*, a poem in which we see the proleptic (and theoretically unlimited) re-production of paradises in historical succession: "Eden raised in the waste wilderness" (*PR* 1.7). Even the Last Judgment returns to and reiterates, with difference, the hallucination with which we began: "for then the Earth / Shall all be Paradise, far happier place / Than this of Eden" (*PL* 12.463–465).

This series of iterations of paradise, if accelerated in the mind, reveal the flickering effect I referred to as *delirium*. Baudelaire captured this experience in *Les Paradis artificiels* when he averred that the pleasure of hashish and other hallucinogens was not so much in the hallucinations themselves, some of which were very unpleasant, as in their rapid succession, in the experience of one hallucination being canceled so that another may arise in its place and be canceled in turn by another. No longer does aesthetic excitement emerge from being agreeably deceived, from entering into a sustained, imaginative world, a heterocosm such as Spenser's Fairyland or Sidney's Arcadia.

We have seen that effect in Milton's concept of paradise, for a *concept* is what paradise becomes in his hands. The physical paradise is not finally important to Milton, which is why he cancels it, using the flood to tear the mount from its foundations and hurl it, like Orpheus' head, down the Euphrates to the Arabian gulf. Even its spiritual reconstitution, as a paradise within, by which Milton means having a clear conscience and the perfect use of reason, though more important to him than its original, is not primary. What is primary is universal createdness, the being of the world as an artifact of God. The physical paradise, situated on a mountain, is intended to serve as an index of universal createdness, pointing in the direction of this Creator, and the paradise within, where the conscience is clear and the reason is free, is ultimately the sense of the presence of God as one's maker. It is this presence that the poet, as a maker himself, must repeatedly cancel and repeatedly restore. But that very instability in Milton's poetry makes room for something that is strikingly new and that belongs to the art of modernity: the phenomenon of emergence. Emergence is very different from its predecessor in the classical tradition, metamorphosis, which remains under the domain of mimesis, or hallucination. We have seen that by undermining the foundations of the imagined world, delirium thrusts the poet, as a creator and a spiritual guide, into the foreground. But delirium also makes it possible for the art of modernity to capture something that is truer than mimesis, truer, that is, than the hallucination of a stable world of real, and essentially unchanging, persons and things.

PATTERNS OF EMERGENCE tend to appear at crucial moments in Milton's poetry. In *Paradise Lost* they range from the emergence of Sin from Satan's head and the emergence of Death from Sin's body to the creation of the universe at God's command and the emergence of history from Eve's womb. The two great works Milton wrote after *Paradise Lost*, *Paradise Regained* and *Samson Agonistes*, show more abstract structures of emergence: the revolutionary bringing forth, in *Paradise Regained*, of a world without transcendence, and the exploration, in *Samson Agonistes*, of what such a world may be like. Less abstractly, the Son in *Paradise Regained* is given his identity when he rises from the stream and is, in the legal sense of the word, *created* as the Son. Samson is brought forth from the darkness of his prison into the light of day, and after his final act, he emerges again, from the ruins, to be cleansed and entombed as a hero. His very death is an emergence: "Samson hath quit himself / Like Samson" (*SA* 1709–10).

That production and emergence should be central to Milton's poetry, and especially to the three great works of his maturity, should not surprise us when we consider Milton's cast of mind, which we have observed at work in the "primal scene" of Adam's birth. Thinking back to first principles and discounting later manifestations (except as things to be explained according to those first principles) is so much a part of our modern intellectual world—a world we inherit from Milton's contemporaries Bacon, Descartes, Hobbes, Leibniz, Newton, and Locke—that it takes some effort to see how very startling such a way of thinking was in Milton's day. Thinkers who are more typical of their age, such as Richard Hooker, Robert Burton, and Thomas Browne, seem much more distant from us now because they considered questions in massively total perspective, using analogy, and regarded the appeal to first principles with suspicion, as too easily misleading. But when Milton proposed to consider the reasons for the failure of the English revolution, he turned directly to the Fall of Man. The Fall of Man is not just about the loss of radical innocence; it is an emergent structure having the potential to explain everything that follows in history.

It is striking, therefore, that a poet for whom the performance of creativity has so much importance should also place God's creation of the world and of us at the center of his ethical vision. Kant referred famously to the starry sky above him and the moral law within him. For Milton, the starry sky above him is an artifact, and the moral law within him is the memory that he, like that starry sky, is a created being first and a creator only after the fact. Yet something in Milton's spirit cannot accept this subordination of creativity to Creation, hard as he works to affirm it. Blake had his own explanation for this: Milton "was a true Poet and therefore of the Devil's party without knowing it." It is perhaps worth recalling that the speaker of this thought in *The Marriage of Heaven and Hell* is himself a devil, although a very Blakean one, which is to say, stimulatingly ambiguous.[8] This subversive impulse in Milton's spirit—we may call it the recognition of human production as the foundation of everything humans can value, including the concept of Creation—is also in the spirit of the age, which is another emergent structure, the continual, restless struggling forth of the new. While this newness is continually emerging across the limit of what has happened just now, it is still always emerging from something else that is on the other side, so to speak, of a veil that is suspended between contrary terms. Milton's creativity, which would be the ground of the shamanistic authority of the poet in the modern world, depends on the hallucinatory creativity of God. But in the end Milton's creativity would destroy that hallucination almost as entirely as Samson destroys the Philistine temple. For there is something in Milton's poetry that lies beneath the hallucination of universal createdness and also beneath the visions of emergence, as it does beneath destruction itself. Rather than something that is thrust forward to seize our attention, this is something that withdraws, that is laid back and hardly to be noticed except at formally designated moments: the process of creating the poem, the underlying hum of its production. I believe that this ground note—this *burden*—is something Milton discovered and that it is what makes Milton for us the very great poet he is. It is the persisting and undeniable sense we have that the poem is an emergent structure, something that feels, even as we read it, still in the process of being created, of excitedly breaking forth from the poet's imagination and passing, even now, through the poet's lips to our ears.

ᔡ 2

Milton's Halo

$\mathcal{I}_{\text{N}}$ The Genealogy of Morals (1887), when the project of overturning everything in culture arrives at aesthetics, Nietzsche observes that Kant, "like all philosophers," understands art through the detached experience of the "onlooker," the *Zuschauer*, rather than through the practical experience of the "artist" or, as Nietzsche adds in a parenthesis, the "creator": "von den Erfahrungen des Künstlers (des Schaffenden)."[1] The word in parentheses echoes the active verb in Luther's translation of the opening words of the Bible ("Am anfang *schuf* Gott Himmel und Erde," In the beginning God *created* the heaven and the earth). This bold comparison of the artist with the Creator was heard for the first time in the Italian Renaissance, when the traditional hostility of Christian thought to the artistic imagination gave way to a new elevation of the artist from the practitioner of a craft to something intensely spiritualized and almost divine: the artist as an *opifex*, a *creator*, like God. Michelangelo himself was called "il divino."[2] Defensively pious as such expressions usually were, placing the artist firmly beneath God, they stood on the threshold of the secularization of spiritual life in modernity and the elevation of the idea of creativity to a new level as something consecrated, magical, and sublime, something shamanistic.

When Nietzsche speaks of the artist as a "creator," he evokes an idea that by the date of *The Genealogy of Morals* had been a commonplace of literary criticism for over a century: that the creativity of the artist is a sort of spiritual power, a nimbus or halo inherited by the artist from a disappeared, or a disappearing, God. Yet it is this poetic badge worn around the head, the sign of his spiritual authority, that Baudelaire, in the comic sketch about the loss of his halo, "Perte d'auréole," describes losing in the tarry muck of the Paris street, "dans la fange du macadam":

> When I was crossing the boulevard in great haste, leaping through the mud in that moving chaos where death gallops toward you from all sides at once, with a sudden jerk my halo slid off my head into the muck of the macadam. I didn't have the courage to pick it up, thinking it less disagreeable to lose my insignia than to have my bones broken. And besides, I said to myself, in every evil there is some good. I can go around now incognito, commit low acts, and give myself over to drunkenness, like simple mortals.[3]

Walter Benjamin made the well-known and now ritually reiterated claim that this scene, the "loss of the aura," is the condition of the artist in the age of mechanical reproduction, when the ability to reproduce the artwork mechanically—by printing and later by photography and film—caused the feeling of spiritual power surrounding the traditional artwork to perish with that artwork's uniqueness. Note, however, that whereas Baudelaire is speaking of himself, as an artist, Benjamin is speaking of the artwork.

For Benjamin, the reproduced object is removed from the realm of *tradition* (of "handing on") to become present anywhere at once. It loses all distance and comes instead startlingly near. This shock of the new and the near displaces the unique presence of the artwork as something that exists in time, passed down through the ages and associated with cult along the way. At one extreme in Benjamin's examples is the Stone Age image of the elk inscribed on a cave wall, where the image is a reservoir of magical power. At the other extreme is the demystifying photograph of the crime scene (Atget's Paris) and, especially, the film, associated (for Benjamin, via the megalomanic theories of the great filmmaker Abel Gance) with the cathartic destructiveness of mass movements and the "liquidation" of the cultural heritage.[4] In yet another contrast, Benjamin says that whereas the traditional artist is a magician, preserving the unique feeling of a distance from what the work of art takes for its subject, the modern artist, of which the film cameraman is the most advanced type, is a surgeon, one who works in the closest possible intimacy with his subject by cutting into it and exposing its structures, thus demystifying it utterly.[5]

Stimulating as these formulations are—we are still reflecting on what Benjamin said after almost seventy years—there is in them more than a little of Marxian pathos, the desire to associate the arts insofar as possible with mass movemants and advances in modern technology. Their crudeness would have disgusted Baudelaire, a passionate, early admirer of photography as an art, though not so much as their envying the arts their spiritual power to disturb and even terrify complacency with magic, substituting for this irrational power the equally irrational (and perhaps equally spiritual) shiver of pleasure communicated by an idea of the arts as engaged in inhumanly ruthless analysis. What would no doubt in time have struck Benjamin himself, who died only four years after the publication of this work, is that the processes he describes—mechanical reproduction in particular, which in the form of printing profoundly transformed, not to say created, in the Renaissance, the very concept of "literature"—led to the opposite effect: the return to the work of art of an ancient aura not unlike that which surrounds the prehistoric image of the elk on the cave wall. "If we have had a renaissance in the twentieth century," the late Guy Davenport said, "it has been a renaissance of the archaic. . . . Only our age has prepared itself to feel the significance of an engraved ox rib 230,000 years old, or to create and respond to a painting like Picasso's *Guernica*, executed in allusion to the style of Aurignacian reindeer hunters of 50,000 years ago."[6]

Mechanical reproduction has actually contributed (it is not by any means the sole cause) to the "re-auratizing" of the work of art and of the artist in modernity. A visit to any of the secular cathedrals of modern art—the Pompidou Center in Paris, the Tate Modern in London, and the new MOMA in New York—or to the shelves of contemporary poetry will overwhelmingly substantiate this claim. The "re-auratizing" of the work of art, and of the artist as a kind of spiritual medium, began in the earliest phase of modernity, when the term *modern* began to be used to refer to the present time: the Renaissance.

Medieval works of literature appeal to earlier authorities leading back to some witness on the original scene, each story inscribing itself in a "tradition" of witnessing that resembles a manuscript stemma: each copy is manually connected to another, from which it is also separated in time, the time of tradition, of "handing on." Two acts of the hand—copying and transmitting—are blended in one. The medieval authors of the most popular stories about the Trojan War, "Dictys Cretensis" and "Dares Phyrigius," represented themselves as combatants on either side. It is in this sense, a sense opposite to ours, that they are *authors*, "authorities," being persons who know and have expertise acquired from fieldwork and study, like a professor or, in medieval terms, a "clerk": "For so the French book saith," says Thomas Malory, telegraphing when he is about to add something of his own to the traditional stories of Arthur. Robert Henryson's *Testament of Cresseid* is presented not as the poet's own work but as another quire, or gathering of pages, which he found in his copy of Chaucer's *Troilus and Cryseyde*, a work already famous and over a century old. It is by claiming that they are *not* original that medieval authors assert their authority.

Once printing came in and a work could be reproduced in six hundred or more copies, as we see in a mythopoeic poem such as Thomas Lodge's *Scillaes Metamorphosis*, the very fact of an artwork's having the ability to be in many places at once makes it seem essentially un-physical, unattached to any particular copy, as if it had descended from the skies, like a vision. This effect detaches the work from tradition, which can be explained in earthly terms as the work of the hand, and gives it its magical, heavenly aura—and also its hallucinogenic power. At the same time the figure of the *author* comes into the foreground not in the old sense of the word but rather as one who *creates*. The author is now one who brings into being phenomena—hallucinatory experiences— that have never existed before. Where formerly the addition of the new had to be concealed as the old, in the Renaissance the addition of the new becomes the *sine qua non* of the author as creative artist. Plato's idea of the poet being in a state of *enthousiasmos*, of "having a god within" and raving in the tripod of the muses (as the priestess of Delphi raves in the tripod of Apollo), is revived in an entirely positive light (which it certainly did not have in Plato) by the Florentine Neoplatonists, by Giordano Bruno in the *Eroici Furori*, by Sidney in the *Apology for Poetry*, by Spenser, who calls on the muses for "goodly fury," and by the young Milton in the poetic raptures and "ecstatic fit[s]" of the sixth elegy, the Nativity Ode, and "The Passion." It becomes possible for the

literary phenomenon of the *invocation*, the calling in of divine power to
one's aid in creating, to carry the astonishing authority it does in *Paradise Lost*.

Although this development, which would deepen in modernity, is
the opposite of what Benjamin claimed to have occurred, that claim has
considerable dialectical force, as it did already in Baudelaire, who said
that *modernity*, the condition of being transitory and contingent, is
"one half of art, of which the other half is the eternal and the immutable."[7] The irony of "Perte d'auréole" is deeper than Benjamin suspected and curves back on its author. Baudelaire did not give up the
aura so easily or contemptuously as might appear. It is the deep paradox
of Baudelaire's poem, and of his career, that in seeming to relinquish
the aura, which had been so unself-consciously and regally assumed by
Victor Hugo, he caused that aura to glisten around him anew, even
from the tar of the streets, as it had never done before.

From the magical and mythopoeic world of Lodge to the performance rituals, or *Aktionen*, of Joseph Beuys (which demanded a photographic and filmic record), to the intensely mystical work of Anselm
Kiefer (perhaps the most important, the most epic, visual artist in the
world today), to contemporary poetry, which exhibits mystery and
near, or complete, unintelligibility as a fundamental demand, we see
one increasingly deepening phenomenon. It is the condition of the artist in modernity to mediate spirit under circumstances in which this
spirit can no longer be named or assimilated to any authoritative ideology, such as medieval Christianity. An idiosyncratic ideological system—for example, Yeats's *A Vision*, or Spenser's "Letter to Raleigh," or
Milton's *De Doctrina Christiana*—must be hallucinogenically conjured
and continually departed from and returned to. I have called this condition *delirium*, a rapid oscillation between some apparently rational
standard (the schematic plans of such artists are often, as in Kiefer's
case, fantastically complex) and the experience of transport, of shamanistic flight into the heavens or into the depths of matter, that the very
effort to adhere to that standard provokes.

➳ RETURNING TO THE transition from the Renaissance to the
Enlightenment and the Romantic period in England, France, Germany, and Italy, we see a dramatic increase in what Paul Bénichou has

called the "secular spiritual power" of the poet, a power that bears striking resemblances to the prehistoric religious practices of shaman-ism.[8] These practices, the most important of which is the investment of spiritual authority in a figure who manipulates signs of his (or her) own invention, constitute an irruption of the psychic energy that has been underlying European culture since prehistoric times, an event that be-gan when the repressive power of a more recent and highly articulate ideological order—that of Christianity and medieval cosmology—be-gan to fall into a state of what may be termed *metaphysical decay*. As Angus Fletcher has remarked, in a reading of the "Cantoes of Muta-bilitie," which is Spenser's final, prophetic vision of ancient powers ris-ing up from below to overwhelm an organized cosmos that had stood, more or less stably, for two thousand years, "irruptions into the estab-lished orders are exactly what to expect when deeper cosmic beliefs fall into disarray."[9]

The cosmic disarray to which Fletcher refers was brought on, of course, by the new science, which tore apart the old, Ptolemaic world order, inspiring Donne to say, famously, "'Tis all in pieces, all coher-ence gone, / All just supply and all relation." This experience of meta-physical decay, of the loss of a stable world order, an order that was once sublimely and benevolently created by God, was by no means a simple one. The experience was complemented by the optimism of a new world that was under construction inside the very ruins of the old: a technological and scientific civilization. In the prophetic text of this new world order, *Novum Organum* (1.129), a "new instrument" for at-tuning nature to human desire, Francis Bacon says that "inventions are like new creations and are imitations of God's creative works."

These incompatible worlds—an old world created by God, now in a state of advanced metaphysical decay, and a new world in the process of creation by humankind—collide at a historical juncture for which Mil-ton alone was prepared. Indeed it was only because the old world order of divine Creation was already a thing of the past that Milton was able to see it so clearly and, in the seventh book of *Paradise Lost*, to represent it as it had never been represented before: with perfect clarity and bril-liance, cleansed of the quaint encyclopedism of his immediate prede-cessor on the theme, Joshua Sylvester's translation of Du Bartas, and cleansed also of the feeling of mystery that accompanies the uttering of a magic command. Milton was able to do so, however, because in representing the Son as the Creator, he was drawing unconsciously (as Blake saw) on the new, Promethean spirit of human technology:

> He took the golden compasses prepared
> In God's eternal store to circumscribe
> This universe and all created things.
> One foot He centered and the other turned
> Round through the vast profundity obscure
> And said, "Thus far extend, thus far thy bounds,
> This be thy just circumference, O world!"
>
>   *Paradise Lost 7.225–231*

When the Creation is completed, the Son returns to Heaven not so much for the purpose of returning home as to gain sufficient distance on what he has made, to see it in its entirety, and to be certain that it has been completed according to plan, "Answering his great idea":

>   up returned,
> Up to the Heav'n of Heav'ns his high abode
> Thence to behold this new created world,
> Th'addition of his empire, how it showed
> In prospect from his throne, how good, how fair,
> Answering his great idea.
>
>   *Paradise Lost 7.552–557*

In these passages we are a long way from the two Creation accounts that open the Bible, the first governed throughout (that is, repeatedly, as in an incantation) by the magic of command ("And God said . . ."), the second by the shamanistic procedure (resembling Daedalus' making of automata) of fashioning something of earth and breathing life into it. Milton shows us a rationally transparent procedure, an image of production in a technological age: an idea is conceived, a plan formed, measurements taken, materials gathered, orders executed, and a survey of the whole taken at the end. This is not to say that nothing survives of the mysterious effects of the Bible: command is present throughout Milton's account. We do not see *how* lions and stags emerge from the earth at those commands, and the later account of the creation of Eve is profoundly mysterious. But the mysterious effects that do survive in the account of Creation in book seven of *Paradise Lost* survive, so to speak, as quotations, as wonders that have been enframed by a wholly technological outlook. Where, then, does the mystery go? It is transferred to the poet who creates. If God creates like a great scientist and engineer, according to reason, the poet's access to God's accomplishment becomes deeply invested with aura.

The underlying argument of this book is that Milton's halo, the fiery residue of the empyrean where he says he has flown and the symbol of his creative power, is partly an irruption of the shamanistic power of which I have spoken and partly an inheritance from the disappearing God of Christianity, whose ways the poet nevertheless strives to affirm or, to use his own word, to *justify*. There is a contradiction, therefore— a productive contradiction, to be sure, as is so often the case with strong poets—at the heart of Milton's project: the more artistically brilliant is the poet's justification of the ways of God to men—in particular, the account of Creation—the more the God he justifies, the Creator with a capital *C*, disappears behind the brilliance of that justification. This is the source of Milton's delirium, the inner rift out of which his creative energy flows as a consequence of his having to alternate rapidly between opposite terms. Following the guide of the *lira* is an ancient symbol of orderly procedure—and of orderly writing, especially poetical writing, in which there is a "turn," a *versus*, at the end of each line. Early Greek writing, which went from left to right across the writing surface and then from right to left, was called *boustrophedon*, "turning of the ox." The image of the turning verse as the turning of the plow is evoked by Spenser at the end of the first installment (1590) of *The Faerie Queene*: "But now my teme begins to faint and fayle, / All woxen weary of their journall toyle: / Therefore I will their sweatie yokes assoyle / At this same furrowes end."[10] *Delirium* (in contrast with *hallucination*) is not an imaginary addition to the world. It is a continual, pulsatile divergence from and return to that guide.

That ideological guide would be for later poets—more broadly, for modern artists—the dynamic, emerging cosmology of modern science, which is continually in the process of making and unmaking itself, according to reason. The authority of reason would be supplemented by the older, more stable moral capital of western European culture, a capital that, despite its relative stability, began to become an affair of politics (of Tories and Whigs, of the "right" and the "left") rather than of metaphysics. But for Milton the ideological guide is given by an inner reason that is our moral conscience, the only portion of the image of God that was not lost at the Fall, the candle of the Lord.[11] Such reason is expressed in everything that follows from the central moral proposition of *Paradise Lost*: that God is the Creator and Man is God's creature. Acknowledgment of our "createdness" is the basis of what we may call Milton's metaphysics of morals, and its clearest statement is the rhetorical question Abdiel puts to Satan: "shalt thou dispute / With Him the points of liberty who made / Thee what thou art?" (*PL* 5.822–824).

ᔫ᷎ Despite the firmness of this point around which, as on a spindle, everything in Milton's system turns—recognize your Creator, praise him, and justify his ways—the poet, as a *poet* (the original, Greek sense of the word means "to produce"), must be a creator in his own right. This second, contradictory imperative—be a creator in your own right—is the peculiar destiny of the modern poet, and modern poetry must therefore be in some sense *about* poetic creativity. We can see that even when representing the Creator in language such as Abdiel uses, the poet occludes the Creator with the material force of this representation, with an artifact in sound. The very representation of the Creator as the Creator of all things introduces a new, artistic phenomenon that escapes the totality of divine Creation, a paradox Giorgio Vasari evokes when describing Michelangelo's great painting, on the Sistine ceiling, of God the Father, venerable and sublime, soaring in the ether and borne up by angels, extending his right hand to give life to the newly created Adam. Michelangelo's Adam is painted with such beauty and perfection, Vasari says, that he seems to come fresh from the hand of his original Creator ("dal sommo e primo suo creatore") and not from the brush of a painter.[12] Vasari did not add that the Creator himself, in what is perhaps the best-known representation of him in Western culture, seems also to have been brought into being by the painter, that is, by one of that Creator's creatures. In the most radical formulation of this contradiction, God and Man create each other, each in the image of himself. "We say, God and the Imagination are one," says Wallace Stevens, adding, amusingly, "How high that highest candle lights the dark."[13] Very high, but not high enough.

The inescapable paradoxicality of this situation is not peculiar to Milton as a religious poet but is rather, as I have said, a fate that Milton alone was capable of accepting because he was a sort of Janus figure, looking at once into the culture of the past, which he mastered and possessed, and into the culture of the future, which he unintentionally prophesied when he made the real subject of *Paradise Lost* the excitement of an epic being made. That destiny, which is to suffer within the self a rift between divine Creation and human creativity, has been stated as follows: Milton is the last great poet in the European literary tradition for whom the act of creation is centered in God, and Milton is the first great poet in the European literary tradition for whom the act of creation begins to find its center in the human. Every enduring critical problem in Milton—from his use of ideologically incompatible classical and Christian imagery to his representations of Satan and God, not to mention what, exactly, occurs in book nine of *Paradise Lost*, at the Fall—springs from the stress of this conflict over who has the authority to create.[14]

⁓ OVER THE COURSE of the seventeenth century, or, to be more precise, from Spenser's "Cantoes of Mutabilitie" to Milton's *Paradise Lost*, a subtle but immense cultural change takes place (it is partly registered in satire) in which a poetics of hallucination gives way to a poetics of delirium. The cultural change underlying the shift in the arts from hallucination to delirium is the change from the imaginary perception that we live in a world created by God to the equally imaginary perception that we live in a world, an environment, created by Man. Spiritual power no longer enters this new, manmade world through the divinely created, natural things that surround us, the signs the Creator has left in Creation. Spiritual power enters the built environment of the manmade world only through artists.

⁓ THERE IS IN *Paradise Lost* something that resembles the violent physicality of Spenserian allegory but that actually has a role in the transition from the poetics of hallucination to the poetics of delirium: Milton's "allegory" (the reason for the quotation marks will be made clear in a moment) of Sin and Death. Death tears himself out of Sin's bowels and immediately rapes her, and from that rape the hellhounds are born. These torment Sin perpetually by going in and out of her womb, howling and gnawing at her bowels from within:

> For when they list, into the womb
> That bred them they return and howl and gnaw
> My bowels, their repast, then bursting forth
> Afresh with conscious terrors vex me round
>   ✒ *Paradise Lost 2.798–801*

Milton is drawing in this passage on the Scylla episode in Ovid but also on the grotesque imagery of the Error episode at the opening of Spenser's *Faerie Queene*. When the Red Cross Knight half strangles Error, a serpentine monster with a woman's head, she vomits not only a black stinking poison full of books and papers but also her young: blind toads and frogs that creep on the ground in the weedy grass. When the Red Cross Knight cuts Error's head off, these young gather round her opened neck, trying to get back into her body. Finding they cannot return to their mother, they drink her "coal black blood," which causes them to swell up, their bellies to burst, and their own guts to spill out on the ground, soiled in the blood of their mother. Such writing—in Spenser's Error episode and in Milton's description of Sin—does the opposite of what we expect when we suppose that allegorical writing grows up naturally out of allegorizing interpretations of Homer and Virgil and that such writing reflects, in an uncomplicated way, the anti-materialist assumptions of the culture of the sign. Allegorical writing negates that negation of the material world which allegorical interpretation implies.

Dr. Johnson condemned as "unskillful" the allegory of Sin and Death in *Paradise Lost* because it is too violent and too material a spectacle for immaterial agents to act in. The disgust roused by the gross physical torment of Sin obscures the status of Sin as a universal. The astounding bridge that Sin and Death build across chaos, "a ridge of pendent rock / Over the vexed abyss" (*PL* 10.313–314), is, Johnson complains, "a work too bulky for ideal architects."[15] Sin's lacerated entrails and Death's vast, seeking nostril, making Death "Sagacious of his quarry from so far" (*PL* 10.281), resist any idealization as meaning. But they produce the effect Milton intended: to force open the rift between the material and the ideal until the ideal disappears altogether, over-

whelmed by the exudations of substance—of blood and guts, of chaotic
slime and rotting flesh—that rise through the crack.

Milton intends to destroy in this manner any possibility of his poem's
being interpreted allegorically. He does so by pressing to extremes the
violent physicality that had been dialectically awakened in his great allegorical forebears, Spenser in particular. In so doing, Milton frees Sin
and Death to become daemonic beings (of the kind he knew from the
pre-classical, archaic worldview of Homer and Hesiod) in an entirely
material world. Death is not the symbol of death but is death itself, the
killer. Sin is not the symbol of sin but sin itself, for she is metonymically, rather than metaphorically, connected, by "secretest convey-
ance," to every sinful act as its cause. By the circulation of the energy of
sin, every sinful act enlarges the principal:

> Methinks I feel new strength within me rise,
> Wings growing and dominion giv'n me large
> Beyond this deep, whatever draws me on,
> Or sympathy or some connatural force
> Pow'rful at greatest distance to unite
> With secret amity things of like kind
> By secretest conveyance.
>
> ᴫ *Paradise Lost 10.243–249*

Despite the popularity and even the authority of the view that
Homer and Virgil concealed philosophical "undermeanings" behind
their literal texts, no philosopher of the first rank accepted this view
(beyond the obvious political analogies in Virgil), and for one reason: because it reduces the brilliance of the mimetic to mere writing, to
letters on the page. The material and physical world of human experience to which literature addresses itself, by mimesis, cannot be so easily
dismissed. But until the development of neo-Aristotelian critical theory
in the Italian Renaissance, from which neoclassical aesthetic norms
would derive, there was no conceptual language for speaking of the
world of human experience as entangled with the senses or the passions.

Man emerges inevitably as the victor in the struggle for the authority
to create because it is a struggle with a disappearing God of whom it
can no longer be said with conviction, "Of old hast thou laid the foun-

dations of the earth: and the heavens are the work of thy hands" (Psalm 102:25). But the victory will have peculiarly constraining effects on the poet as "maker"—the seeker of what another poet, Arthur Rimbaud, with sharp insight, simply called "the new"—when the poet is no longer engaged in the imitation and praise of the cosmos, of what has already been made.[16] The victory will condemn the poet to the role of a shaman, a mediator of a spiritual power that can no longer have any fixed ideological meaning or any clear metaphysical source. What are poets for, Friedrich Hölderlin famously asked, in a time of spiritual impoverishment?[17] The answer is not so mysterious as might be supposed: it is to restore a sense of spiritual contact by drawing on the resources of nature in preference to the traditions of the past. What is meant by these "resources of nature," however, is a psychically complicated question.

჻ IN MODERNITY, humankind recognizes itself as the creator of its built environment. Nature lies both beyond this environment and deep within it, in the interior of our bodies. We have scientific knowledge of this nature but not consciousness of it. When nature is no longer something of which we can have consciousness—consciousness of it as that which has already been made, in six days—it reverts to what it was in pre-classical antiquity: the unconscious realm of the non-made, of pure appearance and mysterious "growth," a resource from which magic can again draw its power. The transferal of nature into this unconscious realm happens when human creative work, considered as a totality, as the entire structure of a built civilization, replaces the consciousness of nature as a cosmos. I have suggested that this occlusion of the Creator by a quasi-magical, human creativity would have unexpected consequences for the imaginative artist in the modern world, imposing on the artist a peculiarly spiritualized role and causing many works of art to resemble shamanistic instruments and incantations. Making art becomes a matter not of creating something in the sense of production but of being creative in the first place, a state for which the object is merely a secondary indication or proof, an evidence. Such a view of the arts responds to what we now expect works of art to be: mysterious concretions of wisdom. The creative artist communicates creativity to us so that we will feel creative in turn.

᭐᭐ CREATIVE GENIUS HAD been a central concern of German romanticism from the outset, in the period of storm and stress or, as it was called, the "Genius Period" (1770–1785), when much of the language associated with the artist in modernity was formed. The language of "creative genius" was commonplace enough to be spoken of by Goethe, in *Conversations with Eckermann* (March 21, 1830). Goethe says that this language is in everyone's mouth now, having been started by Schiller and him and broadcast by the Schlegels. Yet fifty years ago, says Goethe, speaking of the 1780s, notions of creative genius were unheard of. Goethe even parodies this language in *Wahrheit und Dichtung*, in an apostrophe to a baker in Leipzig who "bakes, with creative genius, original cakes" ("Du backst . . . Mit schöpfrischem Genie, originelle Kuchen.")[18] The complex of notions represented by such language—*creative, genius, originality*—was disseminated in France by the writings and, more important, by the personal influence of Mme. de Staël, an influence that bore crucially, for French romanticism, on Victor Hugo: "cette femme de génie," as he called her.[19] The poet, Mme. de Staël writes, feels himself to be at once a created being and a creator, prostrating himself before God and at the same time recognizing, with expanding pride, his own creative powers. The poet sanctifies his own soul like a temple, she goes on to say, so that the angel of noble thoughts will not disdain to enter there.[20] Hugo hardly prostrates himself before God in a delirious poem such as "Ibo" (I Shall Go), in which by the power of his verse he ascends, like Spenser's Mutabilitie, to the conquest of the heavens and of outer space, soaring even to the "visionary doors of the sacred heaven," where, he says, if he is menaced by divine thunder, he will growl:

> . . . Jusqu'aux portes visionnaires
> Du ciel sacré;
> Et, si vous aboyez, tonnerres,
> Je rugirai.[21]

These ideas of the poet came to Germany from England, their principal source being Edward Young's *Conjectures on Original Composition*, which appeared in 1759 and was translated into German the following year. Young expresses in full the proto-romantic idea of the poetic work as a heterocosm and of the poet as a genius who can bring such a world into being: "In the fairy land of fancy, genius may wander wild: there it has creative power, and may reign arbitrarily over its own empire of chimeras."[22]

The figure of Milton stands at the beginning and the end of the development of the idea of the poetic imagination as a divine power and of the poet as a creative genius participating in the glory of the Creator and eventually assuming that glory entirely. Young's unhappy friend William Collins, in the strophe of his "Ode on the Poetical Character" (1746), shows God descending from his "Sapphire Throne" and placing human Fancy there, with the authority to give the *cestus*, or girdle of imaginative power, to the deserving poetical few: "To few the God-like Gift assigns / To gird their blest prophetic Loins, / And gaze her Visions wild, and feel unmix'd her Flame!" The significance of this gesture appears in the antistrophe when, in a vision, Milton is seen in an earthly paradise (situated on a mountain as high as the paradisal mountain of *Paradise Lost*) listening to the music of the spheres and ready to take up, as before, the trumpet of prophecy. As if shaken by the boldness of the claim he is making for the poetic imagination—that by virtue of his creative power the poet achieves radical innocence—Collins closes the ode with the assurance that he cannot follow the high steps of the divinely inspired Milton. The "kindred powers" of God and the human imagination, like the flaming sword of Genesis, have blocked the way to such vision from all future poets:

> My trembling feet his guiding Steps pursue
>   In vain—Such Bliss to One alone
>   Of all the Sons of Soul was known,
>   And *Heav'n* and *Fancy*, kindred Pow'rs,
>   Have now o'erturn'd th'inspiring Bow'res,
> Or curtain'd close such Scene from ev'ry future View.[23]

Eighty-one years later, in Victor Hugo's play *Cromwell* (1827), the preface to which was the canonical statement of romantic ideology in France, Milton is still the symbol of human creative power set into a dubious and troublesome relation to the Creator. But we no longer encounter anything like Collins's fearful palinode. In the preface to *Cromwell*, Hugo says that the goal of art is "almost divine" when it has to do with creation, for the true poet, like God, is present everywhere at once in his work. In the play itself, in a soliloquy spoken by Milton, the relation between the poet and the divine Creator he represents in his poem is more competitive. Hugo's Milton says that a burning genius labors in his breast as he meditates, in silence, an unprecedented design for the sake of which he now lives consoled in his own thoughts. That audacious design is nothing less than the poet's intention to emulate God the Creator by creating an entire cosmos—a hell, an earth, and a heaven—by the power of his own word:

> Car un génie ardent travaille dans mon sein.
> Je médite en silence un étrange dessein.
> J'habite en mon pensée, et Milton s'y console—
> Oui, je veux à mon tour créer par ma parole,
> Du créateur suprême émule audacieux,
> Un monde, entre l'enfer, et la terre, et les cieux.

In the spirit of the pertinacious classical norms against which Hugo revolts, a character who overhears this soliloquy jeers, "risible enthousiaste!" and Lord Rochester—Rochester!—gives Milton an ironical lecture on the inelegancies of *Paradise Lost:* "Vous avez de l'esprit, il vous manque du goût" (You have spirit [or wit] but you lack taste), complaining, among other things, that Eve doesn't lead a lamb on a blue ribbon and that Satan lacks a wig.[24] The real Milton would have been less disturbed by such persiflage than by the Hugolian idea that in creating *Paradise Lost* Milton was competing with rather than celebrating God.

By 1815, in the middle of Wordsworth's three years of frenzied publication, the notion of creativity had already advanced some distance on its path to the unexamined usage of today in the jargon of educational theory and corporate seminars. In his sonnet to the painter B. R. Haydon, Wordsworth, the most self-consciously Miltonic great English poet, consoles his friend for his lack of worldly success in the same language Hugo's Milton chooses to console himself:

> High is our calling, Friend!—Creative Art
> (Whether the instrument of words she use,
> Or pencil pregnant with ethereal hues,)

> Demands the service of a mind and heart,
> Though sensitive, yet, in their weakest part,
> Heroically fashioned . . .
> Great is the glory, for the strife is hard![25]

There is no thought here of a struggle with God, of a power conceded by God, or of a human creative power taking its model from, and subordinating itself to, the overpowering example of Creation by God. The struggle over the authority to create now takes place between the poet and society.

In *The Prelude* that struggle would be between the poet and nature; but it is resolved in the logic of shamanism, by which the poet becomes the medium for transmitting the secrets of nature. Even the shadow of the divine Creator has disappeared and the poet has inherited his glory:

> Of genius, power,
> Creation and divinity itself
> I have been speaking, for my theme has been
> What passed within me.[26]

This is intensely Miltonic language, but it is Miltonic ideology turned inside-out. At the great conclusion to *The Prelude*, near the summit of Mount Snowdon, the poet is suddenly accorded a vision of the clouds stretched out beneath him in the moonlight, resembling a vast ocean at his feet. Through a rift in the clouds, "Not distant from the shore whereon we stood," he hears innumerable mountain torrents "roaring with one voice." The revelatory sound, like a creative Word rising out of the abyss, seems to spread through the entire earth and to rise even to the stars (14.39–62). This (partially acoustical) "vision," as he calls it, in language that grows increasingly Miltonic, "is the express / Resemblance of that glorious faculty / That higher minds [i.e., poets] bear with them as their own" (14.88–90):

> It [the vision] appeared to me the type
> Of a majestic intellect, its acts
> And its possessions, what it has and craves,
> What in itself it is and would become.
> There I beheld the emblem of a mind

That feeds upon infinity, that broods
Over the dark abyss, intent to hear
Its voices issuing forth to silent light
In one continuous stream, a mind sustained
By recognitions of transcendent power
In sense conducting to ideal form,
In soul of more than mortal privilege.

∿ *The Prelude 14.66–77*

No one will miss the bold appropriation of Milton in this passage, by which the Spirit, or Holy Ghost invoked at the outset of *Paradise Lost*, "Dove-like sat'st brooding on the vast abyss / And mad'st it pregnant." It is the Spirit that illuminates the poet from within, giving him the power to create the ideology he has taken it upon himself to affirm:

What in me is dark
Illumine, what is low raise and support,
That to the heighth of this great argument
I may assert Eternal Providence
And justify the ways of God to men.

∿ *Paradise Lost 1.22–26*

The mind of which Wordsworth speaks broods over the abyss not of chaos but of nature. This nature is not the alienated substance of God in a state of violent disarray. It is the place where divinity now resides, a spiritualized nature that speaks in voices—the innumerable mountain torrents—that are also "one continuous stream." The resumptive use of the word "mind" at line 74 ("a mind sustained / By recognitions of transcendent power") slides off the earlier "mind," technically the antecedent of this later one, that "feeds upon infinity." Whatever the earlier mind is, this one is human, although it is "In soul of more than mortal privilege," capable of listening to the voices of nature and of discerning, with their help, ideal forms conducted from the knowledge of the senses. What is most striking about this passage is not how it is similar to Milton's but how it has changed Milton's. The poet is no longer a historical as well as a religious prophet. His voice is a medium of mysterious, unknown spiritual powers, "roaring with one voice," whose source is deep within nature. As Wordsworth says in the closing lines of *The Prelude*, poets have become "Prophets of Nature" (14.444).

வ் How STRANGELY BAUDELAIRE's "Perte d'auréole" seems to parody the magnificence of *Paradise Lost* and its poet! Baudelaire's description of himself leaping through the mud as he traverses the moving chaos of the street suggests Satan's crossing chaos in *Paradise Lost*. The reference to finding some good in misfortune evokes the *felix culpa* mentioned by Adam. Even the reference to having the freedom to get drunk, "me livrer à la crapule comme les simples mortels," seems to mock the temperate bard pictured in Milton's sixth elegy, who, having relinquished such pleasures of the flesh, can sing of higher things. Let there stand beside this poet not wine but pellucid water in a simple beech-wood bowl: "Stet prope faginio pellucida lympha catillo" (l. 61).

Of special interest is the opening reference in "Perte d'auréole" to the poet as a drinker of quintessences, of not only pellucid water but also its opposite, fire. Substances are important in this poem: on the one hand, fiery quintessence, the element of the gods, and divine ambrosia, the food of the gods; on the other hand, alcohol and asphalt. What does the opposition of these substances mean?

Asphalt is a tar-like mixture of hydrocarbons used as a binding agent in road surfaces made of crushed rock. Such a road is named a *macadam* after the inventor of the process, J. L. McAdam (1756–1836), a name that is lost in Benjamin's German translation of the poem, in which "dans la fange du macadam" becomes "in den Schlamm des Asphälts" (in the slime of the asphalt): "Mon auréole a glissé de ma tête dans la fange du macadam." To French ears, to Latinate ears generally, as Milton observes in the sonnet on his book *Tetrachordon* (which was thought to have a hard word for a title and was criticized for that, and other things, by Scottish divines), Scottish names are as outlandish as anything in the exotic diction of the poets: "Those rugged names to our like lips grow sleek, / That would have made Quintilian stare and gasp." Milton's "Petsora" and the "Cronian sea," "Persepolis" and "Susa," "Amara" and "Abassin" are not so trying to the classical ear as is "macadam."

What else would have attracted Baudelaire to this word, apart from its newness and strangeness? Possibly a double pun: in French "macadam" will sound like "mec Adam," *mec* being slang for one's lover or pimp (*Robert* shows *mecque* attested in 1821 and *mec* in 1827) and Adam being, well, Adam. Abel's blood cried from the earth. Are we now to hear a prostituted Eve crying from the slime to which she has been lowered, "*Mon mec,* Adam!"

"Asphaltic slime" is a not unfamiliar substance in Milton. It is the binding agent for the bridge that Sin and Death build across chaos, in a violent, demonic parody of divine Creation:

> The aggregated soil
> Death with his mace petrific, cold and dry,
> As with a trident smote and fixed as firm
> As Delos floating once. The rest his look
> Bound with Gorgonian rigor not to move
> And with asphaltic slime.
>   ↣ *Paradise Lost 10.293–298*

Asphalt bubbles in the lowest, nastiest part of chaos and may provide the substance for the generation of monsters in hell: "Gorgons, and Hydras, and Chimeras dire" (2.628). It certainly burns in the lamps of Pandemonium, and in this connection Milton would have recalled references to it (as bitumen) in Horace and in Virgil, where it is employed in magic spells to make laurel leaves burn. From Herodotus and from the Greek Septuagint version of the Bible, Milton would know that asphalt was the binding agent for the bricks of the Tower of Babel and for the walls of Babylon, a city built on the plain of Shinar, or, as we call it, Sumer, in Mesopotamia. Here, as Milton says, "a black bituminous gurge / Boils out from under ground, the mouth of Hell" (12.41–42). In English, *bitumen* generally refers to this tar when in its liquid form, as when Milton calls the Dead Sea "that bituminous lake where Sodom flamed" (*PL* 10.562).

There were three points along the Fertile Crescent where asphalt boiled up from hell: Babylon and Egypt at either end of the crescent and, in the middle, the plain of Sodom by the Dead Sea: the three most evil places. The evil associations of asphalt are more impressive still if it is the referent of the line in the creation narrative referring to the Son's purging downward "the black tartareous cold infernal dregs / Adverse to life." Although all matter in Milton's cosmos is supposed to have its origin ultimately in God and to return to God at the end of time, recuperated entirely, this one substance appears to stand outside the system, as a heterological, virulent remainder of the kind Georges Bataille theorized, something incapable of assimilation to the world.

Asphalt is associated not only with the plain of Sodom and Gomorrah but also, as Milton learned from Josephus, with the legendary fruit said to grow there, which as soon as touched would change to bitter ashes. A similar fruit (only it is worse, because it changes in the mouth) becomes the instrument for punishing the devils in hell. That the "soot and cinders" (*PL* 10.570) chewed by the serpent-devils are asphalt is confirmed by the passage in *Eikonoklastes* in which Milton ridicules the devotions of Charles I, which he says "are like the Apples of *Asphaltis*, appearing goodly to the sudden eye, but look well upon them, or at least touch them, and they turn to ashes" (*YP* 3.552).

෨ IT SHOULD BE remembered that the classically trained Baudelaire, like Milton, does have a halo to lose, and that he is in the condition of willingly relinquishing the halo rather than of never having had it; this makes some difference. The other poets, not having their own halos, shamelessly ("impudemment") imitate him. There is in the poem a sustained tension between having and losing the halo. It can be cast off into the slime as an outmoded antiquity, but the very slime into which it is cast sticks to the poet and with it a trace of that alienated halo. It is the halo we see shining around Baudelaire's massive, heroic forehead in the canonical photograph of Étienne Carjat (1861); and it is still there, though more furtively, as if he is angry at being caught wearing the thing, in the informal photograph Carjat took of the poet about two years later. No doubt it is an aureola of fumes from bituminous tar, but one that glorifies the poet nonetheless. Not the least of the ironies of "Perte d'auréole" is that the *auréole* of the title, which cannot be recovered in its heavenly form, also can never be lost. Beneath its obvious rhetoric of cynical demystification Baudelaire's poem exposes the dialectic of modernity, one in which his imitators are ridiculed in advance whether they take up his halo or, as they would later, his slime.

෨ MILTON NEVER SPEAKS of a halo, but I think the song that surrounded the blind man as he composed must have seemed an acoustic effulgence, the breath of Jove, as he called it in the sixth elegy, issuing from his breast and his lips. In *Paradise Lost,* in the invocation to book seven, it is Urania, the celestial muse, who inspires him, who breathes through him. Her name is Ourania, "sky girl." He asks her to descend to his aid. Already he has followed her call beyond the achievements of classical verse, symbolized by Mount Olympus, where he says she doesn't dwell. For Ourania existed before all the mountains, before Creation itself, conversing with her sister Euphrosyne (wisdom) in the presence of God. The poet reminds Ourania how she guided him up into the third heaven, where he took in its fiery air, which she apportioned, or "tempered," to him. The careful reader may feel there's a problem with tenses. The poet is still soaring as he speaks and he is already standing on the earth. But the gesture of humility is clear: he intends to concentrate now on human things and on human history, its causes, and its course. In asking Ourania to let him down from on high, the poet is relinquishing a heavenly aura that he really has had, like the speaker of "Perte d'auréole." The passage is a sublime illustration of the delirious movement, of a tendency to excess within the power of poetry itself, of wild, Bellerophonian oscillation:

> Descend from Heav'n, Urania, by that name
> If rightly thou art called, whose voice divine
> Following above th' Olympian hill I soar,
> Above the flight of Pegaséan wing. . . .
> > Up led by thee
> Into the Heav'n of Heav'ns I have presumed
> An earthly guest and drawn empyreal air,
> Thy temp'ring. With the safety guided down
> Return me to my native element
> Lest from this flying steed unreined (as once
> Bellerophon, though from a lower clime)
> Dismounted on th'Aleian field I fall
> Erroneous there to wander and forlorn.
> *Paradise Lost 7.1–4 and 12–20*

What is this "empyreal air" and how is it "tempered"? Editors since Patrick Hume, who published the first commentary on the poem in 1695, sagaciously follow the leader: "He alludes to the air that on some very high mountains is so extremely thin and suttle, that humane lungs are incapable of drawing it." The eighteenth-century editor, Thomas Newton, completes the explanation: "This *empyreal air* was too pure and fine for him, but the heavenly Muse *tempered* and qualified it so, as to make him capable of breathing in it."[27] Modern editors repeat this mistake, supposing Milton to be speaking of the first heaven instead of the third. But Milton is not breathing *rarified* air when he says he has "drawn empyreal air." The "Heav'n of Heav'ns" is the third, not the first, heaven, and the qualifier "empyreal" means that "air" is being used in a more general sense: it is the ambient substance of the highest heaven, the quintessence. For assistance in understanding this passage we must turn to the poet of "Perte d'auréole": Milton is a "buveur de quintessences," at once drinking and inhaling heavenly fire.

"Empyreal" must be understood here in its etymological sense as something that is "in fire"—*pur.* The word *empyreon* is associated in Greek literature with burnt offerings and with the radiant, glowing coals of the forge. When one looks into the forge, one is seeing what it is like in the empyrean, the region of celestial fire in the third heaven. This fire is the fifth element or quintessence to which Donne refers when he says, "And new philosophy puts all in doubt, / The element of fire is quite put out." Earthly fire rises because it is trying to reach through the air to its home above the stars. Milton has done what no ordinary person can do—drink or intake liquid fire and survive—because the fire has been *tempered* or moderated for him by the muse. You do not *temper* or moderate thin air: Milton is describing an *excess* of divine presence, not a defect that would have to be made up.

There is moreover another sense of *temper* implied in these lines, one that is related to *tempus,* or time: a measured division of something into parts, an apportioning. As the word is associated in Latin with poetic meter, we may conclude that Milton invites us to imagine the heavenly muse apportioning the fire that he breathes into poetic lines, into what Milton in his note on the verse calls "apt numbers, fit quantity of syllables, and the sense variously drawn out from one verse into another." We have seen something like this before, in the ludicrous image from "The Passion" of the poet's tears being so "well instructed" in metrics that they fall onto the page in characters making up verse: "For sure so well instructed are my tears, / That they would fitly fall in ordered characters" (stanza 7). In this passage we are to think of Milton not only breathing or drinking *in* the empyrean but as exhaling it *out,* too, in his verse, igniting his words with the fiery breath of the spirit. Like the breath that he speaks of in the sixth elegy, the breath of the spoken poem becomes an aureola that surrounds him.

Yet that is not, finally, the burden of the invocation opening book seven of *Paradise Lost*. The passage I have quoted from continues:

> Half yet remains unsung but narrower bound
> Within the visible diurnal sphere:
> Standing on earth, not rapt above the pole,
> More safe I sing with mortal voice unchanged
> To hoarse or mute.
>
> ~ *Paradise Lost 7.21–25*

At this moment Milton shows us a return from delirium to discipline, as if the image of himself breathing heavenly fire and surrounded with an aureola of that fire has become for him, almost as soon as he dares to imagine it, faintly (to recall Hugo) *risible*. He may be better off changing his halo for something resembling Baudelaire's desire to become like "simple mortals": he is better off speaking to mortals with a mortal, earthly voice. This is a *physical* voice: Milton, being blind, had to work on his poem by speaking aloud. The most remarkable thing about this voice, therefore, is its not having grown hoarse or mute after six books of epic song. This physical voice has six more books to sing. Because the poem is now an action of the physical body—a jointure of sounds and not a soaring flight—the poet's body has become an issue, a body that is not just strained by the effort of making the poem but actually at risk from attack, "In darkness and with dangers compassed round" (*PL* 7.27).

It is this reduction of the poetic voice from a divine, fiery flight to a mortal song that makes the evocation of Orpheus so moving.[28] Milton calls him "Thracian bard" after Ovid's "Threicius vates," and it is the divinity of Orpheus' song, its supernatural power, that the word "vates" marks, a song that has the power to move to rapture even the stones and the trees. Because the song is divine, it has power over the material world. Yet for all its divinity the song has its foundation in the body. The vulnerability of the body is shown when the maenads tear Orpheus to pieces, drowning his song with the noise. It is the *noise* Milton asks his muse to ward off:

> But drive far off the barbarous dissonance
> Of Bacchus and his revellers, the race
> Of that wild rout that tore the Thracian bard
> In Rhodopè where woods and rocks had ears
> To rapture till the savage clamor drowned
> Both harp and voice.
>
> ↣ *Paradise Lost 7.32–37*

Milton adds that the classical muse of epic poetry, Calliope, though supposed to be heavenly, could not defend her son from earthly, material destruction. He asks *his* muse, Urania, who *is* heavenly because she proceeds from the Spirit, to protect him: "Nor could the Muse defend / Her son. So fail not thou who thee implores, / For thou art Heav'nly, she an empty dream" (37–39).

Orpheus' head was thrown into the river Hebrus, where according to Ovid it floated out to sea, still singing, an image Milton renders more savage in "Lycidas": "His gory visage down the stream was sent, / Down the swift Hebrus to the Lesbian shore" (62–63). The head was at last carried to the island of Lesbos and buried there with full honors, in reward for which many of the inhabitants of that island—the most famous was Sappho—were given the gift of poetry. But it is poetry that rises from the earth, from our mortal nature; and poetry is sung with mortal voices, "standing," as Milton says, "on earth." The special glory of poetry is that it sings and in its singing deliriously ascends above the earth and then returns, seeming thus to descend from above. But only in returning to the earth to sing with mortal voice is the sublimity of that ascent felt to be sublime. In its grandest cosmic moments Milton's poetry is sublime because his voice is mortal and his feet are on the earth.

3

Milton and Modernity

$\mathcal{A}$NYONE WHO WRITES is familiar with the refusal that accompanies the choice of the subject. This refusal, an act of deliberate forgetting, is a psychological counterbalance whereby we are able to put something forward in writing only when we withdraw something else, something that seems more fundamental, and which we pass over in silence. This thing is not just an alternative subject. Considered psychologically, it is perhaps nothing more than the refusal itself, a necessary reticence about something that feels like the basis of all possible subjects in the chosen field; for the chosen field cannot also be a subject within that field. But whether we think of this thing we avoid as an empty refusal or as an inarticulate plentitude, it is experienced by the writer as the thing about which one must contrive not to write if one is to succeed in writing at all. Every act of writing is carved from this deeper refusal.

When by means of this refusal the writer is permitted to write, the initial refusal is extended in time as forgetting. Preoccupied with the subject in hand, the writer is now only vaguely aware of having once had something more fundamental to think, something which he, or she, has forgotten. But because the gratification of being able to write something rather than nothing is for most writers ample compensation for this sense of loss, the transition from active refusal to passive forgetting is welcome. Even the writer who has the tenacity, I would even say

45

the courage, not to accept such a loss will repeatedly encounter a moment when it is necessary to withhold and withdraw. It is perhaps this that distinguishes the writer of gigantic awareness from those writers who are less interested in probing the limits, or exploring the boundaries, of orderly, articulate thought. I mean the willingness to oscillate continually between moments of active refusal and periods of controlled forgetfulness during which it is possible to write. Every subject emerges at first from a refusal to articulate its ground; and every elaboration in writing is sustained by a deeper forgetting.

It may seem to us therefore as if our freedom to write depends on this economy of primordial refusal and productive forgetting. And it is this sense of loss, modulating from refusal to forgetting, or, in more self-aware writing, oscillating between them, that distinguishes the experience of writing from that of speaking, which does not seem to activate so powerfully the feeling of having to suppress something in order to "speak." We think of the speech act as a *presencing* of the speaking self to itself, in a state that is prior to writing and even opposed to it. For this reason the metaphysical advantage of the speaking voice is associated with the cadence and pitch of modernity. Both seem peculiarly real because they are happening now.

The chief place of refuge from the sense of loss we experience while writing is therefore the place of modernity, a place where the self is in free possession of itself through the voice. Such self-possession is unavailable to those earlier authorial selves, such as "Milton," whom we regard as being dispersed by intertextual and contextual forces that do not disperse us—except, of course, when we read them. For the law of dispersal applies not just to the authors but also to their writings, which we once thought of (and now refuse to forget) as self-contained works of art. Just as speaking is thought of as being prior to writing and opposed to it, so the self-possession of the modernist self may be thought of as logically prior to the diacritical abstraction of texts. These can be brought to life, we suppose, only by an interpretive ventriloquism that will make those texts speak to us now. But because this contrivance for making texts speak must operate through writing, the ventriloquist must employ a kind of writing that will take to itself the authority of a voice.

The kind of writing to which I refer may be found in a species of critical discourse wherein the presence of the interpreter is contrasted with the absence, the irrelevance, or the non-entity of the author, who has lost his voice in becoming a function within the text. The transformation of the literary work—the work that was once thought of as *poiema*, or "thing made"—into a diacritical system, a text, places the interpreter in a position of authority previously held by the author.[1] The interpreter makes literature speak for us now, as meaning, while we still have our voices inside us. For if it is supposed that the essence of a work is its meaning, then it is the interpreter who is finally empowered to bestow that essence upon it. The interpreter has come to inhabit the place of the maker. Although interpretation is temporally subsequent to what it interprets, by addressing itself to the living it contrives to establish itself at the source. "The survival of literature," we are told of *Paradise Lost*, "as anything more than artifact depends on our ability to extend its original reference into a genuinely revelatory description . . . of the world we inhabit now."[2] With such an assertion the interpreter is freed from the logic of dispersal governing texts, claiming to disclose in those texts a world that is more real by virtue of its standing on the instantaneous edge of the present, the "now," thin as that edge is. To retain the authority of a voice that can make an old text speak of the world we inhabit, the interpreter must appear not to have to suppress something more fundamental in order to write. What interpretation forgets must be deeply forgotten. This forgetting is registered, however, in the deprecating word *artifact*. I have myself used the word *poem*, "thing made," but would like to recall a more embarrassing term for what is being suppressed: the *createdness* of the work of art.

When the interpreter privileges the idea of the work as a *text* over the standing of the work as a *poem*, and is entirely oblivious of the work's createdness, the work is thought of as an artifact in terms that can apply to it only as a text. In its origins the work is essentially an "original reference," a meaning reflected, in Milton's case, to the seventeenth-century reader. In order to forget more completely the being of the work as a poem, the interpreter understands that being as nothing more than the verbal reflection of a meaning that the author conceived from the first, a meaning the author intended to transmit to his contemporaries, but not to us. When the createdness of the work is recalled only as a reflection of a meaning, it is easy enough to refuse to give that reflection itself any serious treatment; for other, more recent meanings press with greater urgency on our attention.

Now, it is obvious that a hermeneutic engagement with the work as a text—an activity belonging to the epistemological sphere of inquiry—must always take into account the recipient of meaning. And it would be not just methodologically futile but quite out of keeping with Milton's ambitions to identify that recipient as the seventeenth-century reader. It is incorrect, however, to suppose that the being of the work as an artifact, its createdness, can be grounded in any meaning whatever, whether its original meaning or its later significance. This mistake proceeds from the widespread assumption that the business of criticism is interpretation. The assumption is an attractive one because, by claiming that the essence or ground of the work is in meaning, it enlarges considerably the interpreter's feeling of power. Once one has settled into the belief that the literary work was always an intentional structure, a being-toward-meaning, one can easily subordinate any original authorial intention to the latest, and hence the most "present," interpretation. For this present interpretation will have more presence for us in the world we inhabit than will any meaning prior to it in time. Like sense-certainty, the authority of the latest interpretation rests in the here and the now.

But there is much more to criticism than the "discovery" of unobvious meaning in texts and the theory of how this is done—or even the theory of how this is impossible to do. Indeed, from Plato to Arnold such questions are of slight importance in comparison with the more fundamental conditions of the literary work: the problem of the literary work's standing with respect to the real (for example, how are fictions, as epiphenomena, tethered to the world?), and the emergence of the literary work, as an artifact, into its worldly existence among other made things. Such problems belong, however, to the ontological sphere of inquiry, into which the interpreter will not venture because that sphere is precisely what every thoroughgoing interpreter needs to forget. What the interpreter needs to forget is the standing of the work, prior to any meaning whatever—to any meaning it can have even to its author—as a thing that is made. In the theologico-hermeneutic frame of our present critical practice, the "madeness" of the literary work is difficult to recall and to think, except in its false character as original meaning, because madeness is what must be refused if our interpretive norms are to remain undisturbed. Hence the necessity of speaking of the work—of the "masterpiece" or of the "great work of art"—in language that has been regarded since the middle of the twentieth century as professionally naïve.

We have no choice, therefore, but to invoke this ontological perspective naïvely by recalling that most readers take up *Paradise Lost* for the first time because they have heard that it is, quite simply, a great work of art. The poem is *the* canonical achievement of English literature outside Shakespeare. However methodically useful it may be to forget the monumental character of the work so that its textual character will come into view, this monumentality can never be entirely obliterated because it is emphatically not, as is widely supposed, a wrong idea of the work that has been superseded by a right one. Monumentality is an idea of the work the active suppression of which is necessary for the interpreter to be able to write. A text disseminates; a monument stands. These modes of acting and existing, though inimical, cannot be detached from each other. I am not saying that criticism that forgets the monumental createdness of a work in order to use it as a text is in every case vitiated by that forgetfulness. I am saying that such criticism is weak if it forgets that it has to forget in order to do what it does. We must take care, however, not to be led to the easy conclusion that the being of the poem as a thing made is caught in symmetrical relationship with its meaning, each living the other's death and dying its life. For the interpretive aspect of the poem, in which we feel the multiplicity of its meanings resides, is a problem that was of the first importance to Milton. Either perspective—that of the work as its meaning and that of the work as a song—amounts to a specular formation of the deeper and more difficult problem of the standing of the poem as a thing made.

To the early critics of Milton, notably Dr. Johnson, this problem was formulated in terms of the second of these alternatives, that is, of poetics understood as the discovery of the true, rational laws for making an epic. Considered from this point of view, the createdness of the work was thought to be apparent in the extent to which it reflected the abstract laws of its ideal form. But this abstract idea is precisely what Milton had to reject before he was able to choose the subject of *Paradise Lost* and before he could associate the createdness of his poem with what his Adam perceives, almost immediately upon waking, as being the deepest truth of the world: that the world is a poem, a thing made. Whereas for Johnson, *Paradise Lost* is an approximation, a very near

one, to the ideal epic poem (it is not the greatest, he says, only because
it is not the first), for the interpreter who would make the poem speak
to us now, *Paradise Lost* transcends the original conditions of its making
because those conditions entail nothing more than the reflection of
a meaning. It is noteworthy that these specular ideologemes of createdness try to escape history by running to its extremes: in appeals to
the earliest and hence (it is supposed) the most urgent expression of a
meaning. I am not so much interested in these arguments for themselves as I am in the way they conceal and then reformulate the problem of what it means for a poem to be a creation.

Although there has never been a significant critic of Milton for
whom the poem does not stand, at the root of all meaning, as a thing
made, it has become increasingly difficult since Johnson to think that
createdness openly. Like all difficulties, however, this one, ours, can be
looked upon as an opportunity. We have simply lost interest in prescriptive criteria and have at least made some effort at clearing out an
obstructive theology of essentialist meaning. It seems possible, therefore, that we have an opportunity now to think of the poem in more
fundamental terms than has been done since Milton did so himself.
This means, given the stature of the poem in question, that we also
have an opportunity to think of poetry itself more fundamentally.

Such an investigation will be unwelcome not only to those who read
Paradise Lost to find out its meaning for us but also to those who would
show why its meaning cannot be found. For the being of the poem as a
thing made, its destiny as a monument of culture (another professionally embarrassing term), actively interferes with the interpreter's need
to make the poem into a text that can be disseminatively read. Although the thing that it is necessary for the interpreter to turn away
from and forget in order to be able to write is precisely this standing of
the poem as an artifact, that very turning and forgetfulness is necessary to interpretive writing. Consider the alternatives. If interpretation
obliterates the work altogether by insisting that it was always already a
mediated meaning, it loses any purpose in addressing itself, as interpretation, to the abyss it has opened. And if interpretation recalls the work
as anything other than a reflection of meaning, it loses the occasion
of having something of an interpretive nature to say. Nihilism is too
strong for the interpreter, poetics too self-effacing. The interpreter
must therefore nurture an obliviousness to the contradiction at the
heart of interpretation itself.

We have now to consider how deeply modernist interpretive discourse is committed to this methodological forgetting, or, to focus the question more sharply, to what extent modernist interpreters of Milton must write strange and "improper" things—things detached from Milton's proprietary control over what he has made—as part of a more general strategy of forgetting what they cannot interpret. For the present we may summarize the argument so far by noting that a truly *critical* interpretive discourse, rather than contenting itself with forgetting, will repeatedly acknowledge the existence of the thing about which it must contrive not to write.

᠔ THE SENSE OF LOSS that accompanies the effort to represent an object of thought in writing is particularly acute in modernist discourse because the linguistic materials of thought are conceived as being emptied of meaning except when applied, as instruments, to an object outside them by a self that is also outside them. This is, I suppose, what is meant by a discourse that is thought of not as mediating ontologically between the self and the object of its attention but as standing between the self and the object without being implicated in either. Unlike medieval exegesis, modernist interpretive discourse is thought not to permeate the object and to share in its being but to turn away from it at the last moment, carrying, like a space probe, its distant inspection of the strange object back to the presence where the self has its home.

Now, this separation of the familiar self of the *cogito* from the uncanny object of knowledge is curiously destabilized by modernist interpretation of those objects we refer to as "texts." For in modernist interpretive discourse there is a tendency for reversal to take place such that the object, converted into a text, must serve as a kind of temporary camp through which the discourse can pass, bringing news of a self that is no longer at home to itself: set a distance from ourselves, the text is made to provide a description of the world we inhabit now. Milton thinks: therefore we are. To understand why this reversal of priority occurs, we need to examine modernity more closely.

Most definitions of modernity describe it as a sense of being released from the social and religious constraints of more primitive times, freeing us as individuals to make ourselves whatever we wish,[3] a sense that appears in the Renaissance, together with the use of the word *modern* to indicate the feeling of the separation of the present from the immediate past. In Miltonic terms, the constraints of tradition give place to the liberty of rational choice so that the self may become to itself an object of planning and control. The sense of being free to construct the self as an "ethical subject" according to the dictates of reason[4] is accomplished by refusing to allow the constraints of the past to extend into the present and by deliberately forgetting not the past itself but its pastness. We do this by "situating . . . texts within a postmodern context"[5] and by claiming that the past is unknowable, sterile, or irrelevant unless we can come to know it on our own terms: "Meaning is an empty ideal when severed from the validity of meaning, *right now,* for those who choose to seek it."[6] In pursuit of this meaning we interrogate the past through what we now refer to as "texts," depriving the past of its voice so that we can insert our voices into its writing. In this way the past is compelled to speak not only to us but for us.

Modernity characteristically produces a discourse that tries, therefore, with the persistence of an obsession, to establish the self inside the present moment by compelling all previous texts to reveal it. There is no end to the modernist interpreting of texts because there is no end, inside modernity, to the narcissistic ritual of confirming the self as existent. But because modernist interpretation cannot penetrate its object, it can give the impression of having left the self only if the object is translated into its discourse—only if the object is its words. To represent the object inside the discourse, however, it is necessary to submit the object to methodological oblivion so that it will no longer stand as a thing outside any interpretation of it. If, to choose a classic example of high modernist thought, I want to interpret a subatomic phenomenon as a particle—that is, as something that makes sense to me—I must forget the underlying receptacle, or place of being, in which that particle could also be known as a wave. If I want to interpret *Paradise Lost* as the manifestation of a sacred complex or of an ideological formation—that is, as something that might have a more immediate Marxian or Freudian meaning for me—I must forget that inarticulate receptacle of its being that makes possible, by withdrawing, my interpretive writing about it.

It is this forgetting that makes interpretation a reflection of the interpreter. For what starts out as a discourse ostensibly concerned with an object set at a distance from the self, *Paradise Lost*, becomes instead a discourse concerning a self that is set at a distance from itself by being passed through an encoded version of the object of study, the object itself being excluded as a mere artifact. The poem as the receptacle of the meanings that are imprinted on it is forgotten as a thing distinct from those imprintings. In this realm of pure textuality or "imprinted-ness" it becomes possible to speak not only of the "author function" but also of an *oeuvre* function, or even, in the case of *Paradise Lost*, a *chef-d'oeuvre* function. Just as we can methodologically refuse a text its independent author, so too can we refuse it its existence as a "thing made." The createdness of the work becomes instead, for methodolog-ical purposes, a special code designed to produce the illusion that the text of which that code is a part was once the scene of an act of creation. When? Even Milton must locate this scene in a place that has existed long before him and his discourse: in the "vast abyss" that is the recep-tacle of Being itself.

This "receptacle" *(hypodoche)* is named first in the cosmological sys-tem of the *Timaeus* as the thing about which, having only a kind of dreamlike existence, it is impossible to think (49a–52c). As a third kind of being which is neither ideal nor material, it is the clearing, womb, or open space *(chora)* in which things are embodied in matter: "the Womb of nature and perhaps her Grave," as Milton calls it in *Paradise Lost* (2.911). The *chora* is not even a geometrical space but whatever it is that enables that space to exist—in the way that a container gives shape to the emptiness it holds. As the place out of which *physis* is born, the receptacle must be forgotten if we are to think about anything else, since it is the underlying, unintelligible place where things grasp their existence.[7]

We must invoke some concept as difficult as this (it is not so much a concept as a mode of refusal) if we are to think the createdness of the literary work without falling back into formalism, or literary history, or both. Under these intellectual habits, formulations of the being of the literary work as a thing made are inadequate not because they fail to address themselves to anything real but because they contrive to avoid what they refer to even as they call it to mind. Indeed, they call it to mind only so that it may be more efficiently forgotten thereafter. For the writer who uses such terms always has a more immediate subject in view, the articulation of which demands the forgetting of this one. I too forget, though deliberately, in choosing as my subject not the being of the work of art as a thing made but rather that forgetting of this being which enables the critic to write. To legitimate this new subject I need only establish that whenever we write about a work of art or study it in some detail, we have the sense of having to forget something more fundamental. It may be that our intuition of this deeper standing of the work in its createdness may be nothing more than an element in the structure of interpretive refusal, just as the structure of the repression in classical psychoanalysis can create for itself the memory of a traumatic event that has never occurred. But we are concerned here only with the feeling that when we interpret, we are cutting out something more fundamental. It is the feeling, droning behind all responses like a background noise, that the work of art is what it is only because it opens a place to itself where it stands as created.

I offer two examples of moments when we tune in this background of noise before tuning it out once again. The first is familiar to teachers of literature, who must meet at some time the complaint that the explication of literature destroys our primary experience of it: we murder to dissect. I have heard some sophisticated answers to this objection, and any dissatisfaction I have felt has not prevented me from making use of them myself. But however we interpret the motives of those who make this complaint, it is not impossible that they do have a point. We know that there is indeed something in the experience of literature that is forgotten, or repressed, once we begin to explicate the work in question and to treat it as a text, or as the expression of an array of intersecting codes. That is perhaps why elaborate hermeneutical gyrations performed on a "text" such as *Winnie the Pooh* are instantly recognizable as satire. It is only the more obvious importance of works such as *Paradise Lost* that allows us to forget our primary experience of the work so that we can preoccupy ourselves with our ideas. And perhaps some of these ideas, when quoted out of context from serious studies of Milton, might be mistaken for satire.

The second example is that of a musical score. When we see a score for the first time, even if we are, like the present author, elementary readers at best, our knowledge of the music is instantly enlarged. We see things that were inaudible to us before, and the rigorous subtlety of musical design is swiftly, unexpectedly apparent. To see the music is the best way to hear it. But I doubt that anyone has had this experience without suspecting that a price has been paid when that first, ignorant rush of enthusiasm is lost. We feel we will never again hear the music in quite the same way—as the voice of the music itself. I am not suggesting that such a feeling cannot be recovered, with interest, after we acquire knowledge of the music. It is sufficient for the present argument only that this be felt as a *recovery* of something temporarily lost. What has been temporarily lost is the primary sense of the work as a made thing and, more important, of the work's participating in a more general continuum of createdness—whence its sounding like the voice of music itself. It is this continuum of createdness that interpretive discourse must refuse to acknowledge in order to get itself talking *about one work in particular.*

To say this, however, is not to say that the createdness of the work is inimical to all writing about literature, even if such writing entails a wholly different kind of forgetting. On the contrary, the createdness of the work informs the most powerful critical discourses, which are always concerned with relationships between works rather than relationships in works. Of these the most formal is poetics. Poetics addresses itself to questions concerning how works are made, how they function according to the principles on which they are made, and what the differences are that make a difference between them. But a discourse as strong as poetics, even as it grows more authentically than interpretation out of the continuum of createdness, has a technical purpose in view that will permit only the briefest of glimpses into what underlies and sustains it. The standing of the work as a thing made, and the struggle of the work to distinguish itself from every similar work, can be better seen in a species of critical activity that is humbler in its aims than poetics.

I refer to the task of glossing, in textual notes, the provenance of various expressions or ideas, as when we are shown how Milton's "liquid lapse of murmuring streams" takes up for its own purpose, and echoes with a difference, Ausonius' "liquidarum et lapsus acquarum" (*PL* 8.263). When we read Milton in Henry John Todd's great variorum edition of the *Poetical Works*, we notice as a physical presence, and in massive detail, what every reader can sense: that a great many verses of *Paradise Lost* are taken partly or entirely from Homer, Virgil, Dante, Ariosto, Tasso, Spenser, Shakespeare, and numerous minor poets in several languages. An unintended effect of an edition that makes these sources typographically present is to cause us to see Milton's epic as an assemblage of earlier texts. None of the early commentators assumed that Milton would have each borrowed verse clearly in mind as he gathered it into his epic. They understood, and they set out to show, how Milton digested his vast reading so thoroughly that the words were, as he spoke them, as distinctively his own as any words could be. But by tracing Milton's phrases back to their heterogeneous sources, the early commentators were able to show, even to dramatize, something of the process of creation itself: a continuing struggle between allusiveness and self-assertion. For the independence of Milton's epic as work is made more conspicuous to us when we can observe it differentiating itself at every moment from its various sources and becoming more distinct with every allusive departure. Each allusion, far from affirming an identity between the verse in which it occurs and the verse from which it derives, opens a rift as the new poem struggles to separate itself from the reservoir of poetic making in general. It is in this struggle of the hidden to remain hidden and of the new work to raise itself out of the hidden—and even to show its dark materials as things properly concealed—that the createdness of the work appears.[8] While the editorial repetition of sources at the bottom of the page may allow us to see more clearly the struggle that is taking place inside every word of the poem, even in an unannotated text that struggle is always faintly audible to us. For the very independence of *Paradise Lost* as a thing made, a *poiema*, is rooted in the hiddenness of the previous texts from which, at every moment of its growth, it seems to be tearing itself free—even as it brings them to light. The sense of opposites struggling in the very language of the verse, of the verse being wrested from the hiddenness of making in general and compelled to stand out above it in a particular cause, characterizes unmistakably the voice we refer to as "Miltonic." I suspect that this point would go some way toward explaining why a poet so closely attuned to Milton's verse as Wordsworth was never captures that voice—while Pope, using the more aggressive instruments of parody and satire, does. But it surely also has something to do with Pope's having translated Homer. Somehow, we know that the Son at the end of the sixth book of *Paradise Lost* would be less tremendous if Milton's creation of him had not been wrested from the terror of Hector's face and the majesty of Ezekiel's wheels.

Now, the createdness I have said is revealed in this struggle is obnoxious to the interpreter not only because it withdraws before every effort of familiar analysis but also because, unlike interpretation, which seeks to overpower the text by conferring meaning on it, it demands an attentiveness, a "listening," that can be distinctly uncomfortable. It can seem to us as if it is not we who are making the work real in the world we inhabit now but the work that is opening to us a reality transcending our ephemeral being. However delusive this feeling may be, there can be no denying that it constitutes something fundamental in our reason for making art and for seeking it out and that it is altogether prior to interpretation. Whenever we have this experience, it seems to us as if it is, at its root, an experience of something that is always the same because it is not, like interpretation, about particular works but about making in general. It was because of this sense of unity in all created things that Milton regarded them as being continuous with the original Creation, which included, of course, the poem spoken through him. For our purposes, we may say that this continuity derives from our sense that there is a common receptacle, or place, in which every work of art grasps its existence. The receptacle or place, which is to be understood here on analogy to the Platonic *chora*, is not just the underlying substance of the literary work, which is language, as Aristotle says in the *Poetics:* it is the very possibility of the literary work's being; it is the decisive condition of the work's being.

Whereas earlier thought, from Aristotle forward, simply forgets this receptacle by replacing it with language, modern thinking remembers it long enough to have to refuse consciously to think it. It is almost inconceivable in an earlier age that the interpreter would acknowledge two distinct bases for thinking about a literary work: as an artifact holding its existence *in itself* as a thing made and as a text holding its existence *for us* in such a way that it is "subject," as William Kerrigan writes, "by its *essence* to endless reinterpretation."[9] Ancient allegorical interpreters of Homer predicate the latter on the former, leaving the essence of the work in its original state as a "thing made" while assuming that Homer somehow obtained prophetic knowledge of future concerns, encoding these into his epics. For the ancient interpreters the work is open to endless reinterpretation only because it was made to be infinitely meaningful by a poet who was infinitely wise. The modernist interpreter, however, recognizes the distinction between the *poem* as a thing made and the *text* as an empty structure open to any meaning that may be worked into its lattice—or pressed through its lattice, as in a silkscreen. It is only after remembering this distinction that the interpreter denies the ontological priority of the poem as a thing to itself so that its essence will be, as he says, "for us." Its status as a thing made is not just deeply but deliberately forgotten. If modernity may be characterized, at its strongest, by methodological obliviousness—the consciousness that to write, as Nietzsche said, it is necessary actively to forget most of what one knows—then modernity poses a distinct challenge to that sort of writer we call *fundamental*. For such a writer will always be aware of the absurdity of having to forget the foundation in order to think it.

Few would dispute Heidegger's claim to have searched this dilemma more thoroughly than anyone else. It may therefore be useful at this stage to review briefly what modernity would mean in Heideggerean terms. Such an approach may seem to be taking an extravagantly circuitous route to its subject, which is, if we have not yet refused it, contemporary criticism of Milton, or, more precisely, the question "What kind of forgetfulness makes critics write such uncanny things about Milton?" It may be that a more sensible approach to the oddness of modern and postmodern criticism of Milton would begin by asking whether or not such criticism corresponds with Milton as he actually was—and whether or not it should try to. It would ask not "Why are things of this kind said?" but rather "How do things of this kind contribute to our knowledge of Milton?" However profitable it may be to write about this second question after having refused or forgotten the first, its results must remain insecure until we have made some attempt at recalling the terms in which the first must be asked. These terms will help us to understand our interpretive relation to old texts as one in which we enact, as in a ritual of the self, our modernity.

꙳ MODERNITY FOR HEIDEGGER IS, in the first instance, our conscious recognition of being thrown into the present moment of a world that offers us no ground on which to secure our being within it. This sense of groundlessness is due to a kind of ontological oblivion by which we fail to distinguish the fact of *Being* as such from particular *beings*. Whenever we inquire into the former, we speak about it as if it were one of the latter, asking what kind of thing *Being* is. We thus commit the elementary mistake, which a rather different philosopher would call a confusion of logical types, of including the totality of things as one thing in that totality. As a consequence of this dilemma, what Heidegger calls the "Being question"—"Why is there something

instead of nothing?"—is a question that cannot be asked without absurdity because of the presence in that question of the word *thing.* De-
generating into the question "What kind of a thing is Being?" its formulation must always take place on our side of the threshold between
Being and beings. The same analysis may be applied to the work of art,
wherein we confuse the work in its fundamental character of createdness with our perception of it as a constituted meaning, mistakenly supposing its essence to be rooted in our experience of it.[10] Just as the naïve
ontologist asks, "What kind of a thing is Being?" so the naïve interpreter asks, "What kind of a meaning is *Paradise Lost?*"—a question
that is little more than a roundabout way of asking (although the
roundaboutness, as we shall see, is necessary to it), "Who am I?"

It was to acknowledge this difficulty that Heidegger proposed in *Zur
Seinsfrage* (1955) to write "Being" under erasure, so that the visible
crossing-out of the word would display its negation as an act taking
place within time. Thus the act of "crossing out," or "through-strik-
ing,"[11] does more than simply negate what has been written beneath: it
marks the place of the stricken word as that which stands on the threshold across which the unspeakable enters a realm of beings that can be
spoken of as things. The crossing-out initiates, therefore, the ontological task of remembering, recalling, and recollecting that which we have
most deeply forgotten.

This gathering is associated with the passage in the *Timaeus* on the
hypodochē, or "receptacle," which, though not itself a thing, is that in
which things and their qualities appear, as in a mirror.[12] According to
Heidegger's view of the history of Western philosophy as the history of
the forgetting of Being, it is in this episode of the receptacle that Plato,
for a moment, heard the call of Being before allowing it to fall back
into oblivion as the thing about which it is impossible to think. After
we have forgotten this primordial being, which is not itself present as a
being, we are able to write a kind of philosophy in which the totality of
existence is conceived of as a presence that may be set before the eye of
the mind and subjected to visual inspection, or "theory." Heidegger
proposed that by his writing "Being" under erasure, it would be possible to remember Being at the moment in which the threshold is
crossed from Being to beings, a moment that is held not in its presence
(since it is just prior to the distinction between presence and absence)
but in its footprint or trace.

Seen in more historical terms, the crisis of trying to think Being as a whole without reference to constituent parts is a reading back into Greek metaphysics of a principle developed in German hermeneutics. We are here undertaking to reverse the direction of this reading of metaphysics through hermeneutics by dislodging from its usual place the question "Why are such strange things written about Milton?" so that we can discern what metaphysical anxieties those writings temporarily allay. For to say that its meaning for us makes the poem stand essentially now, in the present, is just as much a metaphysical assertion as to say that it stands for itself. There is no final escape from the question of the being of the work of art. The question can only be refused, forgotten, delayed, or taken up, if only temporarily, in the quest for an answer.

Whatever path we choose in that quest, our willingness to follow it some distance has the unexpected benefit of revealing an ontological motive behind the insistence on finding modern meanings in old works of literature. Indeed, the exposure of this motive is a necessary first step in any inquiry into what the work is. For to question the work's essential createdness, we must dislodge it from its improper standing in the epistemological sphere, where it has been held captive to the protean will of the interpreter. When we ask what kind of being the interpreter is trying to establish for the work when proclaiming the mobility of its meaning through each generation of readers, we begin to see that the interpreter is concerned not at all with the meaning of the text—either right now or back then—but only with the authority of the interpreter himself, or herself, as the giver of meaning. We speak of ourselves through *Paradise Lost* so as to have a receptacle, or open space, in which to set up our modernity. For modernity, as the instantaneous edge of the present, has no open place in itself in which to contemplate itself and must therefore use something back there in history as a platform on which to set up a mirror. Hence it will seem as if it is not we who are interpreting ourselves but *Paradise Lost* that is interpreting us. For the poem allows us to mediate ourselves to ourselves through its alien system, providing the ontological difference every model requires. This mediation of the self to itself in an action performed through an external structure is called *ritual*.

If interpretation is a ritual by which we assure ourselves of the monumental solidity of our existence and of its openness to self-inspection, we should hardly be surprised that much recent criticism of Milton is concerned with articulating modernist and postmodernist concerns. What is more surprising is the persistence in such writing of the convention that criticism proceeds from a known self to an unknown object of study—Milton—when in fact a familiar body of knowledge about Milton is being used to articulate and explore an unknown modernist self. The *subject* in the old sense becomes the *subject* in the new. To justify a reversal over which we have little control, it is said that the critic's concern is not to recover or to remember what Milton meant but to find out what, at this instant, Milton's "text" means. To do this it is necessary to discredit the image of the great work of literature as a monument, something that opens up its own space, and to substitute for it the image of the literary text as a mirror, something that opens up and monumentalizes the otherwise liminal space of the observer. By making the poem into a textual mirror, we can see ourselves standing in the suddenly more ample space of the present.

Such an alteration of perspective inevitably multiplies versions of *Paradise Lost*, starting with that which appears to us now and ending, at the other extreme, with that which is taken to be a methodological fiction preceding every idea of *Paradise Lost*: *Paradise Lost* as it actually was—or as it *is* outside every context. We have, however, seen that nothing characterizes so perfectly the temper of modernist criticisms as the assumption that to write of the first, it is necessary to refuse to write of the second and even in some sense to forget this second. For if we remember, assiduously, that everything we set out to write will fail to coincide with *Paradise Lost* as it actually was, we are in danger of writing nothing whatever. Only when we choose to forget the priority of the receptacle to the instantaneous spaces created by the poem as mirror can we comfortably write something of an interpretive nature about each of those spaces. Indeed Milton himself, confronting the dilemma of having to forget his ideas of *Paradise Lost* in order to make it, spoke of the poem as being made not by him but through him. Like the sculptor who speaks of releasing the figure from the block of stone in which it is concealed, Milton seems to offer his epic to us as a disclosure of something that already exists. Or does he? What Milton shows us—and this is the true *subject* of *Paradise Lost*—is the drama of an epic being made. Any meaning we can attribute to the poem must have its basis in that.

We have seen how the hermeneutic question as to whether, or how, *Paradise Lost* means anything to us at the present must be approached through the ontological question of the origin, or "primal leaping" *(Ursprung)*, as Heidegger calls it, of the work of art. What kind of being, a being distinct from and prior to its interpretations, can we speak of with respect to *Paradise Lost?* In what mode can we recollect the *Paradise Lost* that existed before it was seen as text in the light of its modernity to each of its readers in each of their moments in time, before the poem was, as it has been since Raleigh, Waldock, Empson, Bush—*Paradise Lost* in our time? Such questions cannot be confronted—they cannot perhaps even be intelligibly asked—until we have worked our way back to them through some preliminary questions about ourselves as interpreters. Of these there are two (or, more precisely, the same question read forwards and backwards): (1) Why is it that when writing about *Paradise Lost* we end up writing about our modernity? (2) Why is it that to write about our modernity we feel it necessary to conduct that writing through the text of *Paradise Lost?* The first may be termed the *modernist* question concerning criticism of Milton, the second the *postmodernist* question.

In considering interpretation as a ritual of integrity in which the modernist self is confirmed in its existence, we have answered the first question. In our condition of thrown-ness, the work of interpreting alien texts seems to give us a footing in the world we inhabit. The modernist interpreter, lacking any secure ground on which to set up a monument to the modernist interpreter, is able to open a modern world in the reflection of texts and to see it, for the first time, as home. Our home is here, paradoxically, in the distant and alien structures of *Paradise Lost*. But of course in trying to appropriate Milton's epic to ourselves we push it even farther away from ourselves, making it strange even as we make ourselves, inside its language, familiar. I have referred to this procedure as *modernist interpretation* because the trick of allusive self-constitution in alien texts is established in the classics of what we call "modernism": *Ulysses, The Waste Land,* and the *Cantos.* And since what we call *postmodernism* submits the absurdities of modernist self-constitution to an ironic analysis, it is appropriate that its question should be a reading backwards of the modernist question. Whereas modernism, feeling too thin, makes the self fat by placing a convex mirror in every previous text from *Gilgamesh* to *Paradise Lost* and beyond, postmodernism reduces the self to an anorectic wisp, dispersing the presence of the self—and, of course, that of the poem—throughout the ecologies of allusion and play.

Insofar as we have recognized, therefore, within modernity, the necessity of writing about ourselves through the alienated texts of our poetic tradition, we have at least partly answered the second question: we need historically distanced texts to serve, in their unacknowledged but powerfully felt createdness, as receptacles or clearings in which we can monumentalize ourselves as existents. Establishing and enlarging ourselves in the places that are opened by all previous texts, we no longer feel reduced to the very limit of thinness, like the sculptures of Giacometti, by our modernity. Ritual interpretation prolongs the fragile illusion that our existence is authentically grounded in what we call, betraying our anxiety on this point, the real world, a world over which man positions himself as the master. But like a dying star that inflates itself before its collapse into nonentity, this enlargement of the figure of Modern Man, of Man grasping his existence in the clearing or place of old texts, is preliminary to his disappearance, either into extinction or into a more authentic mode of dwelling within nature.

⁓ A POEM OPENS a world to itself. Like a Greek temple, a poem discloses to us the receptacle or place of its existing, a place that for the old poets, up to Milton, is unfolded from and constructed around the standing of gods, who have not yet been declared to be dead. Milton himself, in his first thoroughly Miltonic poem, "Ode on the Morning of Christ's Nativity," anticipates the proclamation of Nietzsche by recounting the "dreaded Infant('s)" purging the temples of Moloch, Peor, and Baal. In their place a divine man is to stand, at the climax of *Paradise Regained*, as a living oracle poised on the topmost spire of the temple, from which he will reopen the world as his kingdom. We can discern in this astonishing image, taken by itself, a quintessentially modern ideal, one that is given its first really vigorous expression in the Renaissance: Man is a god serenely poised over the earth, indifferent to the life of the hidden ecologies in it and balancing himself on the one still point where, he imagines, he cannot be touched by the demons of process and exchange.

But how can he see himself in this position? Whereas previously he could enter the temple and look in through the columns at the god standing there at its center, he must now contrive to look in on himself. He wishes, to adapt the relevant Arnoldian phrase, to see himself steadily and to see himself whole, forgetting that he must alienate himself from the very self that he observes. It is not enough for him to enter the windswept, weed-infested sanctuary and to stand in the place of the god. A mirror must be placed there, at the center, so that he can look through the columns from the periphery and see himself poised in the clearing, at home. Subjecting himself to complete visual inspection, he must forget the observer—the subject in the modern sense—who is also himself. The strangeness of his dilemma is familiar to us, and not just as interpreters who use alien texts as platforms for inspecting ourselves at a distance. To catch sight of ourselves we must travel to the farthest place we can reach, feeling more at home on earth when we have taken its picture from space, balanced in one of our hands. As for the poem, as soon as we recognize that we are using it thus as a mirror, it seems as if it is not we who have made ourselves strange but the poem, which withdraws behind the mirroring surface, by a refusal that is symmetrical with ours, more deeply into its exile.

ཤ 4

Why, This Is Chaos,
Nor Am I Out of It

*I*F REASONING IS the imposition of order on what is less ordered than reason itself, then there appears to be something contradictory to reasoning about chaos. This is so at least if we take *chaos* to mean simply "disorder"—disorder as in itself it really is. The branch of applied mathematics called *chaos theory,* so useful for the analysis of super-complex, nonlinear systems such as the weather, appears to non-specialists (of whom, of course, I am one) to be a contradiction in terms. So long as *chaos* means *absolute* disorder (which in chaos theory it does not, I am told), the logic is ineluctable: the more we reason about chaos, the less chaotic this chaos will be and the more chaotic our reasoning about chaos must become. Absolute disorder, if such a thing can objectively exist and is not merely a phantom artifact of reason, is a negative that cannot be engaged dialectically with any objective positive term, such as *cosmos.* The more we look at it, the more it disappears.

Absolute disorder can, however, be dialectically engaged with a subjective positive term from the Hebrew tradition: creation. *Creation,* whether it is human or divine, means decision—the decision that something shall be, and perhaps also the decision that something shall not be. I return to this point at the conclusion of this chapter, where I suggest that the objective chaos of *Paradise Lost*—that "hoary deep" and "dark / Illimitable ocean without bound" (2.891–892)—becomes the subjective chaos of *Paradise Regained* which is symbolized by the desert, the empty place of moral decision in history. There, as it happens, it is the act of refusing to take any action at all that is most creative, thus leaving room in history for the Kingdom of God. But the Kingdom of God is something altogether different from an objective cosmos, an arrangement of things, such as "embryon atoms," or of qualities, such as "Hot, Cold, Moist, and Dry" (2.900 and 2.898). Its ground is not in ontology but in ethics, which is to say, in decision.

꙰ COSMOS WAS THE GREEK WORD for order in general, for arrangement (whence *cosmetics*), before it was the word for the order of the universe as a whole. The word acquired this meaning at the beginning of Greek science, perhaps with Anaximander, when the "limit" or "boundary" (*to peras*, the turning point or goal in a racecourse) is reputed to be the beginning of organized thinking about existence as totality. This limit or frame, the context of all contexts, was contrasted with "the boundless" *(to apeiron)*, which Anaximander called a "certain other nature" *(hetera tis physis)*. "The boundless" was later appropriated to the word *chaos*, from Hesiod's *Theogony*, where Chaos is said to have come into being first and to have generated broad-bosomed Earth, black Erebus, and Night, whom Milton makes Chaos's queen, "sable-vested Night" (2.962).[1] Hesiod imposes on Chaos what is doubtless the oldest human principle of organization: genealogy.

Mingling with later Greek physics, and in particular with the analysis of *things* as combinations of matter and form, chaos becomes the source of Ovid's undifferentiated mass, his "indigesta moles." Ovid's chaos, the chaos antiquity transmitted to the Middle Ages, is the abject substance that lies there before the universe is formed. He says that the great undifferentiated lump of chaos was before the sea and the lands of the earth, and the sky which covers them all, so that the face of nature was the same all around, nothing but a lifeless weight and a congregation of the ill-joined seeds of things:

> Ante mare et terras et quod tegit omnia caelum
> unus erat toto naturae vultus in orbe
> quem dixere chaos: rudis indigestaque moles
> nec quicquam nisi pondus iners congestaque eodem
> non bene iunctarum discordia semina rerum.[2]

This passage may be conceptually unsophisticated, but it is poetically powerful and is the source of most of what is developed in Milton's first description of chaos:

> Before their eyes in sudden view appear
> The secrets of the hoary deep, a dark
> Illimitable ocean without bound,
> Without dimension, where length, breadth and heighth
> And time and place are lost, where eldest Night
> And Chaos, áncestors of Nature, hold
> Eternal anarchy amidst the noise
> Of endless wars and by confusion stand.
>
> ⌐ *Paradise Lost 2.890–897*

Anaximander may or may not have said, as was later supposed, that this "other nature," which is boundless, and which remains hidden from us utterly, "encompasses and steers all things," but in either case the otherness of this other nature cannot be reasoned about because it cannot be divided into parts, into units or things.[3] When you use the word *chaos*, you cannot answer the question "What is it?"—what *thing* does this name *chaos* refer to—for chaos is not a thing but something prior to the separation of being into things.

If this "other nature" "steers all things" and is the generative source of the *cosmoi*, the systems of order (it is significant that Anaximander uses "cosmos" in the plural), then any reasoning within these systems must depend on something that is other to reason—radically other. An analogy in modern cosmological thinking is the *singularity*, the moment of absolute unintelligibility and non-difference just before the universe expands into being. The singularity—infinitely small as it is, yet infinitely large as it is too, because there is nothing outside it—is our chaos, the yawning gap into which our mathematical reasoning cannot go but out of which our reasoning comes.

It has therefore been left to the poets to *imagine* chaos and other originative, anarchic structures, from Homer, whose Tartaros is "steep," to Hesiod, whose chaos yawns like a monster, to Ovid, whose chaos is a gigantic lump, to Bernardus Silvestris, whose chaos—Silva, or Hylē, as she is called—is a tumultuous and slatternly female, to Milton, whose chaos whelms and engulfs, assaulting "Heav'n's heighth" with waves that soar like mountains (7.214–215), and onward to Coleridge's "deep romantic chasm" and the dizzying alpine vales of Wordsworth and Shelley, the same alps in which Milton, returning from Italy, saw a sea of mighty waves of rock. We could continue on into modern poetry, to A. R. Ammons, whose very human chaos is a mountain of garbage, "the origins feeding trash":

> garbage has to be the poem of our time because
> garbage is spiritual, believable enough
>
> to get our attention, getting in the way, piling
> up, stinking, turning brooks brownish and
>
> creamy white: what else deflects us from the
> errors of our illusionary ways?[4]

There is also the hard-edged chaos of modern physics invoked by Jorie Graham, for whom chaos is the event horizon between theoretical blindness and imaginative seeing, "an indentation, almost a cut—a foothold— / Where the dizziness seems to be rushing towards form."[5]

To think about something that cannot be reasoned about means, in the first instance, to imagine it, as a poet does, or rather to listen for it. Thinking about chaos means allowing to appear to the acoustic imagination what cannot be *theorized*, which is to say "looked at." As a geometric visualizing, *theoria* cannot enter into chaos without changing chaos into something other than it is. And if chaos is a phantom artifact of reason, reason's own unstable image of what lies beyond its, reason's, reach, then chaos must haunt the *visibilia* of theory as a sort of low hum. There is indeed something weirdly acoustical about chaos. It is as if, in making itself as different as possible from *theoria*, it stripped itself of visibility and chose to reside within sound. *Chaos* is a word only a poet could invent, at once onomatopoeic of something dreadful, although we know not what, and at the same time productive of metaphors. If chaos is not the opposite of order but rather the source of all possibilities of order, then perhaps chaos is the source of poetry, too, its muddy Castalian fount, its tumultuous and slatternly muse.

᧞ FOR THE GREATER NUMBER of readers of *Paradise Lost*, the most astonishing thing in that astonishing poem is chaos. The very word has a dreadful yet astonishing sound, especially in Greek. It begins deep in the throat, with a harsh, rattling chi, a breathy, vibrating *k*, its only consonant. As it rises in the throat, the sound stops vibrating and opens into a broad *ahhh* sound, which is then narrowed as it gathers itself under the palate and is pooled in a short *o*, an omicron. For a moment the sound is permitted to expand in the mouth, under the dome of the palate, before being flattened as the teeth begin to close and the tongue presses forward, forcing the sound out as a hiss: *kkkkaaaossss!* Milton would know that the word is from a verb meaning "to gape," "to yawn open"—*chaskô*—with its final omega sounding as deep as Tehom, the Hebrew word for the oceanic deep, opening wide in order to swallow before closing its jaws with a hiss. The word *chaos* sounds like what Milton says it is: a *deep*, an *abrupt*, an *abyss*. Nor is it an accident that in those three sounds Milton captures the three physiological places from which the word *chaos* arises: the throat, the palate, and the teeth.

But in the poem *Paradise Lost*, chaos is at least three distinct things: a personification, a narrative scene, and a cosmological concept. Chaos is personified as a king—he of "falt'ring speech and visage incomposed" (2.989)—and is "the power of that place" whose name he bears, as we are told in the argument to book two. Chaos also bears the splendid epithet "Anarch old" (2.988). As a king, Chaos is suitably indignant at encroachments on his realm, in particular the incursion of the rebel angels (and their pursuers), at which he roars (6.871) as they encumber him with ruin (6.874). He is roused to fury at the bridge Sin and Death thrust through him: "Disparted Chaos overbuilt exclaimed / And with rebounding surge the bars assailed / That scorned his indignation" (10.416–418).

Most of all, Chaos is indignant at the three great structures of divine Creation and divine justice: Heaven, the first of the great systems of Milton's cosmology and the source of the other two; Hell, "your dungeon stretching far and wide beneath" (2.1003), as Chaos says to Satan; and, as Chaos also says to Satan, "another world / Hung o'er my realm, linked in a golden chain / To that side Heav'n from whence your legions fell" (2.1004–6).

It is from Chaos that we learn that these three things, which are everything, are formed from the substance in his realm and that heaven, hell, and the world occupy space that is subtracted from that realm—if space can be subtracted from a place where "time and place are lost" (2.894). Like the later Roman emperors, Chaos resides on his "frontiers" (2.998) (whatever *frontiers* means), to defend "That little which is left so to defend" (2.1000), though "little" hardly seems the *mot juste* for what is left: a "dark / Illimitable ocean without bound" (2.891–892). By his last appearance, in book ten, Chaos is like the figure of Triton in Wallace Stevens's poem "The Comedian as the Letter C": a "rebounding surge" melding with the element of which he is the power, a vestigial personification, a baroque allegorical outline disappearing into the element of which he is the power.

Milton's chaos is also a narrative scene, that is, an imaginary place where physical things can occur. Grammar makes Milton make chaos a sort of thing, with semi-things in it, things flaring, noisy, and uncertain: alps of shattered ice, mountainous waves of stone colliding in the nitrous blasts and fogs. Narrative makes Milton make chaos a place. Satan crosses this place on his journey to the created world (the *universe*, as we call it), and Sin and Death, as we saw, thrust their bridge through it. Thus the place that is no place, the place "where length, breadth, and heighth / And time and place are lost," has place, time, height, and breadth during Satan's journey. In the first moments of this journey there is clearly "*heighth,*" an *up* and a *down*—"plumb *down* he drops / Ten thousand fathom deep" (2.933–934)—and as Satan proceeds on his voyage it is clear, where so little else is, that he is moving across some kind of surface, wild, vexed (stirred up), and inconsistent as it is. There is also clearly "*heighth,*" an *up* and a *down*, when Sin and Death throw their "ridge of pendent rock / *Over* the vexed abyss" (10.313–314).

The narrative scene of chaos also has an up and a down when the rebel angels fall through it: "in our proper motion we ascend / Up to our native seat," says Moloch:

> Descent and fall
> To us is adverse. Who but felt of late
> When the fierce Foe hung on our broken rear
> Insulting and pursued us through the deep
> With what compulsion and laborious flight
> We sunk thus low? Th'ascent is easy then.
>
> ᴖ *Paradise Lost 2.76–81*

This chaos, the one that does have direction, time, and place, is the "wasteful deep" (6.862) through which the rebel angels *can* fall for nine days (6.871); it is the "unvoyageable gulf" (10.366) across which Satan *can* voyage from Hell to the universe (2.917–950) and across which Sin and Death *can* throw a "stupendious bridge" (10.351).

Satan traverses one "frith" (2.919) of chaos (a *frith* is a "firth," or fjord) on his journey from hell to the created universe. It is a spectacular voyage, one in which the devil is his own drunken boat:

> At last his sail-broad vans
> He spreads for flight and in the surging smoke
> Uplifted spurns the ground, thence many a league
> As in a cloudy chair ascending rides
> Audacious but that seat soon failing meets
> A vast vacuity. All unawares,
> Flutt'ring his pennons vain, plumb down he drops
> Ten thousand fathom deep and to this hour
> Down had been falling had not by ill chance
> The strong rebuff of some tumultuous cloud
> Instínct with fire and niter hurried him
> As many miles aloft. *That* fury stayed,
> Quenched in a boggy Syrtis, neither sea
> Nor good dry land, nigh foundered, on he fares
> Treading the crude consistence half on foot,
> Half flying: behooves him now both oar and sail!
> As when a gryphon through the wilderness
> With wingèd course o'er hill or moory dale
> Pursues the Arimaspian who by stealth
> Had from his wakeful custody purloined
> The guarded gold, so eagerly the Fiend
> O'er bog or steep, through straight, rough, dense, or rare,
> With head, hands, wings, or feet pursues his way
> And swims, or sinks, or wades, or creeps, or flies.
>
> ⌁ *Paradise Lost 2.927–950*

Milton has introduced into this narrative scene at least one and perhaps two things that belong to his chaos as a cosmological concept: the element of chance—it was by "ill chance" only that Satan would not be falling "to this hour" (2.934)—and the impossibility of any rhythm or method to Satan's progress. If you swim, wade, creep, and fly, making use of both oar and sail, that is, of incompatible methods of propulsion (you row only when you can't sail), then you are never settled into any single rhythm of work. The systematic incoherence in the description serves the purpose of reminding us that chaos, as a narrative scene, is an accommodation to the needs of the story and cannot be true in any stricter, metaphysical sense. For how can something "without dimension" ever be crossed? Even the slightest motion in chaos is impossible (although everything in chaos appears to be moving) because there is infinitesimal division between even the tiniest distances: like Zeno's arrow, which does not move because it travels through infinitely divisible space, nothing in chaos should move. That is why *time* ("time measures motion," says Donne) is lost there.

It seems almost as if Milton is registering the fancifulness of chaos as a narrative scene by the Arimaspian simile plucked from Herodotus. It is the strangest simile in *Paradise Lost* and one of the few that has no thematic significance. It may, however, have a kind of methodological significance, indicating that chaos must be described as a scene, however fanciful, even though it is strictly indescribable. As a narrative scene, chaos is presented as the least real thing in the poem—that is, the most necessarily *accommodated* thing. But paradoxically chaos also seems more real and more direct, perhaps because it is more frightening, than any other scene we see in *Paradise Lost*. Chaos seems to us more real, more near to what we are and what we know, for example, than heaven, the surface of the sun, or even the earth, especially the garden of Eden, which is believable when its soaring trees are seen from a distance—"insuperable heighth of loftiest shade" (4.138)—but which dissolves into the vaguest dreamscape when we are there.

⁊ LASTLY, CHAOS IS a cosmological concept that is in some kind of dialectical relation with the substance of God and the act of Creation. We know that Milton, in *De Doctrina Christiana* (we know it if he is its author, as seems likely), understands primordial matter to be "intrinsically good" and also "the chief productive stock of every subsequent good."[6] Primordial matter is good because its substance originally comes out of God, who at what is perhaps the beginning of time retracts himself from infinity and leaves behind his own substance. From this substance God then creates heaven, the angels, and the world—even the Son, although the Son achieves the status ("By merit more than birthright Son of God" [3.309]) of God's "only begotten" (3.80). The world is made from the alienated substance of God, and this substance must therefore be good. Milton takes pains to construct his metaphysics of monist materialism in such a way that there can be no room either for the (to him) nonsensical idea of creation out of nothing or for the gnostic moral terror of an archaic, independent, and perhaps equal principle of evil concealed in matter. The substance of chaos, God's ancient, abject, alienated body, is the substance from which God creates.

Creation is intrinsically good—in the Bible, God sees that it is good at each stage—and the substance that is employed in creation is good too because it is originally from God. The alienation of the substance from God leads to the higher development of this substance, in Creation, as the appearance of the goodness of God and even of the capacity of some creatures (more than we suppose: flowers, for example) to recognize this goodness and praise it with thanks. The crucial verses from *Paradise Lost* in support of the view of matter that is given in *De Doctrina Christiana* are actually spoken by God:

> Boundless the deep because I am who fill
> Infinitude, nor vacuous the space
> (Though I uncircumscribed Myself retire
> And put not forth My goodness which is free
> To act or not): necessity and chance
> Approach not Me, and what I will is fate.
>
> ↣ *Paradise Lost* 7.168–173

Despite the studied neutrality of the matter for which a place is prepared in these verses, many images of chaos (chiefly those belonging to its status as a personification and a narrative scene) are actively hostile, as Regina Schwartz has brilliantly argued, rather than benign or intrinsically good—or even neutral.[7] This is the mythic idea of chaos, a greedy gulf like Charybdis, a monstrous primordial serpent, like Python, or *Tehom*, poetically associated in the psalms, in the prophets, and in Job with the primordial serpent. "Chaos is evil," Schwartz says, "because what is uncreated cannot be neutral." Falling outside the scope of Creation and failing to perform the only action that can make a being good—the expression of gratitude for being created—Milton's chaos "proves Satanic," and this is true also of his "atomistic chaos."[8] At the Creation, "vital virtue" and "vital warmth" must therefore be "infused" into chaos (7.236) from without, by the Spirit. Living power and warmth are not found in chaos as they are found in one of Milton's models, *prōtē hylē*, the "first matter," which Aristotle refers to as female, an analogy of the blood lining the uterus (*Metaphysics* 1044a.15–35).

More shocking still, if chaos is the alienated substance of God and retains anything of its divine origin, what are those "black tartareous cold infernal dregs" in chaos that must be "downward purged" (7.237–238) by the Son when he creates? For Schwartz, the image of the tartareous dregs is a clue to the truth, exposing "a critical conspiracy to detoxify chaos."[9] For John Rogers, however, those dregs are "the most troubling natural philosophical event in the poem," because they are wholly inconsistent with what Rogers sees as chaos's participation in the benevolent "dynamics of autonomous self-organization that is Milton's creation."[10] For Schwartz, chaos ontologizes evil and is its origin. For Rogers, chaos ontologizes good, being the source of fostering, generative warmth and of autonomous self-organization, which is disturbingly invoked by Satan in his alternative account of how the angels came to be—by "our own quick'ning power" (5.861). Much virtue in that *our*. Those tartareous dregs, inherited from Paracelsus, who scraped them from beer barrels, shouldn't be there. They are, as Rogers says, one of the "systematic lapses in coherence in the organizational discourse underlying all of Milton's poem."[11]

The only sense for Rogers in which these lapses are "systematic," however, is an exogenously political one: what appear to be lapses reflect the changing circumstances of the English revolution, the growing conviction of the successful revolutionary that the people, the masses, are not entirely good and not even capable of correction: the masses must be purged. As Ernest Sirluck argued long ago, partly in response to Arthur Barker's *Milton and the Puritan Dilemma*, Milton, when he is not a poet, is primarily a revolutionary, not a philosopher or a metaphysician. Milton therefore uses ideas not philosophically but ideologically, in the service of revolution. This does not mean that the revolutionary is cynically indifferent to the truth where the continuance of revolution is concerned: for the revolutionary, the revolution *is* the truth. The revolution is the thing in itself, not ideas about the revolution. (This is delusion but not cynicism.) For Milton, God is as surely present and working in history as struggle is for Marx and for Trotsky. A revolution changes, having a logic of its own that is not conformable to any synchronic order to which it must appeal. In its later stages, after the seizure of power is complete and the euphoria is spent, a revolution changes generally in the direction of increasing authoritarianism and paranoia. But even in their extreme realization as terror, as Solzhenitsyn showed, authoritarianism and paranoia are regarded by the revolutionary (sometimes when the revolutionary is himself or herself a victim of terror) as evidence that the revolution is cleansing itself and is moving forward to better times. If the Good Old Cause is not to die, or at least not to grow constipated and ill, those tartareous dregs must be purged.

It may be that the difference between Rogers and Schwartz—and the symmetry of their difference is suggestive—proceeds out of the same initial conceptual move: that of ontologizing chaos, of giving chaos existence as a thing and making chaos the answer to the post-ontological question "What [thing] is it?" What if chaos can never be the answer to any question, and especially the question "What is it?" What if chaos cannot be brought into a dialectical relation with creation as that which creation must defeat (Schwartz) or as that which creation must foster (Rogers)? If Schwartz and Rogers are making the same initial move, however, and coming out with opposite conclusions, it must be said that they are making this initial move *with* Milton, not against him. If there is a difference between Rogers and Schwartz on the one hand and Milton on the other, it is that Milton is less consistent than these exemplary readers of him are. For Milton, chaos is more than one thing— and perhaps also less than one thing.

It is not possible to make Milton's three chaoses—the personification, the narrative scene, and the cosmological concept—consistent with one another, nor is it necessary to do so. Why shouldn't a poet be imaginatively free to blend three different needs into one? But it may also be difficult to make any one of these three things, and certainly the last, consistent even with itself. Nor, again, is there an overwhelming need for the cosmological concept to be consistent: *Paradise Lost* is a poem, not a metaphysical treatise in which the strictest logic is required. In reading a poet there is little to be gained by logic-chopping for its own sake. Yet considering closely how the diverse and incompatible elements of chaos go together can teach us much about what underlies the complexity and grandeur of Milton's art. After all, a certain logical blurring in the "dubious light" (2.1042), a conceptual *sfumato* instead of clear, hard outlines, contributes not a little to the grandeur of *Paradise Lost.* Perhaps what this dubiousness conceals, if there *is* something concealed—something lurking, some dark-walking *sceadugenga*— *also* contributes to the grandeur of *Paradise Lost* but contributes to it by being occluded.

We saw that in chaos, in the midst of it, so to speak, are the three created systems of Milton's cosmos: heaven, hell, and the world. Hell is far removed from heaven and the world but is of course infinitesimally close to them too in proportion with what lies beyond: an ocean extending away from these three systems to infinity. Within that ocean Milton describes the "endless wars" (2.897) of four principles, or *archai*, from ancient Greek science, "Hot, Cold, Moist, and Dry" (2.898). The principles are imagined as generals commanding armies of swarming "embryon atoms" (an intriguing phrase, perhaps an oxymoron: whereas an *atom* is that which has no parts and no principle of development within itself, an *embryon* is that which "swells from within"). The embryon atoms are blasted about like grains of sand in the storms of the Sahara: "unnumbered as the sands / Of Barca or Cyrene's torrid soil" (2.904–905). This state of constant war and indistinction ("neither sea, nor shore, nor air, nor fire, / But all these in their pregnant causes mixed / Confus'dly, and which thus must ever fight"; 2.912–914) is not nature because nature is organized. The war of embryon atoms is the origin of nature.

Milton suggests that this state of war may also be a place, like a womb, from which the organized system of nature emerges after being nurtured there and also a place to which the organized system of nature may at last return: "The womb of Nature and perhaps her grave" (2.911). Robert M. Adams remarks, with some caution, that it is customary to cite as a possible source of this phrase Lucretius' "Omniparens, eadem rerum commune sepulchrum,"[12] although in Lucretius this refers to the earth. But sublime as it is, the phrase "the womb of Nature and perhaps her grave" sorts ill with the notion of creation as the act of God alone, as a decision, not a process. Yet this parental and, more specifically, maternal chaos recalls the words from the invocation to *Paradise Lost*, where Milton addresses the Spirit, the Holy Ghost, as that part of divinity which impregnated chaos:

> Thou from the first
> Wast present and with mighty wings outspread
> Dove-like sat'st brooding on the vast abyss
> And mad'st it pregnant.
>
> ~ *Paradise Lost 1.19–22*

The idea of a fertile and feminine chaos capable, if not of spontaneous generation, then at least of having its own proper generative power is recalled in the Creation narrative of book seven, partly to erase the impression of an independent principle given in the passage just cited. In book seven, the generative power within chaos is "infused" from without, from the Spirit:

> On the wat'ry calm
> His brooding wings the Spirit of God outspread
> And vital virtue infused and vital warmth
> Throughout the fluid mass.
>
> ~ *Paradise Lost 7.234–237*

Rogers and Schwartz differ on the status of chaos itself but not on what is brought from it. Milton's chaos is the origin of that "formless mass," "material mold" (3.708–709), "first matter" (5.472), and "Matter unformed and void" (7.233) out of which the Son creates the universe and all the creatures in it. At the instant when Creation begins, this "Matter unformed" is in a womb again, as "the world unborn" (7.220).

~ But Milton's chaos is also the "wasteful deep" (an appropriation of a Homeric epithet of the sea), the "monstrous sight" of which is disclosed when the crystal wall of heaven opens, rolling inward so that the rebel angels may be expelled. The sight causes the rebel angels to recoil for a moment in horror: "but far worse / Urged them behind" (6.863–864). Chaos is the "wild anarchy" (6.873) that is somehow multiplied by ten when the rebel angels fall through it, when heaven, as Milton says, in a wonderful phrase, is "ruining from Heav'n" (6.868).[13]

When the Son stands at the open gates of heaven, "on Heav'nly ground" (7.210), facing "the vast immeasurable abyss" (7.211) of chaos, it is

> Outrageous as a sea, dark, wasteful, wild,
> Up from the bottom turned by furious winds
> And surging waves as mountains to assault
> Heav'n's heighth and with the center mix the pole.
>   ☞ *Paradise Lost 7.212–215*

We might worry about that "bottom," incidentally. How can an immeasurable abyss (*byssos*, "bottom"; *a + byssos*, "without bottom") have a bottom? This bottom belongs to the vehicle of the simile, to what chaos is being compared to, not to what chaos is. Chaos is being compared to the most turbulent phenomenon visible on earth: the sea. (We might now compare chaos to the violent turbulence at the center of a star.) In referring to the bottom of this sea, Milton is thinking of a groundswell, as in the English Channel, or the Hecate Strait, where the height, pitch, violence, and frequency of the waves is increased by the rebounding effect of the shallow sea floor: "Up from the bottom turned." We note also in this passage that the waves are like mountains. The waves of chaos surge like mountains that threaten—or the mountains would threaten if they *were* waves—to tear the universe apart, mixing its very center with its poles, its extremities. If waves are like mountains, mountains can be like waves. As I suggested earlier, Milton saw such giant waves of rock when he crossed the alps, traveling north from Milan to Geneva. What if those waves were in motion so that their frozen energy were released? They would mix the center of the earth with its poles.

This is the same chaos that the Son commands to be silent and at peace: "Your discord end!" (7.217). He means the discord between the waves, which struggle upward out of the deep, and deepness, or steepness itself (playing on Latin and Greek epithets of the sea, and of chaos, which mean both high, deep, and steep). This is a thought to hold onto in a slippery place: that chaos is steepness. But it is not quite Milton's thought here, although it hovers nearby whenever he is speaking of chaos. Once the Son speaks to chaos, or rather to the waves and to the deep, he launches out from the gates of heaven and rides on the wings of the cherubim "Far into chaos and the world unborn" (7.220).

In the next half verse the causative force of the preposition "For" is unclear: "For chaos heard his voice" (7.221). Are we to understand what is not actually said, that the outrageous sea became calm, so that the Creator *could* ride "Far into Chaos"? Is that the consequence of this "For"? Or does the consequence of "For" immediately follow:

> For Chaos heard his voice. Him all his train
> Followed in bright procession to behold
> Creation and the wonders of His might.
> ⁓ *Paradise Lost 7.221–723*

Whether a consequence follows from or precedes something else is a common uncertainty in *Paradise Lost* and is not made any less so by the many pronouns with uncertain antecedents, especially the pronoun *him*. Most readers will at first take the "Him" of "Him all his train" to refer to Chaos instead of the Son. They will do so especially if they are reading an edition sequaciously punctuated after those of 1667 and 1674, in which "him" is preceded by a colon: "For Chaos heard his voice: him all his train / Followed in bright procession to behold / Creation" (7.221–222).

We initially suppose that this is Chaos's train, even if Orcus, Ades, Demogorgon, Rumor, Chance, Tumult, Confusion, Discord, and, last but far from least, "sable-vested Night" (2.962–967) hardly make a "bright procession" (7.222). We have, for a moment, a baroque procession of Chaos and his train worthy of Luca Giordano's allegorical ceiling in the Palazzo Medici-Riccardi. Milton's dark figures seem suddenly to have been made "bright," joyfully astonished at the moment of Creation and rising from the deep to watch the Son convert the deep into something other. This moment is *perhaps* corrected by the second pronoun, "His"—"Him all his train / Followed in bright procession to behold / Creation and the wonders of *His* might"—which we are likely to assume has the same antecedent as the first pronoun, "Him." But this moment of misreading is never definitively canceled. I mean that it remains possible grammatically, and it also remains more natural rhetorically, for the "Him" to refer to Chaos and the "His" to refer to the Son: Chaos with all his train came to behold Creation and the wonders of the Son's might. Grammar and rhetoric allow Chaos to be present as an observer and even encourage our reading this way; nor can logic alone cancel this vision, although common sense might. On reflection, we may conclude that Milton's meaning is that the "bright procession" is composed of the angels who make up the Son's "train," not of the dark, dazzling followers of Chaos.

 I HAVE ALREADY cited part of the passage on chaos that is most important to any attempt to understand chaos as a consistent cosmological concept. I mean the one immediately following the moment when God the Father ordains Creation and sends the Son, the Word, accompanied by the Spirit, or divine power ("might"), to effect what he ordains:

> And thou my Word, begotten Son, by Thee
> This I perform: speak Thou and be it done!
> My overshadowing Spirit and might with Thee
> I send along: ride forth and bid the deep
> Within appointed bounds be Heav'n and Earth!
> ⁓ *Paradise Lost* 7.163–167

The lines that follow, perhaps the most difficult ones in *Paradise Lost*, begin as an explanation of what is meant by "deep." When God explains himself we are reminded of Byron's description of Coleridge "Explaining metaphysics to the nation— / I wish he would explain his Explanation." The Son has been told to "bid the deep" to do something, and in line 68 we begin to hear why this deep is "boundless": "Boundless the deep because. . . ." These lines are therefore the closest we come in *Paradise Lost* to a formal definition (not a mere physical description, as in book two) of chaos. But within two verses the Father appears to be speaking not of the deep but of himself: "Though I uncircumscribed Myself retire."

> Boundless the deep because I am who fill
> Infinitude, nor vacuous the space
> (Though I uncircumscribed Myself retire

> And put not forth My goodness which is free
> To act or not): necessity and chance
> Approach not Me, and what I will is fate.
>
> ~ *Paradise Lost 7.168–173*

As I mentioned earlier, we are given here a metaphysical history of chaos: it is the substance that was left behind when God retired from infinitude, now abandoned to those two things which have nothing to do with freedom: necessity and chance. Any free decision and act of God's (and all his decisions and acts are free) is *goodness* itself, goodness creating, like grace abounding.

The concessive clause beginning "Though I" bears on the forces of necessity and chance. Although chaos is abandoned to necessity and chance, and although this abandoned substance of chaos was formerly the substance of God—and although God still has such substance in him—God is qualitatively different from his body because his actions are entirely free. Necessity and chance do not come near God's acts or influence them. (Necessity and chance do affect our actions, as they limit our bodies.) What makes chaos *chaos* is not that picturesque mêlée of hot, cold, moist, and dry which we have seen in book two but rather the dual yet contradictory agency of necessity and chance.

This dual yet contradictory agency is already suggested in the passage in book two in which the principles of chaos are first exposed:

> Chaos umpire sits
> And by decision more embroils the fray
> By which he reigns. Next him high arbiter
> Chance governs all.
>
> ~ *Paradise Lost 2.907–910*

The king, Chaos, as *umpire* (OF *nonper,* "not equal," related to L *arbiter*) seems here to hold the position of necessity, since necessity provides the constraints within which the operations of chance take place. (If something rolls off the table by chance, it will, by necessity, fall. But it will by necessity fall down, not, by chance, up. Chance bows to necessity.) Chance, therefore, although a "high arbiter" who "governs all," sits "next" to Necessity, which is here a name for Chaos. The "strong rebuff" of that "tumultuous cloud," which "hurries" Satan "as many miles aloft," encounters Satan at that moment by "ill chance." But both that "vast vacuity" into which Satan falls (and into which he might, by chance, have been falling yet), and the "strong rebuff" that blasts him out again and sets him on his way, are necessary forces that chance cannot change.

We meet then an interesting conclusion at this stage of our journey "o'er bog or steep, through straight, rough, dense, or rare": to the extent that necessity and chance play a part in human affairs, in our individual lives as well as in history, chaos is present among us, not excluded beyond the walls of the created universe. Why then do we not see more of chaos in the created universe? Perhaps we do not because within the created universe chaos is a subjective, not an objective, phenomenon. In our experience, chaos is the presence of choices before any choice is made.

ॐ WE PERHAPS DO SEE chaos in some part of the historical events that will take place in the created universe, in particular events having to do with the technology of war. When Sin and Death build their bridge "by wond'rous art / Pontifical" (10.312–313) they shoal together the lumpy raging substance of chaos and harden it to make their "mole": "Deep to the roots of Hell, the gathered beach / They fastened and the mole immense wrought on" (10.299–300). Here, the "mole" is not Ovid's undigested mass but a military structure, the foundation, or *moles*, for a bridge of the kind Caesar describes in the *De bello civili*.[14] The ocean metaphor continues to hold Milton's imagination— he describes Sin and Death "Hov'ring upon the water" (10.285)—but he uses the semi-frozen ice pack at the pole for his simile because it is not entirely solid or liquid:

> Then both from out Hell gates into the waste
> Wide anarchy of chaos damp and dark
> Flew diverse and with pow'r (their pow'r was great)
> Hov'ring upon the waters. What they met
> Solid or slimy as in raging sea
> Tossed up and down together crowded drove
> From each side shoaling towards the mouth of Hell,
> As when two polar winds blowing adverse
> Upon the Cronian sea together drive
> Mountains of ice that stop th' imagined way

Beyond Petsora eastward to the rich
Cathayan coast. The aggregated soil
Death with his mace petrific, cold and dry,
As with a trident smote and fixed as firm
As Delos floating once. The rest his look
Bound with Gorgonian rigor not to move
And with asphaltic slime.

ᴖ *Paradise Lost 10.282–298*

Apart from such constructions and the "bloody fray" (11.651) they lead to, I see little evocation of chaos in the historical books of *Paradise Lost*, books eleven and twelve, except perhaps in the physical effects of the Flood, in particular the fate of the Mount of Paradise, which is torn from its foundations and washed down the Euphrates to the Arabian gulf, an island buried in guano, "The haunt of seals and orcs and sea-mews' clang" (11.835). That wonderful word "clang," which is Homer's word for the racket of large flocks of birds, is an acoustic chaos that reverberates for us from the noise of chaos itself.

But Milton isn't interested in chaos in history. When he thinks of history, he thinks of the dialectic of sin and providence and of the condition of liberty as it is subject to the first of these and fostered by the second. Where Milton does see chaos, as I have said, is in military conflict, which is best shown in book six: the "ruinous assault / And inextinguishable rage" (6.216–217) of the war among the angels in heaven and, more terrible still, the confrontation of Michael and Satan, which is compared to "two planets rushing from aspéct malign / Of fiercest opposition in mid-sky" so that their "jarring spheres" are "confounded," crushed together (6.313–315). Milton says that their meeting might be compared to this only if we recognize how small that collision would be in comparison to the collision of angels:

such as (to set forth
Great things by small) if, nature's concord broke,
Among the constellations war were sprung.

ᴖ *Paradise Lost 6.310–312*

This possibility—of nature being torn apart from within when constellations make war—has been raised once before in the narrative (although later in the time scheme of the epic), when Satan is confronted by Michael at the conclusion of book four. Satan and Michael are not then in heaven but inside the created universe.

By the portent of the scales God prevents Satan and Michael from fighting. For if they were to fight, the shock of their encounter would tear the cosmos open, allowing chaos to recapture its domain. So, at least, the passage suggests when Milton speaks of the elements going "to wrack." Moreover, the sign by which such ruin is prevented is the sign of the scales, that is, of the Creation, when God "weighed the mountains in scales, and the hills in a balance" (Isaiah 40:12):

> Now dreadful deeds
> Might have ensued. Nor only Paradise
> In this commotion but the starry cope
> Of heav'n perhaps or all the elements
> At least had gone to wrack, disturbed and torn
> With violence of this conflict, had not soon
> Th' Eternal to prevent such horrid fray
> Hung forth in heav'n his golden scales, yet seen
> Betwixt Astraea and the Scorpion sign,
> Wherein all things created first He weighed
> (The pendulous round earth with balanced air
> In counterpoise) now ponders all events,
> Battles and realms.
>   ‿ *Paradise Lost 4.990–1002*

Here it is apparent that chaos is neither a generative principle nor an actively hostile force on Satan's side. It is what we commonly think of chaos being: the opposite of cosmos.

‿ IT APPEARS THEN that chaos in *Paradise Lost* is finally—after the king himself, "the power of that place," has disappeared roaring and the place itself has served its purpose in the story—a cosmological concept that is meant to stand in a dialectical relation to Creation, whether or not it can actually do so. Creation, as it is recounted in book seven, is the great positive event of Milton's epic, the counterpart and development of the living splendor of Achilles' shield, and especially of the dance represented on that shield. From an ethical point of view also, Creation is the fundamental thing in this poem, the recognition that one is created, that one has a Creator, and the feeling of bottomless gratitude (for it seems to go all the way down in the self) for being created. Even Satan sees that gratitude is endless.

It will therefore be necessary to understand Milton's chaos dialectically, by considering creation more closely. For Milton, creation in the most radical sense is not an objective act, like fashioning an oar. Creation is originally a subjective decision, like *deciding* to fashion the oar: "the oar that pulls / against the wave / and with the wave / is everything."[15] Chaos is therefore everything in the objective world, in history as well as in nature, that remains undecided, untouched by the creative impulse to change. Chaos is every situation that is left to develop on its own without our decisive intervention. For the angels in heaven, such an intervention is limited (or so it seems to us) to praise, although for Milton, giving praise musically is the most sublimely creative thing one can do. Small wonder Satan's favorite jest at the loyal angels' expense is that they are minstrels. Praising is creative because it is not just praise but the decision to praise: it is praise as intervention, the angels' spontaneous impulse to transform eternity from within, to make it into song. In the historical world such an intervention, the counterpart of what in heaven is praise, takes the form of struggle and work for the purpose of transforming the world. Creating is making decisions where nothing was decided before.

If this conclusion about creation and creativity is acceptable, however, then there must be an aspect to chaos that we do not see in *Paradise Lost:* indecisive subjectivity, mental blankness, a region in which hallucinations appear and are dismissed and where the mind cleanses itself, to cite Ammons again, of its "illusionary ways." We see the landscape of indecisive subjectivity in the desert of *Paradise Regained.* There, all decisions are at once hallucinatory and possible and are held in suspense. The desert is the scene of an inner moral chaos where a decision must be made, even if it is the decision to refuse to decide. When, ignoring the desert for a moment, Christ "descends" into himself, into the subjectivity of memory, he is only changing mental landscapes in himself. That is why the action of the poem seems to occur in a place to which Christ gives only a part of his attention. The sublime, objective chaos of *Paradise Lost,* that violent and immeasurable abyss, becomes, in *Paradise Regained,* an inner desert. There, the severest test occurs just before a decision is made: "Now enter and begin to save mankind" (*PR* 4.635).

God's Body

CONCEPT AND METAPHOR

*T*HERE ARE FEW POETS, even great poets, whose metaphysical conclusions about ultimate reality we have to take seriously if we wish to understand these poets at all. Milton is one of them. Living in a time of bold and original thought, Milton seems to have felt it to be a matter of course that a great poet should have a fully articulated philosophical system, complete with a logic, a metaphysics, an anthropology, a theology, and a theory of history. I shall turn shortly to some other great epic poets for counterexamples, poets whose metaphysical conclusions, such as they are, we do not have to take all that seriously. For the present, however, and at the risk of some obscurity, I want to try to summarize what Milton's are. The metaphysical conclusions to which I refer, and which I have said we have to take seriously if we are to understand Milton at all, follow from what has been called his monist materialism, the conviction that everything is matter. Milton's philosophical position, as has been recognized for some time, bears a striking resemblance to that of his near contemporary Spinoza, who held that there is only one substance in reality, that this substance is infinite, and that it is God.[1] But Milton and Spinoza came from opposite directions to their common conviction that spirit and matter are not two distinct things but are one and the same. In general, philosophical systems develop either from the outside in or from the inside out: from speculations about the universe to theories about man, or from

speculations about man to theories of the universe; and Milton, as perhaps befits a poet, followed the latter course. Milton did not decide
how the cosmos is put together and then follow through consistently
with a theory of humanity that fits into that cosmos. He decided first,
from scripture, and from his own experience as a poet, what he thought
about Man. Only then did Milton determine, under the guidance of
logic, what he thought about the universe. We might say that he was an
anthropic rather than a *cosmological* thinker.[2]

On the subject of human nature, Milton held that man is not "made
up and framed of two distinct and different natures, as of soul and body,
but that the whole man is soul, and the soul man, that is to say, a body,
or substance."[3] From this notion of Man Milton's metaphysical conclusions were derived. They are as follows: that ultimate reality is one divine substance extending into infinity; that when God withdraws himself from infinity into one place, heaven, he leaves behind a portion of
his own substance, so that space remains full; and that this substance is
matter in the state of chaos.

Milton proceeds thence to his interpretation of the opening chapter
of Genesis, the account of Creation. The universe—the "world," as it
was called in Milton's time—is made by the Son of God, who creates
everything from the alienated substance of the Father. That is what the
phrase "the heaven and the earth" in the opening verse of Genesis
means: the alienated substance of God. The whole verse is one simple
declarative sentence: "In the beginning God created the heaven and
the earth." For Milton this means that the first thing that ever happened was that God, a substance extending to infinity, threw a part of
himself out of himself by contracting, or withdrawing into one place. A
portion of this extruded portion of God was heaven, the place into
which God has withdrawn; and the other portion, "earth," was chaotic matter, which in verse two is called "the deep": "And the earth
was without form, and void; and darkness was upon the face of the
deep. And the Spirit of God moved upon the face of the waters." This
"Spirit" is for Milton the power of God breathed out from the place
where his body now is. But the breath of his spirit, when it speaks, becomes God's Word; and the Word is a person distinct from God the
Father; the Word is God's Son. It is the Son who gives the series of familiar commands that we know as the work of Creation, beginning
with the command in Genesis 4: "And God said, Let there be light: and

there was light." You have perhaps noticed that I seem to have drifted in my account of Milton's system from metaphysics to theology, that is, from an account of ultimate being to an account of the nature and purpose of God. But an important part of what I wish to assert in what follows is that the distinction of metaphysics from theology cannot be rigorously maintained.

ॐ This may be apparent, for Milton at least, in my attempting to capture his entire system in the phrase "God's body." Everything that is is God's body. But it should be made clear at the outset that this phrase, which brings theology and metaphysics together, nevertheless contains an important division. It is a division, however, situated not in ultimate reality or in God but in two contrary actions of the human mind: conceiving, or grasping, and comparing, or releasing. Comparing, or *metaphor*, which means "carrying across," or transference, is more fundamentally an opening of the hand, a releasing of what has been grasped into the limitless realm of analogy. The notion of God's body is both a *concept*, something we can grasp but not imagine, and a *metaphor*, something we can imagine by releasing what we grasp and letting it fall into endless metaphorical change. As a concept, God's body is not a body at all but a substance that extends to infinity; infinite substance is something you can grasp with your mind, by logic, but it is not something you can see in your mind's eye. As a metaphor, God's body is an anthropomorphic image of a king on a throne, even if he is a king the angels themselves cannot see: "Dark with excessive bright thy skirts appear" (*PL* 3.380). You can see God in your mind's eye; but you know when you see him, as you know with all metaphors, that the luxury of seeing is paid at the expense of truth. The tension between the concept of God as a substance and the metaphor of God as a body is at the heart of the system of *Paradise Lost* because it is a system that is formed at the turbulent boundary between metaphysics and theology, between Milton's monist materialism and the Christian idea of God. Every critical problem for the study of the greatest epic poem since Homer flows from this problem of the tension between the conceptual and the metaphorical apprehension of God. And if this claim does not seem sufficiently broad, let me add that a problem so essential to Milton can hardly be irrelevant to the problem of poetry in general. Roman Jakobson famously held that all poetic imagery derives either from metaphor or from metonymy, from figures of similarity or figures of contiguity. I believe it is possible, however, to go deeper than this by supposing metonymy to be a special case of metaphor and by setting this enlarged category of the metaphorical over against the conceptual. If these hypotheses are accepted, then poetry can be seen to happen at an even deeper cognitive level than that at which figural language is patterned, the level at which there is continuous play between attention and comparison. Poetry happens in the clash between concepts and metaphors.

𝒮 IN MILTON'S GREAT predecessors in the epic form, metaphysical assumptions are present but do not bear centrally on what these poets want us to experience and know. The psycho-cosmology we are taught in the sixth book of Virgil's *Aeneid*, where the natural world is said to be leavened by immanent Mind, is sublimely expressed; and doubtless Virgil cared about it personally. But it is only a digression: what really counts for Virgil is the history of Rome, the course of which is determined by gods in whom, as a Stoic, Virgil did not believe. For the Stoics, the gods are no more than an allegory of the system of connections, of points of contact, between the World Soul and the elements of nature. Virgil's message, for he has one, is not metaphysical but moral: it is that the great founding events of history are accomplished by men who are pious and resolute, and that inevitably their achievements exact a high human cost. As to Homer, we cannot without danger of serious anachronism even speak of his having metaphysical conclusions, although he did have notions, images, or representations—it is hard to get just the right word for something so remote from us—about the body, the mind, the soul, the world, time, and fate. In any event, such things belong to Homer's culture, to Greece of the archaic age, and are not peculiar to him. Indeed, the list I have just given is the subtitle of a monumental work of scholarship on that culture, Richard Broxton Onians's *Origins of European Thought about the Body, the Mind, the Soul, the World, Time, and Fate*. Of Milton's other predecessors in the epic form, Ovid, Dante, and Tasso, only Dante's metaphysical conclusions have to be taken seriously if we are to understand him at all.

But Milton's great successor in the epic form, William Blake, is another such poet, one whose characters only really make sense in the aggregate, as parts of a metaphysical system. Blake is interesting to consider in this regard because, like Milton, he goes against the grain of Indo-European thought, which from the Vedas to Freud is governed by dualism. Monism appears in this tradition, of course, but it is always on the defensive. Like his near contemporary Bishop Berkeley, Blake is a metaphysical monist, someone who rejects the division of what is into two radicals—into spirit and matter, mind and body, divinity and humanity, idea and substance. But because monism is on the defensive in the Indo-European tradition, it asserts itself by reducing one of the two generally supported radicals to the other. Accordingly, Blake encloses the physical world within spirit, or, as he calls it, imagination; and the human body, as the fundamental imaginative form, is also the form of the world. As for the concept of matter, it is for Blake the crudest extrapolation from our experience of the five senses, which are themselves the crudest imaginable instrument of knowing. "The world," he said in one of his letters, "is all one continued vision of Fancy or Imagination." Or, as he said in *Jerusalem*, "All Things Exist in the Human Imagination."⁴ The Fall for Blake is the narrowing of the scope of imagination to the dimensions of time and space and to the evidence of the five senses, which he calls "the furrows of death": "The Visions of Eternity, by reason of narrowed perceptions, / Are become weak Visions of Time and Space, fix'd into furrows of death" (*Jerusalem*, plate 49, ll. 21–22). For Blake, everything is holy because everything is imagined.

Milton took the opposite view, believing in the truth of the senses, dimmed as they are by the Fall, and in the reality of the material world as the only reality there is, a world formed into various degrees of substance, including life and what we call "spirit," from "one first matter all." Milton's notion of spirit is not the dualistic opposite of matter but matter's most sublime realization, the perfume of Creation. In the fifth book of the poem, the angel Raphael explains to Adam that angels eat as humans do because spiritual beings need material sustenance: their bodies are real bodies, digesting with what the angel calls "concoctive heat." The explanation brings forth a total picture of the universe that recalls the symbol of the cosmic tree—here, a growing flower—whose roots are in primordial chaos and whose crown is in heaven, breathing odorous spirits, or angels.

> O Adam! one Almighty is, from whom
> All things proceed and up to Him return
> If not depraved from good, created all
> Such to perfection, one first matter all
> Endued with various forms, various degrees
> Of substance and in things that live of life,
> But more refined, more spirituous and pure
> As nearer to Him placed or nearer tending,
> Each in their several active spheres assigned
> Till body up to spirit work in bounds
> Proportioned to each kind. So from the root
> Springs lighter the green stalk, from thence the leaves
> More airy, last the bright consummate flower
> Spirits odorous breathes.
>
> *Paradise Lost 5.469–482*

One sees why Coleridge quoted this in the thirteenth chapter of the *Biographia Literaria*, "On the Esemplastic Imagination," the word "esemplastic" meaning "molded into one": Milton has taken all degrees and divisions in the universe, including the fundamental one between matter and spirit, and molded them into one "first matter": spirit is to matter as fragrance is to flower, being physically continuous with it.

Blake chastises the author of *Paradise Lost* for his monist materialism, which he sees as a "fall" into the material world that is as grave and gross as Adam's original sin—and indeed a continuation of that sin. But Blake also saw in Milton a spiritual ally because Milton was at least a monist like him. To the religious hypocrite who thinks of the body as inherently evil, and who believes God to be everything the body is *not*, Blake preferred a man who had the obstinacy to think about the body of God.

The word *body* bears no single sense: it is an articulate, living structure, an organism; it is a quality of wine, richness; and it is a term in seventeenth-century physics meaning mass, especially mass considered as a totality, as in Hobbes's *De Corpore*. Now, the thought that everything is "body" is certainly a metaphysical conclusion; it is a "concept," or *Begriff*, in the Hegelian sense of that term, a "grasping" (*greifen*) of the whole in a single act of thought. But the thought of the whole universe as *a* body is also a metaphor, an act of transference by which something conceived, that is, something mentally grasped but not seen, is put into something we can see. To take the example of modern cosmology, we can grasp in thought the unimaginable concept of the origin of the universe, but to see it we need the metaphor of an explosion. Similarly, we can grasp the concept of an infinite universe that is filled up with matter; but we cannot picture it. When, however, we take this unimaginable concept of an infinite substance and think of it instead as a body, when we picture a body, we are making a metaphor. But the metaphor is obviously not true to the concept: bodies are by nature bounded, not infinite, and are always engaged with what lies outside them, including other bodies, as of course infinite substance cannot be. When, therefore, we think of the universe as the infinite body of God, we are twisting together two distinct and at least partly incompatible mental acts, conceiving and comparing.

I claimed at the outset that this concept of the totality of being as body is essential to understanding Milton as no single concept is to understanding Homer or Virgil: Homer does not seem to have concepts, and Virgil does not care enough about them. Virgil cares about Aeneas, Ascanius, Dido, and Turnus much more than he cares about the World Soul. Homer cares about Achilles and Hector, about Andromache and Priam, and no understanding of his cosmology—of how deep Tartarus is, for example, or how the ocean flows in a circle—will improve our aesthetic and emotional response to that care. But in *Paradise Lost* we do not care so much about Adam and Eve as characters until perhaps after their fall, more than two-thirds of the way through the poem, in the brief space between the concept of the cosmos and the concept of history, when they appear to us as real people. Adam and Eve are not characters until two-thirds of the way through the poem because before that they have little to accomplish and nothing to endure. We think about them not dramatically but, as it were, environmentally. Adam and Eve are parts of a system of metaphysical conclusions about ultimate reality which, to repeat, we have to take seriously if we are to understand Milton at all.

꙳ WHAT IS MEANT BY that admittedly ample phrase "metaphysical conclusions"? For Hume, any volume of metaphysics should be committed to the flames, "for it can contain nothing but sophistry and illusion."[5] Even the friends of metaphysical inquiry in the Hegelian tradition, such as F. H. Bradley, would say that I mean questions about ultimate reality—about Being, time, appearance, substance, order, and so on—questions that are *not*—repeat, *not!*—questions about God. Being thus assertively distinguished from theology, metaphysics can address questions about ultimate reality without ever addressing the ultimate questions: Is there a God and what is he like? For example, is "he" male? Modern metaphysics will leave it to the credulous theologian to worry about a Father above, about mercy and love and sacrifice and incarnation: they are instead pursuing scientific inquiry, which does not involve them in myth. Of course, there are those who would say that the pseudoscientific pretensions seen in that arrogant prefix *meta-* are nothing other than myth. Metaphysics is nothing more than the skeletal remains of what is embodied in myth; and it was for this reason that Anatole France described metaphysics as "une mythologie blanche," a "white mythology," the title of Jacques Derrida's remarkable discussion of the insinuating and ineradicable presence of metaphor in philosophical texts. Early on in the text we now call the *Metaphysics*, Aristotle says that there are three broad areas of knowledge, of which metaphysics is the highest. There is the mathematical, the physical, and what came to be called the "metaphysical," but which Aristotle calls "theological." While mathematics studies numbers and geometric forms, things that are free from change but that lack independent being, physics studies things that have independent being but are subject to change. Only metaphysics studies things that are free from the respective defects of mathematics and physics: things that are both changeless and independently existing. These things were associated with the heavens above the sphere of the moon, where the unchanging, regular, repetitive motions of the planets and the stars are observable from earth. For Aristotle, and for medieval and Renaissance gazers, looking at the heavens was like looking at mathematics embodied. But Aristotle called this branch of knowledge "theology," believing its most proper subject to be the gods, or to be God. Before any other metaphysical object, God exists and is above change, for he is pure Being, the unchanging origin of change, the unmoved mover.

This identification of metaphysics with theology, which we have since separated, is an identification I believe it is necessary to recover if we are to understand Milton. I suspect we must recover it, too, if we are really to understand metaphysics, but that is another story, and not one I am qualified to tell. I proceed therefore to *Paradise Lost*, where Milton's scandalous notion of God's body is both a concept, the concept of a substance that extends to infinity, and a metaphor, an anthropomorphic image of God as a body.

    ⌁ IN A FAMOUSLY OBSCURE passage of *Paradise Lost*, near the middle of the poem, Milton's God at last tells us something of himself. Because it is the only thing about his being that he ever tells us, it is worth our close attention. The rebel angels have been routed and expelled at the close of book six; and the poet turns from destruction to Creation, the Creation of the entire universe, or, as Milton calls it, the world. The Creation of the world, of earth, and of Man is to be undertaken by the Son, who is God's Word and his "effectual might." God puts his judgments into action through the agency of the Son. The occasion for the disclosure I referred to is God's glossing the noun "deep," which he uses when he asks the Son "to bid the deep / Within appointed bounds be heaven and earth." What is this "deep"? It is certainly based on the "steep Tartaros" of the archaic Greeks, as much as on the passage from Genesis mentioned earlier, and as we shall see the word resonates strongly with the English sense of *deep* as "the sea." But what God appears to think needs explaining first is the deep's boundlessness. Virgil's Tartarus is three times deeper than Homer's, which extends as far below the underworld as heaven extends above the earth. Milton takes this depth inflation as far as it can go when he has God say:

> Boundless the deep because I am who fill
> Infinitude, nor vacuous the space
> (Though I uncircumscribed Myself retire
> And put not forth My goodness which is free
> To act or not): necessity and chance
> Approach not Me, and what I will is fate.
>
>   *⌁ Paradise Lost 7.168–173*

"Boundless the deep because I am who fill / Infinitude, nor vacuous the space." It sounds as if a question has been asked to which "Boundless the deep because I am who fill Infinitude" is the answer. The question is not "What is the deep?" or "Where is the deep?" but "Why is it boundless?" Why? "Because I am who fill Infinitude." This is a mysterious answer. Milton is often difficult, but he is seldom mysterious; indeed, he is one of the least mysterious of poets, especially of religious poets. God's previous speeches in the poem are highly abstract, conceptually challenging, and perhaps, to a hostile ear, occasionally nonsensical. But they are meant to be clear, and they usually are. To such rigorous clarity this passage is the exception. It is rendered mysterious not least by its allusion, in the phrase "I am," to another occasion for question and answer, Exodus 3:14, when Moses sees or rather hears God in the burning bush on Mount Horeb and asks what name he should give to this deity when telling the children of Israel of him: "And God said unto Moses, I AM THAT I AM: and he said, Thus shalt thou say unto the children of Israel, I AM hath sent me unto you." I suppose that what is meant in Exodus is that all other gods are fantasies whereas this God exists, existence being the most important thing about him; and as a reminder of that fact he should be called simply "I AM." But Milton gives this metaphysical pronouncement an even more metaphysical meaning: not only is this god the only one that exists; this god is existence, or Being itself, without limit or bound—in Greek terms, "the all," *to pan*. But he is more than the *all* in any physical sense conceived of by pre-Socratics, as when Thales says *all* is water or Heraclitus that *all* is fire or Epicurus that *all* is atoms. God is not "it is"; God is "I AM," in the first-person singular. He is everything, in the physical sense of the pre-Socratics, but he is also a person. He is boundless, "uncircumscribed," but retired to one place, from which he sends his Son out into the deep, which is himself. He is a concept, the all, and a metaphor, the Father.

There is another mystery in these lines, although that is too strong a word for what I should call a textual crux. I mean the question whether the concessive clause "though I uncircumscribed Myself retire / and put not forth my goodness" should be attached to what goes before or to what comes after. Should it begin the sentence or end it? Here it is beginning the sentence:

> Boundless the deep because I am who fill
> Infinite, nor vacuous the space. [*full stop*]
> Though I uncircumscribed Myself retire

> And put not forth My goodness which is free
> To act or not, necessity and chance
> Approach not Me, and what I will is fate.

Now here it is ending the sentence:

> Boundless the deep because I am who fill
> Infinitude, nor vacuous the space
> (Though I uncircumscribed Myself retire
> And put not forth My goodness which is free
> To act or not). [*full stop*] Necessity and chance
> Approach not Me, and what I will is fate.

To what does that concessive concede? The usual pointing, as it appears in the two editions published in Milton's lifetime, and as it is given in Fowler, puts a full stop after "space." The phrase beginning with "though" begins a new sentence and concedes to what follows it: to the impossibility of necessity and chance approaching God. One of the earliest commentators (Zachary Pearce, quoted in the Todd edition) paraphrased it thus: "Though I, who am myself uncircumscribed, set bounds to my goodness, and do not exert it every where, yet neither Necessity nor Chance influence my actions."

While I have no textual evidence for proposing a change, this reading seems to me either banal or nonsensical: why should God be more subject to necessity and chance once he has retired? Necessity and chance are left to hold the field for a while in the chaos that God leaves behind when he retires to heaven. When the Son creates the world out of that chaos, the empire of necessity and chance will be diminished. It never occurs to us to think that necessity and chance might somehow approach and overwhelm God in his place of retirement, heaven, for they depend for their very existence on that retirement, that is, on the absence of God. Alternatively, the simple assertion by God that his will is fate is a fitting conclusion to his speech: "necessity and chance / Approach not me, and what I will is fate." This may be obvious, but its very obviousness is impressive. We hear it almost as a command, and even as an apotropaic performative, accomplishing by its very utterance the fending off of necessity and chance: "Approach me not, necessity and chance, for what I will, despite anything you can do, is certain to occur."

Let us see what happens when the concessive clause *follows* what it concedes: "nor vacuous the space, though I myself retire." What is being conceded to is space being not empty but filled up, full of stuff. I leave aside the question whether "infinitude" is like a container that can be filled, even by God, and whether space remains space, magnitude, when it is filled to infinity with God or with matter. The point is God's saying that space is not empty even when he retires from it, that is, when he stops filling it with his body and withdraws to one place, to heaven. With God gone from most of it, what fills this left-behind space? The answer, of course, is matter, which is the alienated substance of God. Matter is out there even if God does not put forth his "goodness," the Son, to create the universe or, as Milton calls it, the world. So when we read the passage with the "though"-clause modifying "space" the concept of matter emerges, whereas in the other reading, which puts a full stop after "space," matter does not appear. God says only that the deep is not empty because he fills it up, and when he withdraws to one place, he is not subject to necessity and chance.

One does not oppose such a well-attested reading lightly, or without very good cause. I believe the concept of matter to be so crucial to this moment, however, as to make an attempt at opposition worthwhile and at the very least instructive. Against the usual reading, therefore, I would oppose the following: on stylistic grounds it does not sound like Milton, who generally avoids front-loading subordinate clauses, and it sounds even less like Milton's God, whose syntax is always direct. And if the syntax is weak, the sense is no better: why should necessity and chance be more likely to approach God when he has retired to one place? It would make more sense for God to say that although he has retired from the deep, necessity and chance do not rule *there;* and indeed something like that is expected when we hear the opening subordinate clause: something about the *deep*, not about *God*.

The reading I have suggested, which assimilates the "though" clause to the vacuousness of space, gives the passage a complexity and fullness—a body, shall we say?—that the other totally lacks. Nor am I the first to suggest it. The Columbia edition silently emends the pointing by replacing the period after "space" with a comma. Already in the nineteenth century, David Masson replaced the period after "space"

with a comma and put a semicolon after "Infinitude," further emphasizing the concession to the vacuousness of space; he also put a period
after "free / To act or not," so that the sentence on necessity and
chance is split off in the way I have shown. These changes emphasize
the contrast between God's having withdrawn from the space and the
fact of the space remaining full:

> Nor vacuous the space
> Though I, uncircumscribed, myself retire,
> And put not forth my goodness, which is free
> To act or not.

In his notes to the passage, Masson says that God means this: "Chaos is
boundless because I am boundless who fill infinitude; nor is Chaos
empty of my presence, though I, in a manner hold myself retired from
it and inhabit more peculiarly Heaven." The only point on which Masson appears to err is in supposing that God is talking about his *presence*
instead of a matter that belongs to his body but no longer belongs to
his presence. A. S. P. Woodhouse expresses it another way, by dividing
God's presence into active and passive: "The matter in its disordered
state is indeed in God's presence, but not in his *active* presence. He has
not chosen to put forth as yet his creative power, but, retired within
himself, has voluntarily left the matter a prey to necessity or chance."[6] I
believe that my difference from Woodhouse on this point is merely ter-
minological: I am inclined to separate *presence* from *substance* here, or
from what I have called "alienated substance": God's presence does not
fill chaos, but his former substance does.

Let me then summarize by paraphrasing these verses again: "The
deep is boundless because I fill infinity. When I withdraw from the
deep and withhold my goodness, the space left behind is not empty. It
is full of stuff, matter. Although this matter was once part of me, it no
longer is and therefore is no longer altogether good (though it is not
evil, either). I can make it good by sending my goodness into it, in the
person of the Son, or I can decide not to: I am perfectly free to do either. Necessity and chance now rule over matter, but not over me, so
the fate of everything remains in my hands. Do not suppose that my
withdrawing myself in any way limits my power. My being, my presence, is now circumscribed. But my will remains boundless. I am here,
but my power is everywhere."

The principal virtue of this reading is that it brings forth the concept of matter from which the other satisfying complexities of the passage arise. But so far we have not been able to see it. I have been talking about this chaotic matter as a pure concept, even though matter is in what God calls the "deep," which reminds one of the opening of Genesis, of *Tehōm*, and of the oceanic waters on the dark face of which the "Spirit of God moved." As readers of the poem, we are able to see this matter as Milton wants us to see it when the poet describes the abyss. Accompanied by a multitude of angels in winged chariots, "Celestial equipage," the Son has gone out the gates of heaven for the purpose of creating "new worlds" and pauses for a moment on the edge of the abyss. We see it as they do, through their eyes, as it were. And after what the Father has said, we do not expect the abyss to be empty like the classical one, a space through which the overthrown devils can fall. We expect the abyss to be full, like a sea:

> Heav'n opened wide
> Her ever-during gates, harmonious sound
> On golden hinges moving, to let forth
> The King of Glory in his powerful Word
> And Spirit coming to create new worlds.
> On Heav'nly ground they stood and from the shore
> They viewed the vast immeasurable abyss
> Outrageous as a sea, dark, wasteful, wild,
> Up from the bottom turned by furious winds
> And surging waves as mountains to assault
> Heav'n's heighth and with the center mix the pole.
>   "Silence, ye troubled waves and thou, deep, peace!"
> Said then th' Omnific Word, "Your discord end!"
>   ⤳ *Paradise Lost 7.205–217*

The abyss is full of matter, which in its turbulence is figuratively *compared* to a sea; and by the time the abyss is commanded to silence, the comparison has become a metaphor we know to have been purchased, as all metaphors are, at the expense of the truth. For what the Son and the angels look out on is not at all other to them, as the sea is other to us; it is the alienated substance of God, the very same substance out of which they are made. A metaphor more true to the concept would be a heaving mountain of flesh.

᷒ ONE OF THE VERY earliest theological questions the Christian Church had to settle is also a classic metaphysical question: What is the nature and the origin (if there is one) of matter? Has matter, as Plato and Aristotle thought, always existed? The classical Greek view of matter as eternal was supported by those philosophical Greek fathers Justin Martyr and Clement of Alexandria on the strength of a phrase in the Apocrypha (Wisdom of Solomon 11:17): "For thy Almighty hand, that made the world of matter without form *(ex amorphou hylēs)*, wanted not means to send among them a multitude of bears." If matter has always existed, how and by whom is the world to be made from this eternal substratum? The world will be made by that demiurgic God of the philosophers who imposes forms upon substance and who initiates motion while being unmoved himself. Behind this God, however, is a more ancient prototype of the god as a conqueror who overcomes a monster whose body is the world. If matter has always existed, it is almost inevitably evil.

If, however, matter has not always existed, where does it come from? There are only two places it *can* come from: either out of nothing or out of God. Altogether, we have three possibilities concerning the matter out of which God created the world: matter has existed forever; matter came out of nothing; matter came out of God. It is interesting that the need for something called *matter*, an underlying, undifferentiated substance, was not called into question: the system was a classically dualist one from the start. Milton did call this need into question, however, in *De Doctrina Christiana* when discussing the origin of matter. To make something, he says, always implies a preexisting substance, or matter. Therefore, to suppose that God created matter out of nothing is not evidence of his special power; it is mere nonsense. We can attribute special powers to God; but we cannot attribute to him powers that derive from our own intellectual confusion.

Let me say by way of digression that I believe it is Milton who is intellectually confused on this point. He supposes that the act of inaugurating Being can be understood on analogy to making a thing, an implement. In Heideggerean terms, such thinking forgets the ontological difference between Being and beings. It is illogical to ask what kind of being, or *thing*, Being in its totality is. And to ask how Being itself is fashioned or made is a derivative of this error. In this regard it is helpful to consider the word *creation* as opposed to making. The word, *creatio* and *creator*, giving us *creation*, was adopted into ecclesiastical Latin, and into the Vulgate Bible, from Roman law. The word was taken up by the church fathers precisely to avoid the mistake of supposing the establishing of everything to be at all like the making of a thing. In creating the world, God is less like the maker of a shoe, an artisan, than he is like the founder of a city—Romulus, for example, whom Lucan calls "creator huius urbis," the creator of this city. In addition to founding, *creation* means election to office. But in all cases it is rooted not in the concept of making but in that of decision. By such decisiveness God's creating the world is an act of divine will, not of divine skill. God does not fashion the world, like an artisan; God *decides* that this world shall be rather than not be. Another way to put this, although to do so brings us close to philosophical thinking again, is to say that God elects this world from the multitude of possible but inexistent worlds. Creation is thus an act not of God's power but of his will. By understanding the essence of Creation to lie in a decision, the problem of matter is largely circumvented.

༄ IF I AM RIGHT ABOUT the thinking behind the Christian fathers' adoption of the word *creation* for the first act of God, its brilliance consists in its transferring the terms of the problem of matter, of the substance from which the world is made, from metaphysics to law. To some this may seem to be merely evasive, a trick. But I believe it represents a deeper thinking through of the problem in terms that the metaphysics of the time—or perhaps of any time—could not provide. The legal view of Creation takes the problem of being back behind the question "How was it done?," which is really a question for physics, to the question "Why was it done?" The deepest metaphysical question we can ask is "Why is there something instead of nothing?" Milton does not have any especially original answer to this question; but Woodhouse was surely right when he said, "There is no tenet of orthodox belief to which Milton adheres more tenaciously than the voluntary character of the creative act."[7] When we remember that Milton was a poet who believed he was inspired by the muse who "deign[ed] her nightly visitation unimplored," but only when she felt like it, rather late in his life and then only between the autumn and spring equinoxes, we realize it took some courage for Milton to believe so tenaciously in the voluntary character of the creative act. God creates substance by letting it go out of himself; God creates the world by letting the world go out of the possession of his mind, where it is held as a concept. Milton created the language of *Paradise Lost* by letting the language out of himself, into the external realm of figurative, rhythmical expression. As he composed, the primordial substance Milton drew out of himself was everything he had learned in the past. What is voluntary for the poet, as it is for God, is a kind of release, a letting go.

☙ I HAVE TRIED TO SHOW how the Christian fathers could think about Creation without thinking about matter, that phantasmatic "something we know not what" (Locke) of Greek ratiocination. It must now be considered what is to be done with the concept of matter when that concept is supposed to be inevitable. We saw that there are three possibilities. First, if matter has existed forever, it is originally and essentially, that is, in its *archē*, independent of God. It can thus be a power opposed to God in a struggle for dominance that God need not necessarily win. Matter becomes a gnostic force, a dark side of the cosmos controlled by its own animate demon who is Evil itself. Like Marduk slaying the sea goddess Tiamat or Mithras slaying the bull, God conquers matter and makes a world from what he has subdued: the sea is the blood of the monster and the mountains are its bones. We can catch resonances of this monster in the description of the abyss in the passage just cited: "Outrageous as a sea, dark, wasteful, wild." Obviously, this gnosticism will not do. The independence of matter diminishes the majesty of God, who has to fight to survive, and promotes an un-Christian contempt for the body, a contempt even of suffering and infirmity as manifestations of evil rather than as conditions to be relieved by charity and love.

The second possibility is that God gets this original matter out of himself, as an *excrement*, a word the etymological meaning of which is something that grows out of something else. Such matter must be the opposite of matter that has existed forever: it must be fundamentally, because originally, good. The third possibility, which is the one that Christian theology chose, is that matter came out of nothing, *ex nihilo*. Note that creation out of nothing is consistent with the legal sense of the word *creation*. Creation out of nothing is a disguised way of speaking of the Creation as a decision rather than as any physical event. But it should be added that Christianity favored creation out of nothing because the theologians wanted the resulting matter to be neither evil nor good but strictly neutral; and I think Milton tried hard to obtain this neutrality. To put it technically, I think Milton's concept of matter was hylozoic but not pantheistic: he did not think as a pantheist does, that God is "in" everything, animating matter; but he did think that all matter is in some sense alive, striving to return to its origin in God. He thought this even if he distinguishes, in Raphael's speech, between matter that is not, and matter that is, "indued" with life (5.473–475). For in the speech just preceding this one, Raphael in effect gives us Milton's concept of matter:

> For know whatever was created needs
> To be sustained and fed. Of elements
> The grosser feeds the purer: Earth the Sea,
> Earth and the Sea feed Air, the Air those Fires
> Ethereal and as lowest first the Moon. . .
>
> The Sun that light imparts to all receives
> From all his alimental recompense
> In humid exhalations and at ev'n
> Sups with the Ocean.
>   *Paradise Lost 5.414–418 and 423–426*

Now, from a traditional standpoint, the concept of matter as originating in God diminishes God and destroys the sacraments. It destroys the sacraments by valuing every bodily impulse, and every bodily process, as holy: if everything is sacred, nothing is. Material things are supposed to become sacred by an act of divine will, in miracles and relics, for example, and especially in the celebration of the mass, which makes bread and wine holy. We see how Milton's protestant opposition to all these sacralizing acts was consistent with his monist materialism: everything is holy, unless infected by sin, which, like Creation, begins in decision.

Let us now summarize the alternatives that the Christian fathers rejected and condemned. On the one hand, an independent, uncreated matter, which has existed forever, leads to a transcendental longing for escape into spirit, an uncharitable otherworldliness that is contemptuous of nature, of the body, and of suffering. On the other hand, a wholly dependent, divine matter leads to nature worship, to body worship, and to the conviction that both suffering and sin, the circumstances of the Fall, are not so serious: everything is holy. The Christian fathers saw two kinds of paganism hidden in these concepts of matter and with the potential to infect Christian belief: the first gives us a radical dualism and a transcendent spirituality that could take no account of the material world. This dualism is essentially Neoplatonic. The second gives us a monism that reduces God to nature and that sees minor divinities in everything, in sacred groves with their genii, in streams with their nymphs, in the stars and the ocean; it is a monism that takes so much account of the material world as to deny that there is any other. More important, it denies history. This second kind of paganism, which is close to archaic thought, and which survived in the country religions of the late Roman Empire, bears more than a casual resemblance to Milton's cosmology before the fall, where nature is populated with spirits, where the physical world is a growing totality, like the world tree, and where the elements and phenomena of nature, the sun and the sea, for example, nourish each other by continual exchange or, as Milton calls it, "alimental recompense" (5.424). Most important, it is a monist cosmology that denies the existence of spirit, if by *spirit* we mean a substance that is entirely distinct from body, or matter.

Milton is sufficiently resolute about this to apply it to God. Milton's problem, therefore, is not the usual dualist one of explaining how God becomes involved in the material world—or, for that matter, how angels become involved in the material world, as Aquinas's angels do by putting on bodies of compressed air. Milton's problem is to explain how the Creator is in any fundamental way separate from what he creates.

This problem of separation may seem less intractable to authors than to theologians, for authors have to create otherness, the work of art, from the dark materials of their own lives. I presume that to be the meaning of the figure of the author in *Finnegans Wake*, Shem the Penman, who writes on his own body with his own excrement. Similarly, one feels that the gigantic erudition of *Paradise Lost* is something Milton felt he had to expel from his person, from the lifelong digestive assimilation to himself of all previous literary culture. Left behind after this act of expulsion were the materials of his creative project—his poetic diction, mostly—violently crushed and ready to be given new form.

From a theological standpoint, however, we may easily perceive why the third possibility envisioned by the fathers of the church, creation of matter out of nothing, was preferred. Creation *ex nihilo* was indeed the only possibility consistent with the needs of a theology that had to assert at once the transcendence of God and his concern for human history. God's transcendent power and his love of mankind may thus be expressed eminently in the Creation and the Incarnation, respectively. At the same time, the creation of matter out of nothing may be thought to preserve together human responsibility and freedom. For if the matter of our bodies originates in nothingness, it is morally neutral; it neither provides an excuse for the abandoned sexual indulgences of the gnostic sects—if your body is totally evil, why try to rein in its impulses?—nor a means of evading the freedom to put your bodies at risk in a good cause. Most important, a morally neutral matter, created from nothing, allows us to understand why the body is good, why, in Paul's words, the Lord is for the body and the body is for the Lord (1 Cor. 6: 13). The body is good not because it is of the same substance as God but because it is created by God, formed by God's will, and thus manifesting good in action. The body represents a decision of God.

It must now be asked whether the theological dangers of materialist monism, which I have just outlined, are avoided by Milton. Through most of the eighteenth century Milton was regarded as consistent enough with Anglican orthodoxy. It was not until 1824, with the announcement of the discovery of Milton's theological treatise *De Doctrina Christiana*, that this strange view of the poet was shattered.[8] In his second edition of the variorum *Poetical Works*, in 1842, Henry John Todd expressed his dismay at three unavoidable heresies: "mortalism," "Arianism" (more properly, subordinationism), and "materialism": Milton's conviction that when the body dies there is no soul that is kept in storage, so to speak, until the Last Judgment; that the Son is subordinate to the Father rather than being coeternal with the Father; and finally the conviction from which these others follow, that all Being, and all beings, derive from a single principle, which is the substance of God, from whose body matter is taken before he "puts forth his goodness"—by which is meant his Word, his creative power, in the person of the Son—into that alienated substance with the purpose of shaping it into a world. Let us read again the words we have examined thus far, together with the command that precedes them:

And Thou my Word, begotten Son, by Thee
This I perform: speak Thou and be it done!
My overshadowing Spirit and might with Thee
I send along: ride forth and bid the deep
Within appointed bounds be Heav'n and Earth!
Boundless the deep because I am who fill
Infinitude, nor vacuous the space
(Though I uncircumscribed Myself retire
And put not forth My goodness which is free
To act or not): necessity and chance
Approach not Me, and what I will is fate.

⌐ *Paradise Lost 7.163–173*

We may perhaps now see the reason for the final, apotropaic assertion "necessity and chance / Approach not Me, and what I will is fate." God has alienated his substance from himself so that it is matter; and it has here at last become as neutral as any proponent of creation *ex nihilo* could wish. Matter is now ruled only by necessity and chance, "outrageous as a sea," until the Father sends forth his "goodness," the Son, to subdue it by Creation. But there is something uncomfortable about any substance that once belonged to the body of God being ruled by necessity and chance, however alienated that substance now is from his person. For this matter can in truth never be entirely alienated from God. It is therefore necessary to assert forcefully the contrary of what is actually feared, that necessity and chance may indeed trespass on God and that his will, which he calls "fate," is overruled by theirs. Every determinist reading of the Fall bears out the reasonableness of Milton's anxiety on this point. For him, what God principally "wills" is freedom. Man's fate is to be ruled not by necessity and chance but by his own freedom, which God gives him. Man becomes subject to necessity and chance only when, through the Fall, he gives up this freedom and remains terrified of it ever after. For the terror of freedom is what Milton calls history. In history, necessity and chance approach Man, though they do not approach God; and what God wills, fatally, is the restoration of human freedom. Before the creation of the world, but just after the fall of the rebel angels, God is thinking ahead into history when he says, "necessity and chance / Approach not Me, and what I will is fate." History may be fate for him. For us, it is necessity and chance and, just possibly, freedom.

6

A Bleeding Rib

MILTON AND CLASSICAL CULTURE

*T*HE LAST SCENE of divine making in *Paradise Lost* is the creation of Eve. It is also the first and only time that the impulse to create does not come solely from God the Son but from a creature whom the Son made. Adam, not wanting to be alone in paradise, requests a companion, and the request is evidence that he has been properly made—made, that is, to be a husband and a king. What Adam does not know is that the substance with which Eve will be made is to be taken out of him, out of his body. It comes as a surprise. He is unconscious when this extraction occurs; but while he is unconscious the actual operation is revealed to him, as if in a dream. Up to this time Adam has seen the *results* of creation: his first and most striking intellectual act, a deductive leap, occurs shortly after he first wakes and infers that everything he sees is the art of "Some greater Maker." But when God puts him to sleep, leaving him his "internal sight," Adam sees the process of creation itself, and sees it working out of himself:

> Mine eyes He closed but open left the cell
> Of fancy my internal sight by which
> Abstráct as in a trance methought I saw
> (Though sleeping where I lay) and saw the Shape
> Still glorious before whom awake I stood,

Who stooping opened my left side and took
From thence a rib with cordial spirits warm
And life-blood streaming fresh. Wide was the wound
But suddenly with flesh filled up and healed.
The rib He formed and fashioned with His hands,
Under His forming hands a creature grew,
Manlike but different sex, so lovely fair
That what seemed fair in all the world seemed now
Mean—or in her summed up, in her contained,
And in her looks, which from that time infused
Sweetness into my heart, unfelt before,
And into all things from her air inspired
The spirit of love and amorous delight.

⟁ Paradise Lost 8.460–477

This is a strange and remarkable scene, although it is at first hard to say why. The language is plain. In the range of Miltonic diction it is closer to "for in the inn was left no better room" than it is, say, to "above the circling canopy / Of night's extended shade." The action, too, is meant to seem plain, governed as it is by homely, workmanlike verbs: "closed," "stooped," "took," "fashioned," and "formed." Moreover, the creature Eve appears to act more impressively than her divine creator: her gaze "infuses" sweetness into Adam's heart and causes all things around her to become more animated, to tend toward her with love. Whereas Eve has the power of acting at a distance invisibly, of bewitching people and things, her creator must work with his hands, like a humble craftsman. The scene has none of the spectacular force of the great Creation scene narrated by the angel Raphael, in which are joined the Hellenic architectural symbol of the compasses and the Hebraic power of the spoken command:

Then stayed the fervid wheels and in his hand
He took the golden compasses prepared
In God's eternal store to circumscribe
This universe and all created things.
One foot He centered and the other turned
Round through the vast profundity obscure

And said, "Thus far extend, thus far thy bounds,
This be thy just circumference, O world!"

                   ⌁ Paradise Lost 7.224–231

Yet if we look beneath the calm surface of the scene of the creation of Eve, we can discern large, dark forms of ancient myths and ancient thoughts moving swiftly past one another: Hebrew psalms, Galenic medicine, Aristotelian metaphysics, and even, by the conclusion, the erotic and supernatural "marvels" *(maraviglie)* of chivalric romance. Slowly we absorb the shock of one person casually opening the living body of another and removing a rib; and there is the unforgettable shock of the blood, which is fresh. Next there is the spontaneous healing of the wound, reminding us that powerful forces are at work behind the simple actions that we see performed. This reminder makes the actions themselves, especially the molding of Adam's flesh as if it were clay, resonate with something greater than themselves. Stage actors know the trick of concentrating on something physically small, an action performed with the hands, such as lighting a cigarette, at a moment when something important is said. Milton uses this dramatic trick when Adam's and Eve's hands come apart, when her hand reaches for the fruit, when his hand, going slack with horror, releases the garland he has woven for her, when the "hastening angel" catches them in either hand, leading them to the eastern gate and down the cliff beneath it, and of course when they turn and walk away, "hand in hand with wandering steps and slow" (*PL* 12.637 and 648).

In two verses from the passage we see God's hands twice, once as a craftsman's and once as a sort of magician's. God's hands first remove a rib and then work above it, concealing it, like a covering mantle, as the new creature seems to grow on its own: "the rib he formed and fashioned with his hands; / Under his forming hands a creature grew." When the hands are withdrawn to reveal Eve completed, she seems to summarize and to give a center to everything that has ever been made. Small wonder Adam will make the fatal mistake, just before he eats the fruit that Eve offers him, of calling her "last and best / Of all God's works" (*PL* 9.896–897). He is naturally inclined to think so because he can see her and he cannot see himself: he sees Eve as Eve will see herself in the pool, as an *eidōlon*, a visible thing that is also an illusion, potentially an idol, a "goddess humane" (*PL* 9.732), as Satan, with unerring flattery, calls her. Adam must learn what is best of God's works not by gazing on them but by reasoning about them. Yet it is hard not to gaze and be dazzled.

There is a hierarchy of making in *Paradise Lost* in which the creation of Eve stands third. We can comprehend her creation only when we have a clear understanding of its place. Above and before the creation of Eve is the Son's essentially Platonic creation of the World, "answering his great idea" (7.557). The Son creates the World out of preexisting matter, or chaos; and when he does so, the original of those "cordial spirits warm" that stream from Adam's rib must be introduced—the verb "infused" is employed here as well—from without:

> but on the wat'ry calm
> His brooding wings the Spirit of God outspread
> And vital virtue infused and vital warmth
> Throughout the fluid mass.
> ℘ *Paradise Lost* 7.234–237

When the Son makes Eve, the power of life is already there in the substance he uses, streaming from it freshly. But when the Son makes the world, the universe, the preexisting substance is unformed and lifeless. This more radical, originative act of making is higher than the making of Eve because more must be done: life is not merely translated and refashioned in the new creation but is itself introduced and created. Still further back in time, and at the most fundamental level, we have the Father's creation of matter out of himself by withdrawing from infinity, leaving his alienated substance behind him as chaos. This chaos may be infused with vital virtue or left as it is, his goodness being free, as he says, to act or not. Some of the chaos will be acted on by the Father's goodness when the Son makes the world and some will be left in its original state, in readiness for future acts of making. When the Father says, "Boundless the deep . . . Though I uncircumscribed Myself retire / And put not forth My goodness," his "goodness" means his Son, to whom he has just said, "ride forth and bid the deep / Within appointed bounds be Heav'n and Earth" (*PL* 7.166–171). The entire Creation for Milton is like the garden that is growing just a little too fast for the gardeners to control: it is an open system. There are then, to summarize, three levels to divine Creation. The first is ontological making, where matter, for Milton the ground, if not the bedrock, of being, is produced from the Father. The second is ideal making, where being is now determined as the joining of an *idea* to *life*, the first imposed upon matter, the second infused into matter. The third is translative or, better, reproductive making, in which both the substance and the life are captured and transferred from something previously made. Adam gives his substance and also his life, his "cordial spirits warm, / And life blood streaming fresh," for the creation of Eve. We should note that this last act of making recapitulates both of the earlier, more radical acts of creation. The forming of the rib recapitulates the Son's making of the world by ordering chaos to an idea; and the extraction of the rib recapitulates the Father's production of matter out of himself.

Beneath these three acts of divine making we may place the mimetic narratives made by the angel Raphael; these are the heroic and hexaemeric poems to either side of the midpoint of *Paradise Lost*, the war in heaven and the Creation of the world and of man. Those poems are meant to summarize and also to surpass all previous human efforts in the highest kind of verse: heroic epic, on the model of the *Iliad*, and the epic of origins, on the model of the *Theogony*. The account of Eve's making is itself part of a narrative Adam relates to Raphael in return for what the angel has narrated to him, and each praises the art of the other: "thy words with grace divine / Imbued bring to their sweetness no satiety . . . / Nor are thy lips ungraceful, Sire of Men, / Nor tongue ineloquent" (*PL* 8.215–219). The narratives related by Raphael and Adam are mimetic representations standing apart from the events they describe. They are, like the scriptures, *accommodated* accounts, mediated for the capacity of the hearer in the one case and moderated by the resources of the teller in the other. Raphael speaks in types and shadows—"what surmounts the reach / Of human sense I shall delineate so / By lik'ning spiritual to corporal forms" (*PL* 5.571–573)—and Adam reports not what actually occurred but what he was able to discern in the cell of his fancy, his internal sight. The world the Son creates is in every sense equal, or "answerable" to his "idea." Mimetic narratives, however, carry with them the acknowledgment of an inequality with what they relate. They are creative, but what they create is secondary to what they refer to.

Descending further down the scale of excellence in making, we find the still impressive, not to say titanic, achievements of the devils in building Pandemonium and of Sin and Death in building the bridge across chaos. From these acts of making the principle of adequation is absent. We hear of no preexisting idea or architectural plan. The dominant image is of sluicing liquids and channeling them together until a structure rises almost by chance. Pandemonium rises like an "exhalation," by which term Milton means to evoke mirages created by swamp gas. We hear of veins of liquid fire "sluiced" from the lake of fire in hell, of liquid gold scummed and conveyed from "boiling cells" through tubes made in the ground to various points from which the several parts of the structure arise, "As in an organ from one blast of wind / To many a row of pipes the sound-board breathes":

> Anon out of the earth a fabric huge
> Rose like an exhalation with the sound
> Of dulcet symphonies and voices sweet,
> Built like a temple where pilasters round
> Were set and Doric pillars overlaid
> With golden architrave, nor did there want
> Cornice of frieze with bossy sculptures grav'n.
> The roof was fretted gold. Not Babylon
> Nor great Alcairo such magnificence
> Equalled in all their glories to enshrine
> Belus or Sérapis their gods, or seat
> Their kings, when Egypt with Assyria strove
> In wealth and luxury.
>
> ᗒ *Paradise Lost 1.710–722*

Egypt, Babylon, and Assyria are evoked in case we are in doubt what to think of this structure. It is interesting to note how the poet troubles to mention pillars, architraves, cornices, friezes, and even sculptures without ever mentioning the work of the hand. For the work of the hand implies measurement and planning, an "idea" to which the structure must answer. Rising instead like an "exhalation," the fantastic structure, for all its material solidity, lacks the ontological solidity of a thing that has been thoroughly worked, perfected in the etymological sense of that word, by the close interaction of the brain and the hand. Where divine Creation *produces* what is, and human making, in poetry, *refers* to what is, demonic making breathes out, *exhales* what is not: it is the breath of lies.

Other products of making can be found in the poem: there are hymns, prayers, instruments, and weapons; there is a meal, a bower, a garden that is tended, a marriage that is kept. But these do not raise what is for Milton the central relation in any consideration of making: the relation of form to preexisting substance. That relationship is essentially technological, extending the human practice of making artifacts to everything that exists. Everything that exists, everything we see in the world and encounter in nature, in the realm of growth, is thus supposed to be a consequence of making, or, to use the classical term, of *poiesis*, which means production according to knowledge. In the Septuagint, the Hellenistic Greek translation of the Hebrew scriptures, we read, "In the beginning God poeticized [*epoiesen*] the heaven and the earth." Milton is engaged in a struggle from within with the Christian tradition, a struggle to be a creator independently of the Creator. But as the Septuagint translation of the opening of Genesis reveals, and as Milton himself shows in *De Doctrina Christiana*, it is the Aristotelian conception of the being of things as artifacts, that is, as combinations of matter and form, that exerts the strongest hold on the mentality of the Christian tradition.

There is one conspicuous act of making to which I have not yet referred, although Milton's inclusion of it in *Paradise Lost* was for his early critics a striking and dubious departure from the epic tradition. I refer to the making of *Paradise Lost* itself. The theme is set forth in the introductory passages to books one, three, seven, and nine, in which Milton achieves one of the most powerful effects in his poem, what I have referred to as the drama of an epic being made. In its official presentation—for example, in the invocation with which the poem opens—the drama of an epic being made is one in which the poet merges with God as Creator. The Spirit that brooded on the abyss when the world began to be formed broods now on the mind of the poet, creating the poem that will describe that original creation; and the light that invested the rising world of waters is now investing all that is dark and unformed in the mind of the poet. The invocation tells us that *Paradise Lost* is a leaf on the tree of Creation, but a leaf in which the pattern of the veins recapitulates the pattern of the whole of which it is a part. What we do not hear about, and what this mystique of participation conceals, is how the physical continuity of the poem with divine Creation is mediated by earlier *poems*, such as the *Iliad* and the *Aeneid*. All poetry stands between divine Creation and Milton's creation of *Paradise Lost*, as a barricade against God and as a substance that is available to Milton.

It is, I suppose, easy enough to say that every act of making *in* the poem in some way must reflect the making *of* the poem. In the scene of Eve's creation we may find an inadvertent disclosure of Milton's relationship with the body, the corpus, of heroic poems made in the past. Such a claim may sound a little banal. But is it banal to reduce the astonishing creation of Eve, the confluence of so many diverse conceptual frames, to a reflection of what Milton is doing in *Paradise Lost* with the verse of the past? Comparison of events in any poem to the making of that poem are suspect unless they lead beyond themselves, teaching us to consider how the poet actually works and deepening the ways in which we think about making. Those are hard conditions to meet. I can hope to achieve little more here than to indicate how we might begin to think about Milton and making. Of the importance of the subject, however, there can be no doubt.

An assertion of this kind confronts us with a methodological decision: whether to take as our goal a better understanding of *Paradise Lost*, using the concept of making to get there, or whether to take as our goal a better understanding of making, to which we may be led by attentively reading the scenes of making in *Paradise Lost*. It is not just simple prudence that makes me choose the latter course: it seems the only course that will also lead to a truly new way of understanding *Paradise Lost*, allowing the poem to teach us (as it was originally intended to do, after all) about something other than itself. To look directly at *Paradise Lost*, as criticism of the poem since Addison has done, is to become caught in the toils of interpretive issues—I have called them the antinomies—that will never be resolved. These antinomies revolve around one large question: whether the theological and poetical systems of Milton's epic successfully coincide, or whether they continually irritate each other, creating the sort of friction that anti-theological readers have been quick to exploit. Stanley Fish outflanks such readings by claiming that the friction is intended for a theological purpose: to call forth resistance in ourselves for the very purpose of overcoming such resistance. Resistance is not futile; but it is temporary, leading only to a stronger commitment to what was originally resisted. Yet this maneuver hardly stops the revolution of the antinomies. Rather, it widens the scope of the possibility of their revolution. For the anti-theological reader of *Paradise Lost* can claim that the very design the poem has on its readers, the design of correcting their aberrant thoughts and reincorporating their minds in the poem's theological system, generates in a stronger reader, such as Blake, a stronger resolve to resist, and not only to resist but to re-create.

Considered this way, as a window on things that are in it but that also lie beyond it, *Paradise Lost* has much to teach us about a poetics that eludes traditional modes of inquiry: the theory of things that have the character of having been made, things that are determined in their being by *poiesis*. In poetics, reflection on art is reduced either to a branch of the theory of perception, aesthetics, or to a branch of the theory of meaning, hermeneutics. Artistic making seems too humble a thing to be brought into serious question. *Paradise Lost* belongs in a class with Nietzsche's *Birth of Tragedy* and Heidegger's *Origin of the Work of Art* not because it could have been read as making common cause with either of these texts, but because on its own terms it thinks as radically as they do about art.

❧ TWO POINTS ABOUT the making of Eve are of particular interest: the preexisting material out of which she is made and the waste that is produced by her making. The preexisting material is Adam's rib, which is extracted not, as it seems, from the realm of nature or growth *(physis)* but from the realm of previously made things. For nature, in the Judaic and Christian traditions, is the realm of things that have previously been made. It appears, of course, as if something of the substance that goes into the making of Eve—the cordial spirits and life-blood—is taken from a nature that is independent of the making. The life-blood is "streaming fresh." When we are considering an act of the maker of nature, some confusion of the categories of the natural and artificial is to be expected. But on the whole we are supposed to think of Adam as an artifact that has been torn open and used as material for another artifact. "Torn open" may sound melodramatic, but I think there is in the scene a striking violence that is glossed over by the bland verbs "opened" and "took," and that this violence is essential to Milton's art. Hazlitt was speaking with deliberate exaggeration when he described Milton as a writer of centos, that is, of poems composed of recognizable fragments of earlier poems, the ancient Roman centos, obscene poems composed entirely from lines and half lines taken from Virgil.

This, then, is the first point about making which is suggested by the creation of Eve: that poetic language is not taken from "nature," from the language that surrounds us in the immediate, ordinary worlds of common usage, or, to put it more precisely, from what Saussure called *parole*. Poetic language is instead quarried from the material remains of the past, from written records, from earlier, partly recognizable poems. When we read, in "Lycidas," "Alas! What boots it with uncessant care / To tend the homely slighted shepherd's trade / And strictly meditate the thankless muse?" (64–66), we are meant to hear in the arresting verb "meditate," which is related not only to Latin *meditatio* but also to Greek *mathesis*, the opening verses of Virgil's first eclogue, in which Tityrus is addressed and described lying under the protection of a beech tree's boughs, using a slender reed to study, to practice, and to prepare himself thoroughly (all this is suggested in the Latin *meditare*) in the art of the woodland muse: "Tityre, tu patulae recubans sub tegmine fagi / silvestrem tenui musam meditaris avena." Again, when Milton says, "Things unattempted yet in prose or rhyme," or "Instruct me, for thou knowst, thou from the first / Wast present," we may not immediately identify their sources—which are, respectively, Ariosto and Homer—but we may have a strong sense that the language belongs to the realm of things that have been previously made and that the language has been reworked for this occasion (*PL* 1.16 and 19–20). In this material sense the language of poetry is monumental language not only because it is grand but also because it remembers: it is a memorial to everything pathetic or grand that has ever been said in a poem.

The notion of *allusion*, of a poet deliberately "playing toward" something in an earlier poet, as when we speak of Milton *alluding* to Ovid, is inadequate for two reasons: because it implies a conscious, isolated act of reference rather than a relatively unconscious process of improvisation, and because it has the direction of movement backwards. The poet does not "play toward" something in the past. Things in the past are captured, torn free of their contexts in previous works, and brought forward in time to be worked into something new. Instead of imitating, by mimesis, the poet improvises with what can be captured, improvisation being that kind of making which Aristotle suppressed in order to bring mimesis forward in his analysis. Aristotle remarks that the early tragic poets worked without method, by mere improvisation, to be superseded by poets who mastered "the poetical craft" ("hē poiētike technē"), where *technē* implies the imposition of form on matter. The verb "to improvise" *autoschediazein*, means imposing an outward order, a *schema*, on things and events as they emerge unpredictably in time. Milton was perhaps closest to that great improviser, the poet of the *Iliad*. Although the technical details of the process of formulaic composition in Homeric verse were unknown in his day, Milton would have recognized the highly formulaic, repetitive character of the stock epithets in Homeric verse and the artificial character of Homer's poetic language, which was drawn from a number of dialects and refashioned at a level above them. Milton understood intuitively the improvisatory character of Homeric verse and captured something of its effect in the recycled diction of *Paradise Lost*.

The second point about poetic making which is suggested by the scene of Eve's creation qualifies and troubles the first. It is that there is something left over from the process of making, a waste that cannot be recycled, springing free at the moment the body is opened and the rib is pulled free, "life-blood streaming fresh." I spoke of this blood as belonging to nature only in a secondary sense, since nature in the Christian tradition is already an artifact. The problem cannot be cleaned up so quickly. For even in the Christian framework some things will awaken rumors of an earlier pattern of thinking, and spilled or streaming blood is one of those things, suggesting danger and contamination (Milton would be aware of this sense from the Greek tragedians) as well as power, productiveness, and life. That streaming blood can no more be contained in our minds as an artifact than it can be entirely recaptured in Eve. It is an uncomfortable force, like a flood. Milton does not intend us to imagine some of Adam's blood spilling on the ground, like the blood of Medusa, any more than he would expect us to worry about the clippings that fall when Adam and Eve prune the garden. But we have to make an effort to contain ourselves, to forget the streaming blood, which is, as the tree was for Adam (so Milton described it in *Areopagitica*), a provoking object in our sight.

That provocation troubles the official view of *Paradise Lost*, the vision of human nature which is achieved by returning to the root of our existence in paradise, a vision of everything we might have been and of everything we are. What we might have been is a family of creatures who are evolving on the scale of Creation, improved by tract of time and by degrees of merit raised, so Milton describes it, to take the places of the angels who fell. That is what we might have been. What we are shown is the compulsively self-destructive behavior of the historical beings in the eleventh and twelfth books of *Paradise Lost*, in which history can almost be defined as experience without freedom. Milton's intention is that by learning from his poem what we might have been, we may recover some of our original freedom. For what might have been is never wholly lost but is carried with us through time and remains part of the world of perpetual possibility: "What might have been and what has been / Point to one end, which is always present." This is Eliot, whose meaning I am distorting to suit Milton's more optimistic, not to say revolutionary, temperament. For Milton, what might have been remains with us in our conscience as revolutionary possibility, ready to be ignited by divine inspiration and according to divine providence. That is how we are meant to see *Paradise Lost:* as a mimetic vision of everything we might have been and everything we are, and of the potential for attaining liberty in history itself by letting one of these states, what we might have been, be infused into the other. But a different sort of poem confronts us when we do not so much *look* at the vision of *Paradise Lost* as *listen* to the resonance of other poems in it: when we stop gazing at the poem as an idol and instead hold it up to our ear. What we hear when we do so, beneath the resonance I spoke of, is the violent energy of assimilation that has gone into the making of Milton's epic.

These two ways of encountering the poem, considering its vision from a distance and listening more closely to its composition, are not wholly incompatible with each other. But as I said when I remarked on the methodological choice between reasoning about *Paradise Lost* and reasoning about making, the poem has much to teach us about what lies beyond it. When we expand our horizons accordingly, we see that *Paradise Lost* evokes two perspectives that are struggling with each other for dominion over literary history: the technological and the traditional. The technological perspective is mimetic and is oriented toward the future, which it understands as the inexhaustible substance of the natural world. Its project is to absorb the otherness of nature into the eschatological form of the human. To imitate human action is to do so for an exemplary purpose, to project human conduct forward in time and to absorb nature itself into that exemplary form. From the technological perspective, literary history is the handing down, the *traditio*, of particular skills, such as the right way to compose a tragedy or an epic. Actual monuments, like actual ruins, are left behind in the past, although the monuments at least retain some usefulness to progress, since the rules of art can be deduced from them. Ruins, however, works of art that can no longer be put to any use because they are supposed to be no longer relevant, are left behind in the past, like waste. In their present canonical status *Paradise Lost* is regarded as a monument and *The Faerie Queene* as a ruin. But even the monuments are perpetually falling into ruin and must be sustained by our continual, and increasingly strained, efforts to make them seem relevant to us. It is therefore the other perspective, the one that does not call so urgently for relevance, that turns out to be relevant now. For it acknowledges that waste can never be securely disposed in the past but is always circling around in front of us again, as syringes and cans wash up on the shore. Eliot described it well: "the torn seine, / The shattered lobster pot, the broken oar / And the gear of foreign, dead men." It is only these shattered things, preserving as they do an archaic createdness in them, which can be absorbed into art.

꙳ For MILTON, the preexistence of some natural substance to be formed is a rule of making, derived from Aristotle's analysis of change. To this rule Milton notoriously held even God. To imagine God making something out of nothing, he reasoned, is not to give God any extraordinary power; it is simply to be confused about making, which always requires a prior substance on which the imposition of form can occur. On this subject Milton had not yet got up from the feast of sow thistles and brambles he had been made to sit down to at Cambridge. Just as Euclidean geometry, so convenient to architecture and surveying, could be mistaken for a true representation of space, so Milton mistook the Greek concept of making—the imposition of form on relatively indifferent matter—to be a true representation of making. The more experimental developments in modern art have been largely an effort to take the concept of making outside this Greek paradigm; and it is the radical strain in its thought about making that is modern in *Paradise Lost*. Modern art shows an improvisatory schematizing of circumstances as they unfold in time. A "schematizing of chaos according to practical needs," which is Nietzsche's conception of truth—or one of Nietzsche's conceptions of truth—is what we find in the assimilative energies of *Paradise Lost;* and the verse of that poem is its digestive organ.

With exemplary compression, if not perfect lucidity, Milton described the "true musical delight" of the verse of *Paradise Lost* as consisting in "apt numbers, fit quantity of syllables, and the sense variously drawn out from one verse into another." There is more in this account of the verse than "true musical delight," something that is suggested, perhaps, by Milton's boast that his verse is "an example set, the first in English, of ancient liberty recovered to heroic poem"; for this liberty is the liberty to conquer. Marvell speaks of Milton's "plume" being "so strong, so equal, and so soft," but the impulsive forward force, the careful syntactical balance, and the supple articulation to which Marvell's three adjectives refer are impressive not in themselves alone but for the underlying turbulence they master. A vast reserve of monumental verse is being funneled into *Paradise Lost* in the process of its composition, its "putting together," and this material must be broken down as it is absorbed in the new structure. Unrhymed blank verse, with its greater flexibility between medial pauses and end stops, between the different scales of rhythmical order—monosyllables and polysyllables, lines and half lines, periodic sentences with their suspended verbs, and verse paragraphs stretched or compressed according to the subject in hand— is the most powerfully absorptive metrical system in English. The absence of rhyme sets its violence free. Comparison to *The Faerie Queene* bears out this conclusion. No poet could use rhyme better than Spenser could to capture the material remains of the past. But the texture of *The Faerie Queene* is rougher, its debris and its fragments, which are cemented together in elaborately rhymed stanzas, are less thoroughly digested than are the materials of the past in the blank verse of *Paradise Lost.* The jagged surface of *The Faerie Queene* glitters as it turns in the light. But Milton's epic thoroughly crushes whatever it takes into itself; its smoothness—"so strong, so equal, and so soft"—is the result of an efficient violence that we can still feel in the serpentine rhythm of its motion.

☙ IN GREEK THOUGHT there appear to be two predominating metaphors for prime matter: wood *(hylē)* and blood *(haema)*, indicating, respectively, technological and biological ideas of making. The commonest metaphor for emerging beings is the former, suggesting craftsmanlike working of wood according to a foreseen plan or "idea." It was still necessary, however, to account for living things, which are not fashioned from without and put together in parts, as ships and tables are, and which have the power to move themselves, as ships and tables do not. Living bodies come out of other living bodies, as Eve comes out of Adam, bodies which periodically release blood, except when new bodies are forming inside them. It is not hard to see how menstrual blood becomes an alternative to wood as the metaphor for prime matter, at least when the world is conceived of as an animal. In the male seed Aristotle placed alongside each other two different things: the Platonic idea, which is derived from the metaphor of the craftsman, and the principle of movement, which is derived from the observation of animal bodies. These metaphors bore on theories of the cosmos, causing the inquiry into the first mover and fixing the sphere of the moon as the limit of mutability—not only because the moon goes through phases but also because it seems to govern the menstrual flow. In Aristotle the menstrual flow is attributed to the impossibility, in the sublunary world where form and matter are always falling apart from each other, for the male seed, the plan or "idea" for a body, to be always successful in fastening its grasp upon slippery matter, which therefore escapes as menstrual flow, "life-blood streaming fresh." If women could get above the sphere of the moon, they would stop menstruating and every sexual union would produce issue, as does every copulation of the gods. Menstrual blood thus has a curious double status. In one sense it is waste, natural material that has not been absorbed into production and must be left behind in the past. In another sense menstrual blood is, as Aristotle says of prime matter, pure potential, the raw power of *physis*, which has yet to be absorbed into making. It is blood that is streaming and blood that is spilled. Milton's chaos, which is like a menstruation issuing from the body of God, is similarly divided, lying as it does both before divine Creation, in the future, and behind divine Creation, in the past. The dark materials of chaos eventually come to express this bifurcation: in them are the roots of Creation, as Raphael tells Adam (*PL* 5.479), as well as that which is purely waste and inimical to Creation, as we see when the Son purges "The black tartareous cold infernal dregs / Adverse to life" (*PL* 7.238–239).

It remained for Greek thought to decide whether in the widest possible conception of making—the making of everything, of the whole—a technological or biological metaphor would rule. In Plato a technological metaphor appears to have the upper hand as a demiurge hammers the impressions of the forms into the substance that appears in the "place," the *chora*, although this *chora* is also referred to as the "mother." In Aristotle, as we would expect of a biologist, both extremes of creation, matter and form, are finally conceived of in animal terms: the prime matter is more like menstrual blood than like wood, and the origin of everything is not in a craftsman's idea, as in Plato, but in a first mover.

In keeping with the Christian tradition, Milton usually put the technological metaphor over the biological one, for in traditional Christianity the Son is the only being who is begotten, not made. It is true that the created world as described by Raphael is near to hylozoism, that is, to the theory that all material being is alive, like an animal, a *zōon*. All things must therefore be nourished, like animals, and in being nourished by what is lower, they help to translate matter upward on the scale of being. But they are nevertheless *made* things, which are not originally generated sexually. The denial of one's status as a creature, a made thing, is for Milton the deepest and most radical of Satan's lies, occasioning the most satisfactory rebuke in the poem: "Then who created thee lamenting learn / When who can uncreate thee thou shalt know!" (*PL* 5.894–895).

Vico said that science, which studies a natural world we did not make, may give us an exact knowledge so far as measurement is concerned; but this knowledge is knowledge "from the outside" because we are not the creators of nature. Natural science is less intimate a knowing, therefore, than the knowledge "from within" which the humanities afford, which is knowledge of things humans have made. The study of the history of human institutions, such as Roman law (Vico was a jurist), affords a deeper wisdom than the study of natural science ever can. Whatever the truth of Vico's claim may be, it touches on a deep human instinct, one that probably goes back to the hunter's mimicking of game: the instinct to make oneself like the thing one would know. Such imitation is not Aristotle's imitation at a distance but a conjunction of sympathetic magic and mystical participation that may open the door to alternative conceptions of artistic production, ones suggested by the myth of Actaeon, as interpreted by Bruno, or of Dionysus as interpreted by Nietzsche. The artist is at once the hunter and the quarry, entering bodily into the violence of the scene the artist makes. Suggestions of this appear in Milton, especially when he invokes the myth of Orpheus and imagines his own body being torn as Orpheus' was by the maenads.

When we think of ourselves chiefly as makers, as *Homo faber*, the entire natural world seems more knowable if it is itself a thing that has been made. We might have made it ourselves, or we might make another one like it, a utopia, if only we were better at making. By placing nature in the realm of artifacts, we remove the radical strangeness of nature. What is at issue for Milton is not whether God made the world out of matter, as a *technitēs*, which seemed obvious to him, but where the matter came from in the first place. In supposing matter to have come out of God rather than out of nothing—the traditional Christian view—Milton is only following Greek thought more closely. Apart from Tasso, Milton is the one major Renaissance poet to be philosophically concerned with this problem. Tasso's thought, although it is subtler in its Aristotelianism, is less original that Milton's. In its final form Tasso's epic is to a large extent the result of a theory worked out in prose; the theory comes down to the conclusion that history is a substance to which the epic poet gives form. Milton, however, continued to think in the poem, and he did so in terms that were more daring than what he ventured in prose. This is perhaps to put it too deliberately. In *Paradise Lost*, Milton was able to free the poetry from the poet's limitations, to let the poem think for itself about making.

An assertion of this kind, if it is to escape being merely a mystification, will lead us either into psychology—for example, into speculation about what Orpheus meant personally to Milton—or into Milton's poetic practice at the most unconscious level, its diction, phrasing, and meter. Both routes are promising. But if we are to follow the second, we could do worse than to take up once more the suggestion that was thrown out by Hazlitt, that Milton was "a writer of centos," though "scarcely inferior to Homer."[1] What does this mean?

Hazlitt meant that Milton's poem seems to be made up entirely of fragments translated from earlier heroic poems in Greek, Latin, and Italian, but that Milton nevertheless achieves nearly the power and originality of Homer. The writing of centos, originally done as a joke, was taken up by Christian authors, such as the noblewoman Faltonia

Proba, who used fragments of Virgil to tell stories from the Old and New Testaments, thus attacking the material foundations of an idolatrous culture. That is the effect intended by Prudentius in the *Psychomachia*, the first, and for some centuries the only, Christian long poem in the heroic tradition. The *Psychomachia* is not a cento, but about 30 percent of its phrases are taken from Virgil. Christian poetry has its origin in the capture and redeployment of the materials of a hated but undeniably brilliant pagan culture.

Two commonplaces governed Christian attitudes toward this culture: Saint Jerome's interpretation of the captive bride in Leviticus, who is stripped, shaved, and shorn in order to be purified and made a member of the Hebrew nation, and Augustine's commentary on the "spoils of Egypt," the gold and silver implements which the Hebrews took from the Egyptians when the Hebrews went into the wilderness. Both commonplaces emphasize favorably the violence of an act of cultural appropriation. The violence has a positive role: to make idolatrous seduction by the alien culture impossible and to sharpen the line of distinction across which the materialized goods of that culture are transferred. The effect can be seen in what are called *spolia*, columns and other architectural ornaments which were taken from Roman temples and placed in Christian churches, where they stand out as alien, captured elements. Milton's training as a poet was in writing Latin verse, and Renaissance Latin verse is to a large degree an exercise in spoliating classical phrases.

Milton remarked in *Areopagitica* that the law under the emperor Julian forbidding Christians to be educated in classical culture was considered a severe persecution, for it deprived the Christians not only of the eloquence they needed to promote the Christian cause but also of the knowledge they needed to separate themselves from paganism. It was important that the riches of classical culture be seen as having been captured and turned to purposes alien to their original cultural context.

No poet has ever been more deliberate than Milton in appropriating the resources and materials of classical culture for Christian ideology. He felt he could surpass the greatest of the classical poets, even Homer, not because of any purely artistic superiority in himself but because he had "this advantage over and above of being a Christian" ("Reason of Church Government," *YP* 1:812). He is in possession of the truth and the pagans—"their gods ridiculous and themselves past shame" (*PR*

4.342)—are not. Milton therefore uses the materials of classical culture as *spolia* which are put on display to show that they have been, like Adam's rib, torn free of their original contexts and reincorporated in another system. I have already suggested that Milton shows us why we need to think differently about the concept of allusion. Nothing could be further from the truth than to say that Milton merely "plays toward" passages in classical texts: he pillages those texts and drags away parts of them into his own.

In the verse quoted from Christ's rejection, in *Paradise Regained*, of the temptation to mastery over classical culture, Christ tells his tempter that classical culture is worthless, its vaunted wisdom a chaos of "Conjectures, fancies, built on nothing firm" (*PR* 4.292). The "first and wisest" of its philosophers, Socrates, was just wise enough to know that, and nothing more: "The first and wisest of them all professed / To know this only, that he nothing knew" (*PR* 4.293–294). To sentimentalists the passage seems an ungrateful renunciation by Milton, near the end of his career, of the culture that had sustained him throughout that career, as if Milton were ever an uncritical worshipper of classical culture, like Winckelmann. He learned it; he derived pleasure from it; but he always held it in contempt. Particularly arresting are those lines on classical poetry—especially on Pindar, as I suppose—in which Milton has Christ say that beneath the poets' extravagantly figurative language there is little substance to be grasped and little pleasure to be had, unlike in the Hebrew psalms:

> Remove their swelling epithets thick-laid
> As varnish on a harlot's cheek, the rest,
> Thin-sown with aught of profit or delight,
> Will far be found unworthy to compare
> With Sion's songs, to all true tastes excelling,
> Where God is praised aright.
>
> ᕯ *Paradise Regained 4.343–348*

Apologies are made along one of the following two lines: that this is not classical culture in itself but classical culture as offered by Satan, and that this is Christ, not Milton, who is doing the rejecting. These apologies do not sit well together. Perhaps Milton was careful to insert the unbiblical temptation to classical learning so that there would be at least one temptation in the poem he himself would have found hard to resist, although after forty days in the wilderness without food, surely even Milton would have turned stones to bread, were he able to, and surely even Milton would admit this. But the passage needs no apology to explain it away. It says what Milton always thought: that in itself classical culture is worthless. Of course, classical culture is experienced "in itself" only when it is contemplated passively, by a mind that does not bring to its reading of the classical texts a vigorous, decisive judgment. Such a reader will be "Deep-versed in books and shallow in himself, / Crude or intoxicate, collecting toys / And trifles for choice matters" (*PR* 4.327–329). Note the phrase "collecting toys / And trifles." This supposititious reader also is extracting things from their contexts, fine phrases and noble sentiments, but is supposing these things to be "choice matters" in themselves, apart from any predetermining judgment. Milton collected toys and trifles too, but he knew them to be such and collected them for a higher purpose, subordinating them to higher-order processing.

With this thought in mind we may look again at the phrase in which he says, "Remove their swelling epithets thick-laid / As varnish on a harlot's cheek." Literally this says that were you to remove from classical poetry all of its literary ornamentation, and there is much to remove, you would find beneath it little of value and much that is diseased. But the phrase also points toward what Milton has been doing all along: removing these swelling epithets so as to incorporate them into his own verse. That is what classical culture is for: to be pillaged for its most outward, material phenomena. When the Son in book six of *Paradise Lost* drives toward his foes, "Gloomy as night" (*PL* 6.832), the expression recalls Heracles in the underworld coming forward "like night" (*Odyssey* 11.606) and, more famously, Hector's breaching the defensive wall protecting the Achaean ships, his face like swift and inevitable night (*Iliad* 12.463). In the *Iliad* we are at the high-water mark of the Trojans' successes; in *Paradise Lost* we are at the height, or just past it, of the rebel angels' success. But the similarity is largely irrelevant because Milton is not alluding to the spirit of the earlier context; he is tearing the substance of its language away.

The same observation may be made about Satan's resemblance, at several points in book four of *Paradise Lost*, to Turnus in the *Aeneid:* his crest with "horror plumed" (*PL* 4.989) may recall Turnus' crest bearing an effigy of the monster, Chimera, with flames of Aetna breathing from its mouth; and Satan's flight, at the end of book four, "murmuring," recalls with gloomy brilliance the final line of the *Aeneid*—"vitaque cum gemitu fugit indignata sub umbras"—all the more so for their being no precise verbal connection; a groan that is indignant is a murmur. Gavin Douglas's splendid Middle Scots translation says as much: "The spreit of lyfe fled murnand with a grane, / And with disdeyn under dyrk erth is gayn." As I have said of other classical phrases Milton uses, it is wrong to suppose that he is alluding to the *Aeneid*, that he is inviting us to think generally about Turnus' futile resistance to the will of Jove, and that he is also inviting us to apply the results of that reflection to Satan, as if such an application would make us wiser about Satan. Milton is seizing the best effects of his predecessors in the classical epic and putting them to use in his own, though in such a way as to make it obvious that those "swelling epithets" have not been invented by him but forcefully dislodged from an alien context. Everywhere we have the feeling of the material of the epic being taken not from language, as it were, in the wild, from *parole*, but rather from a language that has already been cultivated by artifice, in the realm of made things. The language of *Paradise Lost* gives the feeling of having been twice made. We thus observe in the very diction of *Paradise Lost* an oscillating, delirious effect: one of images and shadows from earlier poems being preserved only so long as it is necessary to see that they have been canceled.

꙲ IT MAY BE OBJECTED that to speak of Milton's art as a spoliation, an act of continual vandalism directed at the works of the past, is to suppose real damage being done to the originals. It is true that nothing is missing from Homer or from Virgil as a result of Milton's depredations; but I think that Milton intended us, as a result of reading *Paradise Lost*, never again to see the classical works as un-defaced wholes. We would never see anything other than a Turnus who is inadequate to Satan and a Hector, that failed savior of Troy, who is inadequate to the Son. Even so, what justification is there for speaking of Milton's relation to previous works as a material one? Milton's relation to previous works is material in the dialectical sense that their original contexts and meanings—we may even say their very spirit—is negated and crushed so that what survives in the new work strikes us as a brilliant collocation of images and sounds, of "swelling epithets" captured for a better use than that to which they were originally put. Nor is the individuality of the fragments preserved: they are heaped together in one nervous, energetic mass. Occasional fragments protrude, to remind us what the whole is composed of. But so long as some of the verse can be recognized by us as borrowed from previous works, and so long as even more of the verse sounds familiar, though we cannot say why, we will suppose that every phrase the poet uses has been quarried from the work of the past. The very violence with which Milton captures, crushes, and redeploys those material remains has the sublimely dialectical effect of becoming the afflatus of his own epic's spiritual power.

꩜ WHEN THE RIB IS taken from Adam's side, there is a moment when we see it as terribly exposed: "with cordial spirits warm, / And life-blood streaming fresh." For the place from whence the rib was taken has been filled up with new flesh and healed. The rib is now incapable of living on its own. For Milton, classical culture is like this exposed rib. It is as good as dead, or rather it would be better if it were dead, since its inner impulse, idolatry, still springs to life, like the snake-generating blood of Medusa, in such things as the veneration of saints and a stipendiary clergy. And classical culture itself is always in danger of becoming an idol, as we learn when Satan employs it to tempt Christ. That does not mean—nor, for Milton, could it ever mean—that classical culture is to be shunned. If works of the past are to be truly and usefully preserved, they must be engaged in a spirit of mastery and proprietorship, with a "spirit and judgment equal or superior" (*PR* 4.324) to them. That spirit may seem, to the historian or philologist who would reconstruct the past as it actually was, as shocking a violation as removing a rib from a man. As to the rib, the blood is running out of it and the "cordial spirits" by which it is warmed will soon cool and expire. As we observed, the wound through which the rib came has closed behind it, barring all return. Its only hope of survival is to be cut off from the source of its life, to be fashioned into something other than what it was.

7

Milton's Choice of Subject

*T*O ASK HOW MILTON chose "man's first disobedience" as
the subject for his epic is to address something too large, and too fundamental, to be contained by the form of the question. Choice is a mysterious thing, and if we are not to be led too far from Milton, some reli-
able, if admittedly crude, assumptions are necessary. There appear to
be two kinds of choices: those that are relatively specialized and can be
directed from above, as it were, by a metadiscourse of rational selection: what move to make in a chess game, for example, or which muse
to call on when telling of actions forepast. Then there are those rarer,
self-defining choices that engage all parts of the mind in a complicated
exchange from which the faculty of reason cannot escape to become a
detached referee. In this class one may place the choice whether or not
to enter the priesthood, a problem Milton confronted at Cambridge,
or what subject to choose for an epic. It is no simple matter to choose
the subject of a poem one has been preparing all one's life to compose.

I do not mean to suggest that the first kind of choice is less important
than the second: a specialized, rational decision on a matter that seems
perfectly clear to the chooser can have consequences far greater than a
decision taken slowly, deliberately, and after much anxious self-search-
ing. But because the second kind of choice places the identity of the
chooser at stake, it can arouse deep anxiety as to what one will become
after the choice has been made. We could not face such choices all the

time. Which of several possible selves shall I choose to be in the next instant? Only in the state of innocence, as Milton conceives it, can one confront such a question continually without being mad. For the rest of us, radical change, and the liberty that goes with it, is economized by rites of passage, public or private.

There is a tendency, therefore, to think of one's life as a chain of relatively stable selves linked together by points of transition, or thresholds, where one is changed into a new self that, while continuous with the old, is also radically changed. In this way, the anxiety we would otherwise feel about gradual, disorderly, unmanaged change is allayed by a double strategy: we *restrict* change within the narrow bounds of a sudden transformation, at a threshold, and we *define* change in ritual terms as passage from one stable state to another.

In relatively complex, heterogeneous societies like our own, where the self is not so closely identified with a role determined by the group, the transforming power of ritual is in some measure taken over by the idea of individual choice, a private rite of passage in which change is restricted to a point of decision whence a new self emerges. But the complementary task of defining change in terms of a stable identity requires the selection of a new self from alternatives that the original self can know only on *its* terms. In kinship societies this logical problem does not arise so starkly because social values are imposed on the person from birth: the transition is governed from above. The group, or some numinous power (which is much the same thing), provides the superordinate perspective on what one will be, and the individual is spared much anxiety by accepting the authority of that perspective.

In modern societies, by contrast, choices about the whole of one's life must be made as if they were practical ones, that is, by taking a superordinate perspective not on a task but on oneself. The difference entailed in the modern elevation of practical choice onto the existential plane may be one of degree. We have our rituals and role models too. But it seems fair to say that modern individuals are required, to a degree unprecedented in human history, to make existential choices in a practical way. We are forced to imagine a true, essential self looking down on the actions of an implemental self that is engaged in the world; and the essential self decides what new existence the imple mental self will engage in next, what role it will play. Yet we suspect that if this division becomes too sharply defined, breaking the connection between the essential and the implemental selves, we will lose the ability to choose altogether. We therefore have a compensatory habit, and a compensatory discourse, of well-timed impulsiveness, thus warding off the threat of paralysis. I mean the paralysis that would ensue for the implemental self in the world if the connection between it and its superordinate other were broken.

We can see that paralysis expressed, I believe, in the words that are fastened on Samson by Milton's chorus, even if Samson appears to have no further choices to make: "Thou art become (O worst imprisonment!) / The Dungeon of thy self" (*Samson Agonistes* 155–156). The chorus means only that he is blind. But Samson is entombed in himself because he is in an ecstasy of self-condemnation: he looks down on himself from above, as it were, and sees his actions in the past as the walls of a prison. The last choice he makes, which will be practical and existential at once, is a liberating act of well-timed impulsiveness. The ethical world of Milton's poetry is founded on a hierarchical linking of selfhood with self-inspection from above, as we see, for example, in the conclusion to "Mansus," where Milton imagines himself applauding himself from Olympus. But the most powerful moments in the poem may come, as they do in "Lycidas," when that ethical hierarchy is smashed and remade, thus restoring to choice the experience of ritual change. Milton, as we know, is the poet of radical choice. He seems also to be the first major poet to discover life-defining choice as we experience it now, looking down on ourselves from above. Eve envisions a new, powerful self that will emerge after eating the fruit; Adam envisions himself, if he refuses to eat, alone and in pain.

᠅ To ESCAPE THE anxiety aroused by the logical problem of choice—referring for information to the self as it is now in order to decide which of several possible new selves that self should become—it is natural to appeal to an external principle that will transcend the sequence of selves, linking them in a continuous whole. Such a principle should do for the modern person faced with a life-defining choice what the community and the spirits had done for people in the deep past. This is what Milton habitually did by referring any important question, no matter how personal, to a suprapersonal code he called "Reason," whose voice is, as Richard Hooker said of law, "the harmony of the world."[1] Yet Milton's use of this principle takes a ritual form: the task of *restricting* change to a threshold is internalized by him as choice; and the task of *defining* change as movement from one discrete state to another is externalized by him as reason, the universal law that is written (we might now say "copied") on the heart. When Milton says that "reason is but choosing" (*Areopagitica*, YP 2:527), he is speaking of universal reason at work in our actions, an articulation as ample in scope as that of microcosm to macrocosm. The underlying separation—of the universal law from the particular act—is clearer still in *Paradise Lost*, when God says that "reason also is choice" (3.108), which means that choice is *one* of the things—though among the most important—that reason is. Reason operates in different ways throughout all things, in man and in woman as choice. Choosing should therefore be as natural to rational creatures as growth is to a tree or as heaviness is to a stone, these being actions of divine reason as well.

That choosing is not so easily done is, for Milton, a result of the Fall. In this attribution the anxiety aroused by the logical problem of existential choice is understood as a problem of history, for history begins with the destruction of natural choice (choice ritualized as the inward expression of natural law). If Milton is the first great poet to confront the problem of modern, de-ritualized choice, he is also the last to try to re-enchant choosing by placing it in a theodicy. But the greatness of *Paradise Lost* lies near the failure of this effort at re-enchanting choice, as the word "lost" in the title proclaims. Redemption redeems, but it does so without diminishing the tragic extent of the loss; it offers hope, but not for us now. Only with the subject he chose could Milton have given this truth its full force.

৵ It goes without saying that for an epic poet the choice of a subject is life-defining: none of the greatest epic poets, with the remote exception of the first, wrote more than one major epic. The epic is therefore a more radical expression of the self than even the lyric can be. If the lyric is a personal form, the lyric poet nevertheless wears a succession of masks, *personae*. The epic poet, by contrast, virtually becomes what he makes as a consequence of what he decides. Yet the choice of an epic subject, engaging as it does complex and contradictory impulses at all levels of the mind, makes it impossible to direct from above. The ideally disinterested faculty of reason therefore becomes but one interested force among many, sometimes even a negative force, as we shall see. For such decisions, voluntary reason often serves only the ritual purpose of artificially restricting change to a threshold and of retrospectively defining an inscrutable complexity as transition from one state to another. Hence a creative decision that appears to the chooser as something attained in a moment of rational choice, or as something inspired, may be nothing more than the recognition of a choice that has already been made.

Consider, for instance, Milton's remark to Thomas Ellwood on the subject of *Paradise Regained:* "This is owing to you," Milton said, showing Ellwood the poem, "for you put it into my Head by that Question you put to me at Chalfont: which before I had not thought of."[2] That final, emphatic relative clause is perhaps called into question by the "pleasant tone" in which Ellwood says it was spoken. But we saw that Milton declared more than once his conviction that choosing is not just rational but an expression of Reason itself. Ellwood's remark after reading *Paradise Lost*—that something might now be said of paradise found—proved highly convenient to Milton. It gave him a clearly marked threshold from which he could date the beginning of his rational deliberations on the matter, cutting off as irrelevant any earlier, half-conscious stirrings: "which before I had not thought of." By drawing arbitrary boundaries of this kind, Milton turns choice into reason.

ॐ WE COULD THEREFORE expect Milton to ask himself what subject he should choose for his epic by referring that question to an external framework of theory that was shared by other Renaissance poets. His choice would be an instance of universal reason mediated through the more specialized framework of theory. Such a framework was available in the new discipline of poetics, which promised, after the dissemination in the sixteenth century of Aristotle's rediscovered treatise, to get the untidy business of imaginative writing firmly established on a rational basis. For critics of the period the most pressing task of the new discipline was to derive laws for constructing an epic poem— "that critical abstraction of the century," as F. T. Prince called it—that would be as rigorous as those geometrical laws, discovered in the same period, for constructing a dodecahedron.[3] The new poetics was "a sublime art," as Milton did not hesitate to call it, "which teaches what the laws are of a true epic poem" (*YP* 2:404–405). The "true epic poem" was not only a critical abstraction, however; it was also a major cultural desideratum of the period, in a class with, for example, the monumental dome of Brunelleschi in Florence, the first of its kind in the West since the Pantheon. For the Italian theorists of the Renaissance, the composition of a *true* epic poem in the modern world was perhaps desired simply to confirm that a renaissance had occurred.

Milton's enthusiasm for the new critical theory was at its height, not surprisingly, shortly after his return from the Italian academies and libraries, in 1639. In the somewhat depressed intellectual world of Italy at the time there nevertheless continued the debate, or "famosa questione," as his friend Giovanni Manso had called it, over the epic poems of Ludovico Ariosto and Torquato Tasso, the romantic *Orlando Furioso* and the classical *Gerusalemme Liberata*. At issue in much of the debate was the theoretical problem of the relation between historical and mimetic truth in what came to be regarded as the greatest classical epic of the modern age, Tasso's *Gerusalemme*, a poem Milton would have seen himself as being in competition with, for religious as much as personal reasons.[4]

The point to be brought out of this complicated debate is that, in general, Renaissance critical theory understands the *subject* of any poem to be analogous to the principle of matter in Aristotelian thought. This is in keeping with the Aristotelian cast of mind in the greatest of the theorists, Tasso himself. Accordingly, the technical treatment of the subject matter of an epic poem was analogous to the principle of form; and the actual event on which the poem is based—the siege and conquest of Jerusalem in the Second Crusade—was relegated by the poet himself to the status of "bare matter."[5]

These terms were mobilized in defense of Tasso's poem in a volume of critical essays by various hands (including Tasso's) on the theoretical structure of the ideal epic poem or, to give the concept its full statement, "the idea, or portrait of heroic poetry, realized in examples from all the heroic poets."[6] Actual poems, such as the *Gerusalemme* itself, have the authority to call themselves epics to the extent that they resemble this form. They are thus required to stand in a relationship of *similarity* to it. This relationship becomes, in the generalized, Jakobsonian sense of the word,[7] a "metaphorical" principle of authority of which the most obvious consequence is the privileging of formal treatment, of mere technique, over what the reader of a story will care about most: the wrath of Achilles, the return of Odysseus, the trials of the Argonauts, the founding of Rome, the conquest of Jerusalem, the voyage of Vasco da Gama, the Fall of Man.

◯ In the Italian debate on the heroic poem, the partisans of Tasso were at once neoclassical and theoretical, attending mostly to questions of structure (due subordination of the episodes to unity of action, and so on), while the partisans of Ariosto defended him for the superiority of his verse, the fertility of his imagination, and the pleasing variety of his narrative. But the essential difference between the two poems lies deeper: in their contrasting claims to the authority of truth. We saw that from Tasso's Aristotelian perspective the truth of the poem lies in mimetic verisimilitude based on historical fact, a *metaphorical* principle. Ariosto, by contrast, inscribes his narrative in the medieval tradition of stories that claim to have been copied down from earlier copies that lead back in a chain to some imaginary witness, such as Archbishop Turpin, who is also the principal authority in Boiardo, Ariosto's immediate predecessor in the tradition of Carolingian epic.[8] Boiardo says that his book ("novella") of Orlando in love is known to few because Turpin had hidden it, perhaps out of shame that the knight who vanquished all was in the end vanquished by love. Boiardo claims to be following Turpin almost to the point of copying ("la vera istoria di Turpin ragiona . . ."), but it is just as plain that he is commenting on the tale in his own way. I would draw attention to the deliberate blurring by the author of the distinction between his work and the work of a predecessor, suggesting that they are continuous with each other in a tradition. Malory's frequent allusions to "the French book" operate in the same way, and Henryson begins his *Testament of Cresseid* by claiming that the poem comes from an additional quire found in a copy of Chaucer's *Troilus*, which in turn is connected to the general matter of Troy reaching back to those imaginary witnesses, Dictys and Dares, who were there at the time.[9] The relations among all these stories, and even between them and the events they report, are relations of contiguity, a *metonymical* principle.

This difference between Ariosto and Tasso reflects the alteration in European sensibility that was brought about by the change from a manuscript to a print culture. Manuscripts, each copied by hand from another, are metonymically connected in stemmas; books, in contrast, appear to stand entirely alone, though in numerous identical copies, and to capture the truth by resemblance. One consequence of the change is that imaginative structures gained much freer rein, seeming to burst forth everywhere at once, as in Thomas Lodge's *Scillaes Metamorphosis*, in which the world of Ovidian demigods and gods, unsecured by any chain of witnesses, is continually breaking into ours through etiological and allegorical portals. "Literature," understood as experience apart from the truth, formed around the self-contained, multiply reproducible book, which could seem a world to itself.

I have been describing how the root metaphor for the literary work gradually changed in the sixteenth century from that of a branch on a tree to that of a body harmoniously integrated in all its parts, from the open structure of the radiating plant to the enclosure of an organism. The difference became encoded in Renaissance critical theory in the terms *varietà* and *unità*, respectively. "Variety," like a plant, is traceable back metonymically to an original stem. "Unity," like an organism ("quasi animale," as Tasso says in his allegorization of the *Gerusalemme*), demands a rhythmical proportioning of structure by which the tale becomes a model of general truth.[10] Tasso attempted to reconcile the two principles, making unity the horizon containing variety within its bounds, but the change was as irreversible as the larger cultural change it reflected. We see this in Ariosto's defenders as in his detractors. Betraying the change of root metaphors, Tasso calls the *Orlando Furioso* "an animal of uncertain nature," and Ronsard condemns the structure of that poem as a monstrous animal too large to be perceived all at once.[11] Those who defend Ariosto do so on conceptually similar grounds, arguing that the poem does in fact achieve organic unity if rightly—which often means allegorically—interpreted.[12]

꙳ THESE WERE THE CIRCUMSTANCES Milton encountered when he visited Italy and absorbed, we may reasonably suppose, some of the latest speculations on the theory of the heroic poem. Upon his return, as he tells it in "Epitaphium Damonis," he applied his lips to a new set of pipes that fell apart when their fastening broke, unable to bear the weighty sounds of his theme:

> Et tum forte novis admoram labra cicutis,
> Dissiluere tamen rupta compage, nec ultra
> Ferre graves potuere sonos . . .
>
> ꙳ *"Epitaphium Damonis," 157–159*

The theme carried by these sounds includes, among other things, the coming of Brutus to Britain and Arthur's mysterious birth, in other words, the legendary materials of the "Briton moniments," as Spenser had called them, that were thought indispensable to any national epic. I think it is possible to regard Milton's "novae cicutae," new pipes, as a specific reference to his theoretical conception of "a true epic poem." Their failure to hold up under the strain is blamed not on any inadequacy in the chosen subject, however, but on the poet's lack of technical competence to do justice to such a high theme.

We see the fracturing consequences of the theory of the heroic poem in that astonishing passage of *The Reason of Church Government* in which Milton compares his situation to Tasso's, when the Italian poet offered to his patron the choice of the subject of his poem:

> And lastly what King or Knight before the conquest might be chosen in whom to lay the pattern of a Christian *Heroe*. And as *Tasso* gave to a Prince of Italy his chois whether he would command him to write of *Godfreys* expedition against the infidels, or *Belisarius* against the Gothes, or *Charlemain* against the Lombards . . . it haply would be no rashnesse from an equal diligence and inclination to present the like offer in our own ancient stories. (*YP* 1:813–814)

The passage is astonishing because it shows Milton actually considering shunting off onto someone else what he has not yet recognized as his most important creative act. He has not recognized this because of the influence on him of the view of history promoted by the new critical theory, in which he seems eager to show himself expert. The neo-Aristotelian formalist, looking at history, sees independent episodes instead of a whole.

But from the Nativity ode on, Milton is a poet who is excited by the conception of history as an organized whole, encompassing what a church father described as the beginning and end of the cosmos and those things of time that lie in between.[13] Even relatively minor poems, such as "On Time" and "At a Solemn Music," betray Milton's fascination with the presence of history as an organized whole within an eternity that does not efface it. And "Lycidas," to speak of a very major poem, concludes with an eschatological vision of Lycidas bodily in heaven, cleansing the ooze from his hair while his drowned body remains lost in the sea. Such a harsh collapsing of perspectives (we see others in the Nativity ode) is possible only for a poet who thinks of history as a whole that is bounded. Some of Milton's most impressive effects are achieved by forcing that whole up against an eternity that at once overwhelms and preserves it. As for *Paradise Lost, Paradise Regained,* and *Samson Agonistes,* they are partial realizations of the vision of history, a vision they awaken in us by an effect not unlike that of the Gestalt, where the mind completes shapes presented to it only in parts. We are shown war in heaven, the Creation, the Fall, the temptation in the desert, and the agony of Samson, and these things call forth a vision of the beginning and the end of the cosmos and those things of time that lie in between. The center of the vision is in *Paradise Regained,* while its circumference, or part of it, is in *Paradise Lost;* and what it feels like to live within such a vision while being imprisoned in the self is shown—but again, only in part—in *Samson Agonistes.* In the major poems, and in no small number of the minor poems too, Milton's vision of history is so insistently comprehensive that separation of the poems from one another, and of all the poems from the vision itself, seems almost illusory. Small wonder such an imagination would be paralyzed by a theory that reduced history to a substance and cut it into manageable and essentially identical portions.

LOOKING AT THE EVIDENCE from this period for Milton's thoughts on an epic subject, I think he suspects that he is coming at the problem of choosing from the wrong direction and knows that he needs time to think and to grow. If so, we may imagine him giving up on Britain's indigenous kings ("Mansus" 80) with the words he attached, roughly at the same time (in the *Poems* of 1645), to the youthful failure "The Passion": "This Subject the Author finding to be above the yeers he had, when he wrote it, and nothing satisfi'd with what was begun, left it unfinisht." Unlike the subject of the Passion, however, it is not the awful grandeur of the theme that defeats Milton but the strange absence of grandeur he senses in secular themes taken from history.

Notwithstanding this difference, it is instructive to compare the circumstances of "The Passion" in Milton's creative development with what might be inferred of his British epic. Like most ambitious failures, "The Passion" tries to build upon something too easily taken for granted, in this case, perhaps, the depth of the poet's commitment to poetry, a commitment that was not, until "Lycidas," to be tested against what is contrary to it. In "Lycidas," Milton violently disarticulates the conventions of pastoral elegy to get at the terror those conventions conceal. A similar process of negative testing may well have absorbed Milton in confronting the failure of his epic about early Britain. For Milton, the real problem with an *Arthuriad* is not its doubtful basis in fact, nor even the royalist appropriation of Arthur as an icon of kingship. The problem is that tales of Saxon phalanxes, Uther's disguise ("Mansus" 82–84; "Epitaphium Damonis" 162–168), and so on are consigned to the realm of "mere matter," in this case the matter of Britain. And matter requires—in Aristotle it actually desires—the imposition of a form that is alien to it. When Milton rejected the prescriptive structure of rules for making an epic, the question of the choice of subject moved in from the periphery (where theory had officiously placed it) to become his central concern.

Another consequence of Milton's techno-theoretical perspective at the time was the emphasis he laid on the concept of *decorum*, which he called "the grand master peece to observe" *(Of Education, YP 2:405)*. Decorum is the rhetorical principle of unity in identity: it demands that all parts of a discourse hang together consistently and that they do so in a manner appropriate to the place of the discourse in the hierarchy of abstract literary kinds. It is a peculiarly Renaissance cultural concept, demanding the rejection of all improvisatory methods in favor of a rational procedure supposedly derived from the ancients and illustrated by examples, also derived from the ancients, of that procedure applied. Yet the ancient examples seldom conform very well to the ancient rules, such as they are, or to later massive elaborations of those rules by Italian theorists. From the Renaissance to the Enlightenment most of the debates in critical theory proceed from the disjunction between critical rules and ancient examples.

Now, it happens that critical rules and ancient examples, for all their prestige, are of no use to the epic poet in choosing a subject. Ancient examples, of course, can be of no help unless one intends simply to develop (as minor poets in later antiquity did) some untold part of the story from the epic cycle. But unless the development is as original as Virgil's, such a practice hardly deserves the name *choice:* it is mere selection. Virgil does not develop the Homeric story of Troy; he chooses a great, independent story, the founding of Rome, which he links to the story of Troy. It would therefore seem that the problem of choosing an epic subject lies in the realm of critical theory, which places the chooser in a superordinate position from which to judge the available possibilities.

Yet none of the possibilities seems very good. Those who follow history too close at the heels, as Walter Raleigh observed in the preface to his *History of the World* (an epic poem in its own right), are liable to be kicked in the teeth. That is what happened with Abraham Cowley's royalist poem on the Civil War, parts of which were actually worked up from royalist newspapers. It became impossible to continue after the defeats suffered by the cause to which he had committed divine providence.[14] But the problem goes deeper than this because any episode chosen from history for heroic celebration will be unintentionally ironized by our knowledge of what is to follow, our knowledge, that is, that in history nothing heroic is definitely achieved. Thus Trissino's *L'Italia Liberata da Gotthi* concludes with the capture of Ravenna and of the Gothic king, allowing the hero Belisarius to return to Byzantium, "having placed Italy in liberty, in which she would remain as long as God pleased. For the things which are done on earth all depend on Divine will."[15] It would not please God very long. But for intense, even painful irony one should turn to the final stanza of Camões's *Lusiads*, in which the poet exhorts King Sebastiano to conquer North Africa, promising that he will be as great as Alexander without having cause, as Alexander did, to envy Achilles his Homer. Just six years later the king mounted such an expedition to Alcacer-Kebir, where, "in a four-hour engagement with the Moors, under an African sun," as William C. Atkinson describes it, "he laid the might and prestige of Portugal in the dust."[16] None of what Milton had once fervently hailed as "the deeds and triumphs of just and pious nations doing valiantly through faith against the enemies of Christ" (*YP* 1:816–817) will bear very close scrutiny, as Milton learned in his study of British history and in his study of the hitherto idealized early Christian Church. Milton was working toward the recognition, which appears in the final books of *Paradise Lost*, that to see the hand of Providence working in history, history must first be taken as a whole—and in its full, disillusioning power.[17]

⌒ THE TECHNICAL THEORY of the heroic poem therefore could not indicate to Milton, or to any other poet, what he should choose as his subject. Nor could the influence of such theory on the process of choosing have anything other than a negative effect. But negative effects can be useful when they turn us around. Milton knew, as did everyone, that the structure of critical theory could not indicate a subject directly; it could only point away from itself. We saw, however, that by accepting the authority of that act of pointing, Milton was saddled with a paralyzingly abstract conception of what it was he had to choose from: a class of distinct historical events, each member of which would be suitable for enlarging into a unified, self-contained action. Which subject one chooses is a matter of contingency. The epic hero mentioned in "Epitaphium Damonis" is "Brutus" because the poet is British, but it could just as easily be "Lusus" or "Francus" if he were Portuguese or French. Likewise, the poet could consider with an equal mind Arthur fighting the Saxons or Alfred the Danes, or, if a tragedy were wanted, "Hardiknut dying in his cups an example to riot" (Columbia Edition 18:244). The point is that the subject is regarded as of secondary importance to the technical frame into which it is drawn.

Whatever its subject, therefore, an epic had in some way to refer to an aesthetic ideal drawn from the example of Homer and Virgil or understood by the abstract, neo-Aristotelian "laws" of poetics, these being the alternatives in the critical debate between "ancients" and "moderns," respectively.[18] We can observe the idealizing tendency common to both sides in Trissino's claim, in his preface to *L'Italia Liberata da Gotthi*, to have synthesized them on a higher level, taking Aristotle for his master and Homer for his "guide and idea."[19] The poem still went largely unread, for all its theoretical correctness—and for all its metrical skill, being composed in unrhymed hendecasyllabics, which established a modern epic precedent for Milton's writing unrhymed iambic pentameter. It is said that Trissino realized too late the importance of the choice of a subject over all abstract theoretical questions, and cursed the day that he chose not to sing of Orlando. But doubtless the poem's lack of success (since it *is* a good poem) had more to do with its periodic *longueurs* (twenty-seven books, in three volumes), made less endurable still by Trissino's crackpot orthographical theories: Greek omega, for example, is used to represent the long Italian "o," and "h" is supplied where there is no breathing in Italian, thus rendering "Omero" (Homer), as "Hωmηrω."

Notwithstanding this relegating of the epic subject to a secondary place, as outside the purview of theory, the historical character of that subject played an important role in providing the pearl of theory with the sand grain of factual truth. Around this grain of truth could be grown the metaphorical truth of imitation, making the whole epic, in Castelvetro's telling expression, a "similitude of history."[20] But for the epic to become a similitude of history there had to be a point of contact with actual history, thus reproducing in an interesting way the classical problem of *methexis*, the participation of the forms in their instances. Any "third man" mediating between mimetic and factual truth, between the Godfredo of history and the Godfredo of Tasso's epic, will open an infinite regression, since the mediator must be mediated in turn, and mediated to each of the two kinds of truth: there will always be a rift, mobile and elusive but insistently felt, between fact and invention.

⌘ WHEN A LOGICAL PROBLEM goes unrecognized, even as its presence is felt, the resulting uneasiness is often allayed by setting forth a technical program of research, envisaging a solution that can never be attained on that technical level. This is precisely what we find announced in Orazio Lombardelli, who identifies as central to the discipline of poetics the analysis of the manner in which historically true things are to be combined with inventions ("di tal modo le cose vere son con le favole mescolate"). The "third man" that is found for this purpose is the concept of *fable*, the sense of which is altered from that of the passage just quoted, where it means simple invention, to something that has a double foundation, in the truth of fact and the truth of imitation, or verisimilitude ("favola fondata su 'l vero, e su 'l verisimile").[21] The entire complex of theory we have been considering is brought together in a passage from Tasso's *Discourses* in which he reduces history, even the history of great events, to the status of mere matter "before it comes under the epic poet's art": after the poet "has disposed and treated it and clothed it with diction, it forms the fable, which is no longer the material, but the form and soul of the poem; and such Aristotle judged it."[22]

Finally, it is worth noting the brilliant distillation, in Spenser's "Letter to Raleigh," which was appended to the first installment of *The Faerie Queene*, in 1590, of the analysis interminable which is Italian critical theory on the heroic poem. Milton, of course, would have known Spenser's statement, reprinted in the folio editions of the early seventeenth century, better than any of the texts cited thus far. The abstract truths of moral philosophy are to be instantiated in a "historicall fiction" concerning Prince Arthur, the imaginary ancestor of Queen Elizabeth, as Aeneas is for Augustus. But Spenser also asserts that Arthur is only one in a class, any of the members of which could be used to anchor the abstraction of a "good governour and a vertuous man." Homer splits this abstraction between Agamemnon and Ulysses; Virgil and Ariosto unite it in Aeneas and Orlando respectively; and Tasso "dissevers" it again, forming, as Spenser learnedly declares, "both parts in two persons, namely that part which they in Philosophy call Ethice, or vertues of a private man, coloured in his Rinaldo: the other named Politice in his Godfredo."

The critical theory of the heroic poem in the Renaissance stood at odds with the nature of poetry itself, which derives its strength from purely imaginative structures rather than from the truth as understood by history or as understood by philosophy. In the "Letter to Raleigh" Spenser invokes both of these species of truth because he is writing a critical treatise of sorts and following critical fashion. The very phrase "historicall fiction" suggests a grain of historical truth that is not only amplified by fiction but regularized by fiction, according to the philosophical standards of ethics.

But in its most fundamental form, poetic discourse is closer to cosmogony than to history. Whereas historical discourse must support itself by the critical investigation of facts, cosmogonic discourse—the metonymical discourse of the origin and the descent from the origin—is grounded in purely imaginative structures. These are imaginative structures, moreover, that seem physically contiguous with one another, rather than having to stand as representations for something altogether outside them, that is, as imitations of history or imitations of moral philosophy. For Milton to see the poetic vitality in a subject involving the origin and the descent from the origin, he had to break the hold on his mind of the commonplaces Spenser (with far less danger to himself as a poet) sets out in the "Letter to Raleigh."

ᔐ IT IS OF COURSE TRUE that other things had a bearing on Milton's choice: his disappointment with the revolution, his repugnance at the celebration of kings in dynastic epics, his skepticism about British legend, and especially his demonstrated interest in accommodating biblical materials to classical forms. For such a poet, to attempt making a heroic poem out of the Bible would be irresistible. Milton's first important poem is a classical ode on the Nativity, his last work (as is generally supposed) a tragedy of Samson. He concurred in the durable if bizarre commonplace—he even put it in Jesus' mouth—that the Bible has earlier and better examples of all the classical forms. The Book of Job is a brief epic, for example, the Book of Revelation a tragedy, and the psalms surpass all the Greek hymns and odes (*Reason of Church Government*, YP 3:813–815; *Samson Agonistes*, preface; *Paradise Regained*). At the very time he was seeking a theme, Milton was pricked on by the dramatic experiments of older European contemporaries to search the Bible for episodes that might be formed into tragedies. These tragedies' titles (which, but for *Samson Agonistes*, is all they ever came to) suggest by their violent yoking together of heterogeneous materials the struggle for an impossible synthesis—impossible, at least, at this theoretical level.[23]

The synthesis was impossible at this level not just because the imaginative worlds of the Bible and of Greek and Roman literature are so very distinct, for that distinctness is lost if all possible subjects are in essence the same. It was the concept of a subject in Renaissance poetics that played a negative role, having in its turn to be negated before Milton was ready to choose. Essential to this concept, as we saw, is the absurd notion that the epic subject is that which lies outside theory while being officiously pointed to by theory. The structure of theory, in the very act of acknowledging its impotence with respect to the choice of a subject, presumes all the same to know where the materials of the choice lie; and by further presumptuousness it subordinates that choice to its own concerns, thus defining a subject as "matter." The question of the choice of a subject is thus appropriated for theory in the very act of placing it outside theory. So long as theory could insidiously determine in Milton's mind what an epic subject *is* while disqualifying itself on the very question of choice, he could do little. The paralysis one senses beneath the hectically confident activity recorded in the Trinity manuscript must have been bewildering indeed. This was the attitude to history—as entirely subordinate both to technical expertise and to moral abstraction—that Milton had to get past. For history in this sense offers a plethora of subjects between which it is impossible to choose except by choosing at random. One is hardly free to choose when it makes no difference what one chooses.

Put in the simplest terms possible, the obstacle to Milton's choice of a subject was the trivialization by critical theory of the very act of making the choice. When Milton rejected the assumptions leading to that trivialization, the epic subject was changed in his mind from a theoretical abstraction of relatively contingent importance to something fully embodied and real. This real, embodied thing demanded that he no longer worry about technique and decorum, for these were to be taken for granted, as consummate technical skill must always be taken for granted in performing at the highest level. Instead, Milton had to concentrate single-mindedly on the potential he saw in the story of Adam and Eve. He was at last free to choose the one subject with which he could be great.

᠔ GREATNESS—THE GREATNESS, for example, of Milton—is as mysterious a thing as choice, the mystery with which I began. The final task of this chapter is to see where these mysteries meet and to discover why their encounter is necessary. By a "necessary" encounter I mean one that, once it has occurred, shows itself to be anything but accidental. The parties to the encounter are so occultly bound up with each other in advance that when they meet they are revealed to be different aspects, or faces, of an underlying truth. Melville, writing with a condor's quill and Vesuvius for his inkstand, said of *Moby Dick*, "To produce a mighty book, you must choose a mighty theme."[24] In this apparently simple remark lies the secret of the greatness of *Paradise Lost*: the poet's choice of his subject. The magnificence and sweep of the vision, the variety of scenes and the delighted particularity of their realization, the direct and yet full presentation of character, the moral intensity beneath the restraint of the narrator, the hypnotic power with which the epic tradition is absorbed into virtually every line of the poem, the almost physical force of the thought as it unfolds, and above all the glories of the verse, verse that remains in its hypnotic power almost unsurpassed since in English poetry—all these are incidental to the greatness of *Paradise Lost*, which springs from a moment that is apart from these things and anterior to them. Nor is the greatness of the poem to be found in some demiurgic scene where the forms are imprinted in matter, or where the rules of the heroic epic are imprinted in the substance of history. The greatness is in the moment when Milton decided that this thing shall be.

The first statement, therefore, to be made about greatness is that it is achieved only where it is greatness itself that is meant. Greatness at its origin is choice, the choice of itself, and thus begins in a decision. The greatness is sustained by the courage of that decision throughout the execution of the poem, rousing us with the excitement of an epic being made.

Although the decision for greatness appears to be subjective ("I choose to be great"), it is in truth profoundly objective too, because it is accessible to oneself only through the choice of a mighty theme. Indeed, so objectively distant is that theme from all that is most familiar to us that it will appear to a lesser artist to have nothing to do with him or with her, which is of course true. The great is deeply alienating and foreign. But when a mighty theme is chosen by one who has the power of such choice, it elevates the chooser to its heights. To choose the small is to remain apart from, and free of, what you choose, and to remain a self. To choose the great is to tie yourself up with what you choose and almost to become it (as we saw that epic poets do). It is to put yourself at risk, to feel at once helpless and empowered, diminished and enlarged, abject and elevated. That is what we are shown in *Paradise Lost* when Milton announces his chosen theme:

> what in me is dark
> Illumine, what is low raise and support,
> That to the heighth of this great argument
> I may assert Eternal Providence,
> And justify the ways of God to men.
>   ⌁ *Paradise Lost 1.22–26*

Observing that performance of vocation, we are so caught up in its power, so astonished at the brilliance of its execution, and, if we are

critics, so busy in the shallows of its meaning, that the originative courage of the sustaining decision—the decision simply to take on such a
theme—is imperceptible to us. At the level of performance exhibited in
Paradise Lost, the poet's decision to be great is identical with his decision on a theme. Only the choice of the most radical theme can fuse in
this way the subjective and objective aspects of choice, the questions
"Who shall I be?" and "What shall I do?" To choose such a theme is to
feel you are chosen by it. This is the complex meaning of the simple
statement that Milton was inspired by what he chose. He blends his
own voice with that of the voice speaking through him—"thou from
the first / Wast present" (*PL* 1.19–20)—but there is no point along
the line of this speaking where we can divide the two voices. Milton's
choice is Milton's muse. For the myth of the Fall is now, as Lévi-
Strauss would say, thinking through him.[25]

8

Revolution in Paradise Regained

$\mathcal{W}$ HEN DESCRIBING THE works of a great artist with a
long career, one often finds it necessary to maintain a perspective that
allows each of the works to be two things at once: a separate creation in
its own right and a part of the total movement in the artist's imagination toward a larger, inexhaustible vision. From the latter point of view,
each work will seem to be at once incomplete in itself, since it is only a
part of the whole, and yet virtually complete inasmuch as it envisions
that whole and moves toward it. In the language of the political eschatology of Ernst Bloch, the work possesses, even in its smallest details,
the spirit of "utopia." For even in small details—in an eccentricity of
diction or in an unexpected and mystifying image—the work seems to
know what its completeness would be and to gesture toward what it
knows. To choose only two examples, the Father in *Paradise Regained*
speaks of the Son in the wilderness laying down "the rudiments / Of
his great warfare," echoing Virgil's reference to training in the "hard
rudiments of war" ("dura rudimenta belli"); and when Satan's fall, at
the end of the poem, is compared to that of the "Theban monster," the
Sphinx, whose riddle Oedipus solved, Jesus is implicitly compared to
Oedipus. Jesus is briefly a Roman general and a polluted Greek tyrant.
Moments such as these, in their very discordancy, suggest a completeness that the work has not yet achieved. The vast pagan culture from
which the images of power and of pollution derive would itself be com-

148

pleted, *perfected*, which is to say, "worked all the way through to the end," when reconciled to, and incorporated within, the grand biblical opus that the present work invites us to imagine.

Similarly, the feeling we have that the canon of an artist's work forms a totality, however disjointed the relations between its parts appear to be, is an effect of the larger imaginative vision that the works themselves can only ever realize in part. When certain other conditions are met, this sense of a larger totality can actually be strengthened by formal incommensurabilities among the works in the canon. In Milton's case, the incommensurable forms include psalms, occasional verse, victory odes, sonnets, masques, funeral monodies, a full-scale epic, a brief epic, and a tragedy. Of the conditions necessary for the blending of the works into a single project, the most important is that of a strong ideological background. The very difficulty of imagining such diverse works as Milton wrote composing a unity impels us to seek that unity on a higher plane, where the early poems fall into a narrative of *Bildung* preparing for the achievement of *Paradise Lost* and *Paradise Regained*, which poems transcend their formal differences in the shared work of vision. It is well known that in the *Poems* of 1645 Milton did something like this in arranging the early poems for publication, notably in the reordering of the Latin elegies to suggest that the poet's muse is growing purer with time. But the impulse to make each poem seem a preparation for something larger than itself is a reflex in almost all Milton's early poems, from the greeting of the English language in the "Vacation Exercise" to the farewell to pastoral with which "Lycidas" concludes.

This sense the reader has of breathing a larger atmosphere in which all the works stand is present even in the more occasional poems, such as the "Epitaph on the Marchioness of Winchester." The poem concludes with the apotheosis of the marchioness, "Far within the bosom bright / Of blazing majesty and light" (69–70), where she joins Rachel in glory. The sight we are given of the noblewoman joining the saints, "clad in radiant sheen / No marchioness, but now a queen," draws no small part of its impact from the way the poem seems to open into a larger imaginative realm, a realm of which future poems will have more to say. This opening is effected also by a slightly mysterious detail: Rachel is designated by the epithet "That fair Syrian shepherdess" (63). For a moment it is not heaven but, with sublime irrelevancy, biblical

Syria that is brought before our eyes. That peculiar evocation of Syria is but one example of how the feeling of transcendental reference is created within each of the works by a certain incoherency within, by imperfections and distortions arising from a background of noise—a "buzzing," or *bourdonnement*, as Rimbaud called it—which we interpret as the yet unapprehended totality of which the work before us is a part.

I offer one last example of how dissonances become harmonies when referred to a higher-level code. At the end of *Comus* there is an odd, irreconcilable contrast between two mythical couples: Venus and Adonis, who are situated by the poet in the western paradise of the gardens of the Hesperides, and, far above them, in the "spangled sheen" of the heavens, Cupid and Psyche. From Psyche's "fair unspotted" side the twins, Youth and Joy, are to be born as constellations, "so Jove hath sworn." Beneath them, and in a disturbing anticipation of Psyche's "spotless side," Adonis reposes in those western gardens, "waxing well of his deep wound / In slumber soft," as Venus meditates nearby: "and on the ground / Sadly sits th' Assyrian queen" (998–1001). Editors point out that Pausanius says Venus was first worshipped by the Assyrians, just as editors will point out that by the "Syrian shepherdess" the biblical Rachel is meant. But the epithet of Venus is deliberately strange, not only because of its exoticism but also because "Assyria" is in the east, not in the west. It is as if Venus' very passion for Adonis has followed the course of the sun, rising in biblical Syria, where "smooth Adonis from his native rock / Ran purple to the sea" (*PL* 1:450-451), blazing with its full midday heat over the Mediterranean isles, and setting in a Graeco-Celtic western paradise. My point is not to offer this as a convincing interpretation of the epithet "Assyrian queen," any more than I could fully reconcile an evocation of Syria to the meaning of the "Epitaph on the Marchioness of Winchester." My point is rather that all such incongruities give pleasure by virtue of their rising out of that undeveloped chaos of possibilities which we seem to hear faintly in all directions, as the buzzing of Syrian flies. Without these eccentricities of diction and these mystifying images, and without a relatively coherent ideology to which a reader may appeal in attempting to account for them, each poem in the canon would remain closed within itself but also incoherent in itself. This tension between, on one level, incoherent moments and, on a higher, more inclusive level, an ideology that can only promise to recuperate those moments, is the essence of biblical poetics. The Bible is a vast social product that accumulated over more than a millennium from an influx of texts far more diverse than can be found in even the most formally promiscuous of authors. For Christian interpreters, the Bible achieves the feeling of being organized in a great code by means of a structure of imagery deployed in a general system of apocalyptic deferral and visionary anticipation. Literary works that attach themselves to the Bible, or rather to the biblical code, acquire through this attachment the eschatological feeling of opening out, even in their smallest and most eccentric moments, into something greater than themselves.

შ THE IMPORTANCE OF seeing such works in double perspective is especially clear when we consider the relation of *Paradise Regained* to *Paradise Lost.* It is among the oldest critical issues in Milton. The earliest critics of *Paradise Regained*—those whom we hear about through Milton's nephew Edward Phillips—complained that it was inferior to its predecessor, a complaint, Phillips tells us, which the poet could never hear with patience. Later criticism has defended *Paradise Regained* by emphasizing its formal distinctness in the genre of the "brief epic," which was widely practiced in the Renaissance, especially in Latin; and another school has drawn attention to the thematic harmonies between *Paradise Regained* and the poem that was published with it in the same volume in 1671, *Samson Agonistes.*[1] Although both lines of approach have illuminated the poem splendidly, neither fully accepts the critical challenge of Milton's own words on *Paradise Regained.* Milton must have known that, in the nature of things, *Paradise Lost* would always be the more popular work. But the quieter, less extravagant tone of *Paradise Regained* reflects the confidence of a poet who has demonstrated his powers in *Paradise Lost* and now can focus intensely on the intellectual problem in hand, which is the nature of true heroism and its relation to the divine. It is a problem that is raised in *Paradise Lost* simply by the act of composing an epic poem on a biblical theme. But apart from asserting that patience and obedience are more truly heroic, which they are not, the earlier epic does not think the problem through. The later epic does, as far as it can.

Paradise Regained also shows real intellectual development beyond *Paradise Lost* in its ability to engage with the social, political, and moral problems that confront us in the world. If *Paradise Lost* is about how we got into those problems, *Paradise Regained* is about how we get out of them and how we go forward in time. This going forward in time does not mean simply moving away from the past, from the Fall. It means a complete transformation of the past by a future in which our freedom is restored. It means a revolution, not only in history but in consciousness as well. In short, *Paradise Regained* opens up questions that *Paradise Lost* treated as closed.

Indeed, it seems to me likely that once Milton completed *Paradise Lost*, he was bored by the very brilliance of what he had achieved. In any sense Milton would have cared for, the poem leaves one with little to think about beyond Adam's dull summation of what he has learned: "Henceforth I learn that to obey is best" (*PL* 12.561). Obedience, when it is coupled with loyalty and sustained by a sense of one's own worth, is not ignoble. But obedience is hardly enough to define what it takes to be human in the best sense of the word. Milton's term for that is a classical one, *heroism*, which he had identified already on the last occasion in *Paradise Lost* when he reflected on his task and, in so doing, subverted the traditional meaning of the word:

> Since first this subject for heroic song
> Pleased me, long choosing and beginning late,
> Not sedulous by nature to indite
> Wars, hitherto the only argument
> Heroic deemed, chief mast'ry to dissect
> With long and tedious havoc fabled knights
> In battles feigned, the better fortitude
> Of patience and heroic martyrdom
> Unsung.
>
> ᦁ *Paradise Lost 9.25–33*

Both terms denoting this "better fortitude"—"patience" and "heroic martyrdom"—carry nuances of meaning supplied partly from their ancient roots and partly by the events of the Restoration, which were still recent. *Patience* means the ability to suffer under torture, as did the surviving leaders of the English revolution and the surviving judges who condemned Charles I; *martyrdom* means bearing witness to the truth in extreme adversity, as many of the executed leaders also did. This is true heroism for Milton.

It is not, however, the subject of *Paradise Lost*, which is, as we are told in its opening line, "man's *first* disobedience." There was a tendency in Protestant thinking to look too far into the past, to apostolic times, to find a model of the church in its pure state, uncorrupted by idolatry and enslavement to tradition. Like Richard Hooker, who in *The Laws of Ecclesiastical Polity* had attacked such nostalgia, Milton was learned enough in the fathers to know that apostolic times were not what they were cried up to be. But whereas Hooker concluded that Christianity must therefore be thought through as a historically projected phenomenon, regarding non-scriptural traditions of the church as having at least potentially some value, Milton drew the more radical methodological conclusion: to go back to the root of the entire Judaic and Christian traditions in the opening chapters of Genesis, which describe the only time when humanity was in a pure and uncorrupted state. Milton's purpose in so doing was to investigate the deepest causes of the failure of the English revolution; but it was also to submit Christianity to a revolutionary transformation from within, based on a new interpretation of human nature and of history. The Greek father Origen glossed the Hebrew word *Eden* as *hēdonē*, which is Greek for "pleasure." This interpretation reflects the tendency to think that the perfect state of human nature is the enjoyment of happiness and that when things are hard or unpleasant something is wrong—something which perhaps history can explain. But Milton, who preferred hard liberty to easy servitude, believed that the perfect state of human nature is freedom, which means (in Aristotelian terms) the vigorous exercise of one's powers to the fullest. The original sin is the surrendering of this liberty to protect one's enjoyment of happiness, that is, out of fear of losing one's enjoyment of happiness. The original sin is the surrendering of liberty to one's own selfishness and fear, which sins will awaken a third, cruelty. In the final two books of *Paradise Lost*, Milton reveals the driving force of history to be the tendency to repeat compulsively these original sins—selfishness, cruelty, and fear—on a vast scale and in monstrously distorted ways, in the realm of high politics.

To some readers, therefore, including Ellwood, it may have seemed as if Milton had given insufficient attention in the final two books of *Paradise Lost* to the redemptive counterforce working in history through the covenants, through the prophets, and through the Son, who is both the source and the perfection of these things. But Milton says as much as can be said consistent with a deeply historical and non-mystical reading of the Bible. Note, for example, the manner in which the messianic promise made to David is worked into the impulsive forward motion of the narrative, a motion into which David himself enters by way of a relative clause:

> By judges first, then under kings, of whom
> The second both for piety renowned
> And puissant deeds a promise shall receive
> Irrevocable: that his regal throne
> For ever shall endure. The like shall sing
> All prophecy: that of the royal stock
> Of David (so I name this king) shall rise
> A son, the woman's Seed to thee foretold,
> Foretold to Abraham, as in whom shall trust
> All nations, and to kings foretold—of kings
> The last, for of his reign shall be no end.
> But first a long succession must ensue.
>   ᷍ *Paradise Lost 12.320–331*

To an inexperienced ear this may sound like one of the more workman-like passages in *Paradise Lost*. But the very looseness of the passage, imitating the back-and-forth movement of oral discourse relating a complex process through time, captures the inner strain in temporality between the meaningless flow of events and the eruption of singularities in the midst of those events.

Milton omits to describe the long succession of the kings of Israel, and of the separate lines of kings after the division of the kingdom, except to say that those kings are "Part good, part bad, of bad the longer scroll" (*PL* 12.336). Even the good kings, such as Josiah, whom Milton mentions elsewhere, and bad, idolatrous kings, such as Ahab, whose prophets' mouths Satan mentions having filled with lies (*PR* 1.371–376), are here beneath notice. Of special interest, however, is Milton's describing the Son as being "of kings / The last," since this implies that *all* kings since Jesus, not omitting the English kings, and especially the Stuarts, lack legitimacy. One may try to evade this conclusion by saying that the poet is referring to the Son's kingship at the end of time, when his eternal reign is established. But there is no escaping the suggestion

Milton is making by the phrase "of kings / The last": that the eternity of Christ's kingdom makes every subsequent king a usurper. It is a brilliant inversion of the principle of the divine right of kings: kings do not receive their legitimacy from Christ, as his regents; Christ's coming into the world deprives all kings after him of their legitimacy. Although Milton frames his narrative in a providential view of history, he is preoccupied with demonstrating how history is driven by our compulsion to repeat the Fall by surrendering our freedom, and perhaps especially our freedom to think clearly.

It was therefore with some sense—more than has been attributed to him—that Ellwood asked whether Milton might now say something about paradise found, having said so much already about paradise lost. The remark hardly justifies the charge that Ellwood failed to understand the final two books of *Paradise Lost*, especially if we suppose he emphasized the word *much*. Most of the epic *is* about the loss of paradise, and quite properly so. The Redemption is assured in book three and briefly described in book twelve, but Redemption is a subject that calls for a treatment of its own. Redemption is moreover a subject Milton had been writing about all his life, from the early psalm translations to *The Ready and Easy Way* and the *History of Britain*. Milton believed that virtuous, bold, revolutionary action is our necessary contribution to Redemption, which, if it is perfected by Christ, must nevertheless be initiated by us. In turning to the story of how paradise was lost, rather than resuming the theme of how a free commonwealth is won, Milton might be seen as having, if not deserted the cause, then retreated from the immediate fight in order to understand its circumstances better. It was now time to return to the fight, to apply the wisdom he had gained about the Fall to the revolutionary work of true restoration. Seen in this light, Ellwood's remark is anything but naïve; nor should we expect naïveté from a man continually in trouble with the authorities for his beliefs, and who had gone to prison for them: it was provocative. Without admitting any aesthetic flaw in *Paradise Lost* as it stands, one finds it easy to imagine the remark alerting Milton to a structural imbalance not in the poem itself but between the poem and the larger vision of history that the poem partly reveals.

A glance at the invocation to *Paradise Lost* shows how Milton's imagination continually reaches forward, seeking its thematic center beyond the narrative bounds of the poem he is actually composing: "man's first disobedience" does not occur until book nine; the coming into our world of "death" and "all our woe" does not occur until book ten; the "loss of Eden" is completed only in the final lines of the poem; the "one greater man" does not appear until the next epic Milton writes, *Paradise Regained*; and the achievement of this greater man, who restores us to our original state of innocence and regains paradise for us, is of course anticipated in *Paradise Regained* but actually occurs nowhere in Milton's major poems. In the Nativity Ode we are brought by anticipation to the threshold of this state when the poet speaks of the Last Judgment and of the bliss to follow, events that are assured by virtue of the nativity which occurs in the "now":

> When at the world's last session,
> The dreadful judge in middle air shall spread his throne.

> And then at last our bliss
> Full and perfect is,
> But now begins.
> ᴥ *"Ode on the Morning of Christ's Nativity," stanzas 17–18*

In the invocation to *Paradise Regained*, Milton clearly announces that both his epics, despite their stylistic differences, are to be read as parts of a single, historical vision in which heroes come together as "one man":

> I who erewhile the happy garden sung,
> By one man's disobedience lost, now sing
> Recovered Paradise to all mankind,
> By one man's firm obedience fully tried.
> ᴥ *Paradise Regained 1.1–4*

The total experience of humanity which these lines emblematically describe does not fall into a linear narrative, although such narratives can be drawn from it. That is instead projected into one revolutionary moment when every positive human action is gathered to every other and perfected by what Christ does in the wilderness and by what Christ symbolizes when he stands, balanced in time, on the pinnacle of the Jerusalem temple. So habitual is Milton's tendency to reach beyond the action at hand to the meaning of that action in the future that he seems almost unconscious of the way the chorus of angels describes what Christ has achieved as if it were identical with what Christ, as the returned Son, will achieve at the apocalypse:

> now thou hast avenged
> Supplanted Adam, and, by vanquishing
> Temptation, hast regained lost Paradise.
> ᴧ *Paradise Regained 4.606–608*

That triumphant major chord contains not only the titles to both Milton's epics ("regained lost Paradise") but also the heroes of both epics (Christ is spoken to, Adam referred to) and the single theme that the epics share: the central struggle of human life, which for Milton is temptation: the temptation to make oneself less free.

ᴧ THE DRAMATIC INTEREST of the temptations in *Paradise Regained* does not turn on any uncertainty whether Christ will fall; there can be no uncertainty as to that. The interest turns rather on how much Satan will discover about the Son by subjecting him to the temptations and how much the Son will discover about himself. On this point the biblical narratives (Matthew 4:1–11, Mark 1:12–13, Luke 4:1–13) are silent. They are also impersonal. Mark disposes of the wilderness episode in two verses and as many sentences: Jesus was suddenly thrust by the spirit into the wilderness for forty days to be tempted by Satan; he was with the wild beasts; and he was ministered to by angels. In the King James version: "And immediately the Spirit driveth him into the wilderness. And he was there in the wilderness forty days, tempted of Satan; and was with the wild beasts; and the angels ministered unto him." The emphasis here is on the Son's magical power. In Matthew and Luke both, though there are other differences between them, the encounter between Jesus and the devil is business-like. The business in hand is temptation, or "testing" *(peirasmos)*, and the emphasis is on the Son's mastery throughout. There is no interest in character or motive. So little is the sense of a personal confrontation that Satan in both versions seems more like a purely narrative function of the kind described in Vladimir Propp's *Morphology of the Folktale.* In Matthew, the devil is referred to four times simply as the "diabolos," once by name, "Satana," and once, with impulsive narrative force, as the "tempter," "peirazōn". The functional character of this term—which means "the one tempting"—can be seen when we translate literally "and coming forward the tempting one said . . ." ("kai proselthōn ho peirazōn eipen"). Only at the end does Jesus address this tempting one by name, Satana, after which the devil immediately breaks off the temptation: "Then the devil leaveth him." Again, as in folktales, it is Jesus' ability to *name* his adversary that gives him power over his adversary. In Luke, with that gospel's more self-conscious, participial style, the action seems almost to flow around the actors, but with the purpose ultimately of bringing the Son forward as master: "And Jesus being full of the Holy Ghost returned from Jordan, and was led by the spirit into the wilderness, being forty days tempted of the devil" (Luke 4:1–2). Only at the end—and it is Luke's account that will end on the pinnacle—do we see any hint of a psychological response in the devil. We hear that having exhausted his temptations (note again the resemblance to folktale), the devil retreated until the next opportunity (if that is the meaning of "achri kairou"). This is a suggestion, a very subtle one, on which Milton would seize for his climax, when Satan "smitten with amazement fell" (*PR* 4.562).

Milton's innovation in retelling the story is to throw the emphasis not on the ability of the Son to withstand temptation but on the larger story of the conflict between Satan and the Son. By framing the temptation within that historical and apocalyptic conflict, we are able to make the issue one of discovery: of Satan's effort to discover who the Son is and, more remarkably still, of the Son's discovery of himself. The result is to alter the entire feeling of the biblical narratives so that the characters, and especially the devil, are no longer subordinated to the action as functions within it. Satan does what he does not simply because he is "the one tempting," as in Matthew, but because he has a motive: to find out who this "Son of God" is; to find out what the proclamation at the baptism means; and to discover whether this son is the "seed" prophesied in Eden. Throughout history Satan has been watching for signs of the prophecy's imminence, "With dread attending when that fatal wound / Shall be inflicted by the seed of Eve / Upon my head" (*PR* 1.53–55). He has observed Christ's baptism; he has seen the sign of the dove, "what'er it meant" (1.83); and he has heard the voice from heaven proclaim Jesus "my son beloved" (1.85). Given the prophecy in Eden, Satan somewhat illogically takes comfort in the knowledge that at least the Son's mother is mortal. But the reason why he takes comfort in this is soon disclosed: the fear that this Son might be, or might be like, God's "first-begot," who drove Satan and the rebel angels out of heaven:

> His mother then is mortal, but his sire
> He who obtains the monarchy of Heaven,
> And what will He not do t' advance His son?
> His first-begot we know, and sore have felt,
> When his fierce thunder drove us to the deep;
> Who this is we must learn, for man he seems
> In all his lineaments, though in his face
> The glimpses of his father's glory shine.
>
> ∞ *Paradise Regained 1.86–93*

That is what he will discover, and it is the worst news possible: that "Son of God" means God's "first-begot."

When Satan returns to middle air to give a preliminary report on his temptation of the Son, he seems to deliver the news of his ill success honestly and directly. But he does so in the manner of someone who discloses one thing in order to keep another concealed: the man he is now tempting, he tells the devils, is far more difficult to corrupt than was Adam. They knew this before the first attempt was made. Continuing this show of empty candor, Satan admits that "Adam by his wife's allurement fell" (2.134) rather than by Satan's direct effort, and yet Adam is "to this man inferior far" (2.135). But the superiority of the Son to Adam is not at all the point: at issue is not the Son's vulnerability to Satan but Satan's vulnerability to the Son: "such an enemy / Is risen to invade us, who no less / Threatens than our expulsion down to hell" (2.126–128). The very thought of being driven out of the world and back into hell recalls the first time the devils were driven to hell; it also recalls the "first-begot" who drove them there. Is this the same Son as the last? The question is not explicitly asked. It is in fact scrupulously avoided; but it hangs in middle air. The question is still impending when Satan says to the Son that he hopes the Son's "gentle brow" portends some good for him, that the Son's reign may stand between Satan

and the wrath of the Father, as a summer's cloud stands between us and
the beams of the sun:

> though to that gentle brow
> Willingly I could fly, and hope thy reign,
> From that placid aspect and meek regard,
> Rather than aggravate my evil state,
> Would stand between me and thy Father's ire,
> (Whose ire I dread more than the fire of hell)
> A shelter and a kind of shading cool
> Interposition, as a summer's cloud.
>
> ☙ *Paradise Regained 3.215–222*

The question Satan was evading when speaking to the devils—"is this
the Son who threw us out of Heaven, who *is* the wrath of God?"—is
evaded here too. Satan is not so much tempting the Son as tempting
himself to believe that the Son may be the opposite of what he is: a
means to hide from God and from the truth.

Only uncontrolled rage can bring the truth out of Satan or provoke
him to admit the truth to himself. When it does, we see how closely Satan has studied the Son, how carefully he has gone over what evidence
he could glean from the prophets and from Jesus' life up to now, and
how near he has come to recognizing Jesus not as one of the "sons" of
God, meaning an angel, as in Job 1:6, but as the first-begotten Son:

> To whom the Fiend now swoll'n with rage replied:
> Then hear, O Son of David, virgin-born,
> For Son of God to me is yet in doubt,
> Of the Messiah I have heard foretold
> By all the prophets; of thy birth at length
> Announced by Gabriel with the first I knew . . .
> Till at the ford of Jordan whither all
> Flocked to the Baptist, I among the rest,
> Though not to be baptized, by voice from Heaven
> Heard thee pronounced the Son of God beloved.
> Thenceforth I thought thee worth my nearer view
> And narrower scrutiny, that I might learn

> In what degree or meaning thou art called
> The Son of God.
>
> ⤳ *Paradise Regained 4.499–517*

Narrower scrutiny of the actual phrase, "Son of God," brings him no nearer to the truth, since to him it "bears no single sense":

> The son of God I also am, or was,
> And if I was, I am; relation stands;
> All men are sons of God; yet thee I thought
> In some respect far higher so declared.
>
> ⤳ *Paradise Regained 4.518–521*

Therefore, he says, he has shadowed the Son since the baptism, following him into the wilderness, "Where by all best conjectures I collect / Thou art to be my fatal enemy" (4.524–525).

Such a conclusion, after he has sifted all his "best conjectures," is unremarkable. What Satan needs to know is not whether the Son is his enemy—he has no doubt of that—but what the stature and power of that enemy is. How dangerous is this enemy? His efforts to find out can tell him only what his enemy is *not:* a man who can be tricked or maneuvered into damaging himself through any show of weakness which would compromise his perfect freedom:

> And opportunity I here have had
> To try thee, sift thee, and confess have found thee
> Proof against all temptation as a rock
> Of adamant, and as a centre, firm
> To the utmost of mere man: both wise and good,
> Not more.
>
> ⤳ *Paradise Regained 4.531–536*

Other men have resisted temptation. Satan wants to know what makes Jesus, who seems entirely a man, more than a man; for Satan knows he cannot be hurt by a man. What can hurt him is whatever hidden thing makes Jesus more than man:

> Therefore to know what more thou art than man,
> Worth naming Son of God by voice from Heaven,
> Another method I must now begin.
> >> *Paradise Regained 4.538–540*

The English word *method* was a new and fashionable one in Milton's day, recalling the system of rigorous deduction promoted in Descartes's *Discours sur la méthode* and suggesting, etymologically, a path or means of transit. All Satan's temptations have led to this moment to be revealed for what they are: attempts to find out who or what the Son is, to know the worst: "I would be at the worst; worst is my port, / My harbour and my ultimate repose" (3.209–210). These lines are in their quieter way as terrifying as those Satan speaks in *Paradise Lost*, on the top on Mount Niphates. There we learn that the worst thing about being in hell is the knowledge that hell is always getting catastrophically worse. There is no end to the experience of falling through the bottom of one hell into the flames of the next:

> Which way I fly is Hell, myself am Hell,
> And in the lowest deep a lower deep
> Still threat'ning to devour me opens wide,
> To which the Hell I suffer seems a Heav'n.
> >> *Paradise Lost 4.75–78*

No wonder Satan says "worst is my port." But even that is a haven into which he will not come; or, rather, his not coming into the haven of the worst is what the worst is.

I have spoken so far of Satan's effort to discover Jesus' identity as the Son of God. Jesus has little difficulty discovering Satan's; or rather, he seems indifferent to Satan's identity, taking little notice of it until Satan proposes that Jesus worship him, in return for receiving the kingdoms of the world. Yet when Satan first tempts Jesus, inviting him to turn stones to bread, Jesus replies with a quotation from scripture and parenthetically remarks that his interlocutor, though disguised as an illiterate desert dweller, knows the relevant text:

> Think'st thou such force in bread? Is it not written
> (For I discern thee other than thou seem'st)

> Man lives not by bread only, but each word
> Proceeding from the mouth of God.
>
> ~ *Paradise Regained 1.347–350*

Jesus then says to Satan, "Why dost thou then suggest to me distrust, / Knowing who I am, as I know who thou art?" (1.355–356). At this Satan gives a full and astonishing disclosure of his identity, seen in its entire historical extent from his rebellion in heaven:

> Whom thus answered th'Arch fiend now undisguised,
> 'Tis true, I am that spirit unfortunate,
> Who leagued with millions more in rash revolt
> Kept not my happy station, but was driven
> With them from bliss to the bottomless deep.
>
> ~ *Paradise Regained 1.357–361*

Jesus' response to Satan's effort to enlist his sympathy is threefold: a refutation, a reproof, and a prophecy. The last is the basis for Satan's fear that the Son has come to drive him and the rebel angels out of the world: "No more shalt thou by oracling abuse / The Gentiles; henceforth oracles are ceased" (1.455–456).

These lines reveal what might be supposed to be a slight inconsistency in Milton's poem. Here, Jesus is in no doubt who Satan is. Later, Jesus indicates that only when Satan has proposed that Jesus worship him is it evident who this tempter is: "Get thee behind me; plain thou now appear'st / That Evil One, Satan for ever damned" (4.193–194). It is, I think, a justifiable inconsistency. Milton needs the early recognition of Satan by Jesus to show the Son's swift discernment and immediate authority. Milton also needs both the magnificent speech in which Satan discloses himself and Jesus' still more magnificent reply. But Milton does not want to pass up the opportunity given him in Matthew when, after the temptation of the kingdoms, and after Jesus has been invited to worship his tempter, Jesus calls the devil "Satan" and commands him to retire: "Get thee behind me, Satan." In the Authorized Version, the phrase is in Luke 4:8. In the Greek original, the phrase is not in Luke but in Matthew 4:10 only. Yet the phrase as it appears in Luke in the Authorized Version is a closer translation of the Greek original, "Hypage, Satana"—"back off" or "get down"—than the corresponding phrase in the original text of Matthew, "Get thee hence, Satan."[2] Milton reads this moment in Matthew as if it were in a Greek tragedy, as a moment of recognition, of *anagnorisis*, occurring between adversaries one of whom is unknown to the other. For this reason Milton has Christ sarcastically compare this "bolder attempt" to Satan's cowardly temptation of Eve. Note that Jesus pointedly does not mention Adam, whom Satan lacked the courage to tempt:

> dar'st thou to the Son of God propound
> To worship thee accursed, now more accursed
> For this attempt bolder than that on Eve,
> And more blasphemous? which expect to rue . . .
> Get thee behind me; plain thou now appear'st
> That Evil One, Satan for ever damned.
>   ↝ *Paradise Regained* 4.178–194

"Plain thou now appear'st," Jesus says to Satan; but he is not so plain to Satan.

↝ WE COME NOW TO THE issue of Jesus' discovering his own identity as the Son of God, or rather his discovering the full meaning of the phrase "Son of God," which is not completed for him until the angel chorus at the end. When Jesus goes into the wilderness, he recalls his mother's account of his birth and his own reading of the scriptures in the light of what she told him. From these sources he realizes that he is himself the fulfillment of the Messianic prophecies. In the final words of this sentence, "I am," there is a hint that his unconscious is already telling him that he is also the God who spoke to Moses in the burning bush:

> This having heard, straight I again revolved
> The Law and prophets, searching what was writ
> Concerning the Messiah, to our scribes
> Known partly, and soon found of whom they spake
> I am.
>   ↝ *Paradise Regained* 1.259–263

Lewalski describes well the limited state of knowledge the Son is in: "He does not yet understand the full meaning of the prophetic meta-

phors, or of the divine Sonship proclaimed at his baptism, or just what
his "God-like office now mature" will entail (1.188)."³ Nor do we understand it ourselves. Yet Jesus' uncertainty as to the precise meaning
of his identity as "Son of God" raises little or no anxiety in him. He is
confident that what he needs to know of himself will be revealed when
he needs to know it:

> And now by some strong motion I am led
> Into this wilderness, to what intent
> I learn not yet, perhaps I need not know;
> For what concerns my knowledge God reveals.
> ⌁ *Paradise Regained 1.290–293*

The phrase "strong motion" captures the feeling of Mark 1:12, in which
Jesus is "thrust forth"—the verb is *ekballein*—into the wilderness. Its
analogue will appear in *Samson Agonistes* at the critical moment when
the hero feels those "rousing motions" (1382) which drive him to the
temple of Dagon as forcefully as Christ is driven into the wilderness.

   The issue of Jesus' recognition and naming of Satan is a secondary
one, a splendid effect Milton has achieved by fishing a suggestion of it
out of Matthew. Of much greater importance are Satan's efforts to discover the identity of Jesus in the meaning of the phrase "Son of God,"
efforts that culminate in that other "method" which Satan employs on
the pinnacle of the temple, the last of the temptations in the sequence
in Luke. The Matthew sequence—bread, pinnacle, kingdom—seems
the more logical of the two, ascending as it does from an appeal to
the physical weakness of hunger to an appeal to self-importance, and
finally to an appeal to the lust for power. What Milton saw, however, in
the Luke sequence—bread, kingdom, pinnacle—was the way the scriptural quotations in it made a sequence of their own, with the final one,
from Deuteronomy 6:16, directed menacingly at the tempter himself:
"Thou shalt not tempt the Lord thy God" (Luke 4:12). The command
in Deuteronomy in turn refers to Exodus 17:7, when the Israelites seek
to "test" God. The verb in the Septuagint, the Greek version of the
Hebrew scriptures known to the authors of the gospels, is *peirazein*, the
same verb used in the three New Testament accounts of Jesus' temptation. Because the Greek word for "temptation," *peirasmos*, means to put
to the test, the rebuke is especially appropriate to the nature of the final
temptation as Milton understands it. For in that temptation no attempt

is made to draw Jesus into sin: its entire purpose is to conduct a test to find out more about the meaning of the title, Son of God. In his searching out the identity of the Son, what Satan discovers is beyond his worst fear: that this Son is not something new in God's plan but something very old, the Son whose lightning left Satan and the rebel angels "Exhausted, spiritless, afflicted, fall'n" (*PL* 6.852). When the wall of heaven opens for their expulsion into chaos, the rebel angels recoil in horror from the sight of the abyss. But the terror of the lightning is even worse; it impels them to leap for refuge into what they fear:

> The monstrous sight
> Strook them with horror backward but far worse
> Urged them behind: headlong themselves they threw
> Down from the verge of Heav'n. Eternal wrath
> Burnt after them to the bottomless pit.
>
> ✤ *Paradise Lost* 6.862–866

This is what Satan recognizes when Jesus says, "Tempt not the Lord thy God" (*PR* 4.561). More important still, as critics have often pointed out (although the matter has been one of contention), is Jesus' recognition that he is, without having intended it, the referent of the phrase "the Lord thy God." What this climactic revelation means to Satan is different from what it should mean to us. For the climactic revelation is not a revelation of God, a theophany, but rather, so to speak, an anthropophany, a revelation of the human as sufficient to the struggle with evil, without metaphysical aid. What the phrase should mean to us is not that Jesus is ontologically one with the Father, the full expression on earth, in human form, of a transcendent God. It should mean that the full authority of a transcendent God has been taken into the human and resituated there ontologically.

✤ NORTHROP FRYE HAS NOTED that much of the dialogue between Jesus and Satan has to do with time.[4] I would add that in *Paradise Regained* the issue of time is really the issue of politics, of timing, and of improvisation, the ability to seize occasion as occasions arise. As Frye observes, all Satan's assaults may be understood as attempts to provoke the Son into acting prematurely, into improvising, upsetting the delicate balance of history which for a moment in this poem comes to rest upon Christ at its still point: "Thy years are ripe, and over-ripe . . . but thou yet art not too late"; "Zeal and Duty are not slow, / But on Occasion's forelock watchful wait"; "each act is rightliest done, / Not when it must, but when it may be best" (*PR* 3.31 and 42; 3.172–173; 4.475–476). Although in politics it may be necessary to seize occasion when occasion can be seized, a point Milton himself, in his political writings, showed he appreciated fully, for the transcendental politics of saving the world, the sense of timing is not so much political as it is poetic. If Jesus were to succumb to the temptation to seize worldly power and liberate Israel, he would be falling into politics as usual, which occurs within the flow of history and may at most alter the course of that flow. But Jesus' transcendental politics will revolutionize the very conditions in which the political exists in the world. He shows he has the strength to bide his time—"My time . . . is not yet come" (3.396–397; cf. 3.440) —and to endure the anxiety aroused by the temptation to seize power impulsively, an act which would be tantamount to worshipping Satan even without the formal gesture of falling down: "But I endure the time," he says, "till which expired, / Thou hast permission on me" (4.174–175). Such timing can be called inaction only from the loser's point of view.

This political argument over whether it is best to wait on God's time or to seize occasion and liberate Israel now comes to a head at the end of the third book. To what are derisively called Satan's "politic maxims" and the "cumbersome / Luggage of war," Jesus opposes an inward understanding of liberty which has been the burden of Milton's political writings, although it is nowhere more clearly stated than in the opening of *The Tenure of Kings and Magistrates:*

> If men within themselves would be governed by reason, and not generally give up their understanding to a double tyranny, of custom from without and blind affections within, they would discern better what it is to favor and uphold the tyrant of a nation. But being slaves within doors, no wonder that they strive so much to have the public state conformably governed to the inward vicious rule by which they govern themselves. For indeed none can love freedom heartily, but good men; the rest love not freedom, but license; which never hath more scope or more indulgence than under tyrants.

It is by the light of this understanding that Jesus says what he says about liberating the "captive tribes" of Israel at the present time. (He is referring particularly to the ten tribes of the idolatrous northern kingdom, founded by Jeroboam, which were carried off by the Assyrians before the conquest of the southern kingdom, and of Jerusalem, by Nebuchadnezzar.) To liberate a people who are enslaved morally to their own pride and spiritually to the idols of their enemies is only to confirm them in their enslavement to both, giving pride and idolatry a specious legitimacy: "let them serve / Their enemies, who serve idols with God" (3.431–432). After stating this hard but necessary maxim, Jesus resumes the possibility of a transcendental politics by which one remains open to the call of a truly revolutionary action. It is a call that makes a fundamental change in the self as well as in the world:

> Yet he at length, time to himself best known,
> Rememb'ring Abraham by some wondrous call
> May bring them back repentant and sincere,
> And at their passing cleave th'Assyrian flood,
> While to their native land with joy they haste,
> As the Red Sea and Jordan once he cleft,
> When to the promised land their fathers passed;
> To his due time and providence I leave them.
>
> ᴈ *Paradise Regained 3.433–440*

Jesus' fullest reply to the temptation to improvise politically shows the union of his will with that of the Father, giving him the perfect sense of timing in action which is manifested precisely in his active restraint, his refusal to move. I would go so far as to describe this poetic sense of timing as having its spatial counterpart in the athletic act of staying physically balanced in a difficult place, on the pinnacle of the temple:

> All things are best fulfilled in their due time,
> And time there is for all things, Truth hath said:
> If of my reign prophetic writ hath told,
> That it shall never end, so when begin
> The Father in his purpose hath decreed,
> He in whose hand all times and seasons roll.
>
> ᴈ *Paradise Regained 3.182–187*

By the active power of restraint Jesus is concentrating his energy so that at the moment of opening rightness, of *kairos*, his action will be intense and perfectly aimed, felling Satan with a single verbal blow.

⟋⟍ WHAT HAPPENS ON THE pinnacle of the temple? A surprising amount has been written on this question, both as it pertains to the scriptural accounts, where Jesus is taken and stood by the devil "on the roof-peak of the temple" ("epi to pterugion tou hierou"), and as it pertains to Milton's account.[5] In the latter, Jesus is taken to the temple, which appears, as in Josephus, as "a mount / Of alabaster, topped with golden spires," on the highest of which he is placed: "There on the highest pinnacle he set / The Son of God" (4.548–550). It should be said right away that the word in both Matthew and Luke in the King James version, "pinnacle," cannot be the same word, as John Carey maintains, as the word used in the Greek text of Matthew and Luke. The Greek word *pterugion* is related to *pterux*, "wing," but is generally used for things that have a fold along a central line, such as a shield, or even the lips. In architecture, *pterugion* is used for the peak of the roof as it forms a ridge where two inclined planes meet; it is possible for a person to stand on such a ridge, if not for very long. Taking hints from Josephus (as Carey shows) as well as from the King James version, Milton makes the episode dramatic by having Satan set Jesus on the highest of the temple's golden spires, the pinnacle. This augmentation of visual and dramatic effect introduces the first question: whether Jesus balances on the pinnacle using only his human powers. The second question is whether Jesus' quotation, "Tempt not the Lord thy God" (4.561), refers only to God the Father, or whether it refers to the Father and the Son.

The event on the pinnacle requires careful reading, but nothing in it quite amounts to a crux, to anything as uninterpretable as that famous crux in "Lycidas," the two-handed engine at the door. Yet it is unlikely, and perhaps undesirable, that critics will ever perfectly agree about precisely what happens. The reason for this lies not in the event itself but in the centrality of the event in Milton's total poetic vision. The event cannot quite be reduced to the facts of a literal reading because its meaning is the meaning of Milton's work as a whole, the place where it comes into its center. Everything is at stake on the pinnacle.

As Carey observes, Milton's calling the pinnacle Jesus' "uneasy station" (4.584) is decisively against the theory that any miracle or out-right theophany occurs. The phrase implies "that the standing was not miraculous but a balancing feat."[6] In the same note Carey goes on to quote Josephus' description of the view from the royal portico over-looking the valley of Kedron: "The valley was very deep, and its bot-tom could not be seen if you looked from above into the depth . . . if anyone looked down from the top of the roof to those depths he would be giddy, while his sight could not reach down to such an abyss."[7] I sup-pose the point of Carey's quoting this is to remind us that balancing in a difficult place is not just a physical but a psychological challenge, for the slightest fear will cause giddiness and throw one off balance. But the physical challenge of balancing on a single point, the apex of a pin-nacle, perhaps with one foot resting on top of the other, and for an indefinite length of time, is also very great. It is reasonable of Satan to suppose, as he does, that Jesus will fall. Once Jesus has fallen, Satan plans to observe him so as to determine whether the prophecy he has quoted refers to the man he is observing:

> For it is written, He will give command
> Concerning thee to his angels, in their hands
> They shall uplift thee, lest at any time
> Thou chance to dash thy foot against a stone.
>   ᕽ *Paradise Regained* 4.556–559

If Jesus falls and dies, then he will not be the referent of this prophecy and he will pose no further threat to Satan. If Jesus falls but is uplifted on the angels' wings, then Satan will at least know more about Jesus' identity, gaining by this knowledge some limited tactical advantage, for he has had none as yet, not even the advantage of knowing his adver-sary. Hence when Satan tells Jesus to choose to stand—"There stand, if thou *wilt* stand" (my emphasis)—he is purely ironical.[8] Satan never supposes that Jesus has a choice in the matter. I have said that Satan's assurance that Jesus will fall is a reasonable supposition because Jesus is a human being, and no human being who has not been trained to it could perform the feat of balancing on the pinnacle for any length of time. As Carey points out, balancing on the pinnacle is described as an "uneasy" but not an impossible feat. Jesus balances on the pinnacle only long enough to utter ten words and watch Satan fall, whereupon

he is immediately rescued by the angels: "So Satan fell and *straight* a
fiery globe / Of angels on full sail of wing flew nigh" (4.581–582; my
emphasis). I mentioned that a great part of the difficulty of the feat resides in the psychological terror of having to balance at such a height,
and of having to do so, it should be emphasized, without knowing when
or if one is going to be rescued. The perfect mastery over fear which
was witnessed in Jesus' going unprepared into the wilderness is shown
here in his mastery over the terror of balancing on a point with no
knowledge of how he will get down. Jesus is subject to human physical
weakness—a fall from the pinnacle would kill him—but he has none of
the human psychological weakness that is a consequence of the Fall.
Adam fell because he was *afraid* of what would happen to Eve and of
what would happen to him without Eve. Jesus does not fall because he
is the first man since Adam who hasn't any fear, or rather who is entirely the master of any fear he has.

I might as well say that Jesus has Herculean psychological strength
and Oedipal concentration of mind, since these comparisons are the
ones Milton chooses to glorify what has been achieved: Jesus' victory is
like Hercules strangling Antaeus in the air and Oedipus causing the
Sphinx to throw herself from the acropolis at Thebes, the acropolis being not only the highest place but the spiritual and political center of
the city:

> As when Earth's son Antaeus (to compare
> Small things with greatest) in Irassa strove
> With Jove's Alcides, and oft foiled still rose,
> Receiving from his mother Earth new strength,
> Fresh from his fall, and fiercer grapple joined,
> Throttled at length in the air, expired and fell;
> So after many a foil the tempter proud,
> Renewing fresh assaults, amidst his pride
> Fell whence he stood to see his victor fall.
> And as that Theban monster that proposed
> Her riddle, and him, who solved it not, devoured;
> That once found out and solved, for grief and spite
> Cast herself headlong from th'Ismenian steep,
> So struck with dread and anguish fell the Fiend.
>
> ✗ *Paradise Regained 4.563–576*

It is important to note that the heroic labors to which Milton here refers are not miracles. So too with Jesus' balancing on the pinnacle. The answer to the first question, then, is that Jesus uses only human powers.

꙳ THE SECOND QUESTION, it will be recalled, is whether Jesus' quotation from Deuteronomy, "Tempt not the Lord thy God" (4:561), is ambiguous. When he refers to "the Lord thy God," does Jesus mean God the Father or does he mean both the Father and himself? This question will take more time: it goes to the center of the most difficult theological problem in Milton, his Christology, although I must say that I think Miltonists evince far too much faith in theological concepts and theological language. These can be useful in a general way (it is useful, for example, to know that Milton is not a Trinitarian and that he does not believe in the soul as a substance entirely distinct from the body), but are at best crude templates when we try to understand Milton's poetry through them—or, worse, when we merely substitute theological concepts for understanding. Since theological concepts are relatively easy to understand, even when they are meant to express mystery, and can be divided into clear and detachable units, one can get naïve satisfaction out of reducing the poetry to them. They seem to represent positive knowledge in the light of which the poetry may be grasped. The literary-critical results of this procedure vary in quality, from the best Milton criticism to the worst, but the underlying assumption on which all such results depend is that theology may be used instrumentally to grasp what is more subtle, mobile, and living: poetry. Theology is useful, even indispensable, up to a point; but it is not the key to understanding Milton's poetry. (I am convinced by the defenders of Milton's authorship of the theological treatise *De Doctrina Christiana*. But I wonder why the issue arouses such passion. Is it that without *De Doctrina Christiana* we fear we cannot ever know what Milton's poetry means?)

When we consider what Jesus says on the pinnacle, it is less important that the scene goes to the center of Milton's Christology than it is to feel how what Christ says goes to the center of Milton's poetic vision of what it means to be human. The question, as I have stated it, is whether, by the phrase "the Lord thy God," Jesus means God the Father alone or God the Father and himself, in the latter case affirming that he, Jesus, is "the Lord thy God." Part of the problem here is with

meaning. If "meaning" is centered in the subject, denoting a precon-
ceived intention in the mind of the speaker, then I think what Jesus
meant to say is "Don't tempt the Father." That is what he says and
means to say in Matthew and Luke, both of which quote verbatim from
Deuteronomy 6:16 in the Septuagint translation: "Do not put to the
test the Lord your God" ("ouk ekpeiraseis kurion ton theon sou").
There was a minor tradition of scriptural exegesis which held that in
Matthew and Luke Jesus is referring also to himself. But most commentators properly reject such a reading: Jesus is referring only to the
Father. Similarly, in *Paradise Regained,* there is no warrant in the text
for the claim that Jesus intends to reveal himself as the Father by saying, "Do not tempt me, the Lord your God." To intend to reveal himself as the Father would be tactically inconsistent, for his strategy is
never to give Satan any positive knowledge. Instead, Jesus makes everything he discloses rest on hypotheses marked by recurring uses of the
word *if:* "If of my reign prophetic writ hath told, / That it shall never
end, so when begin / The Father in his purpose hath decreed" (3.184–
186). Also, to intend to reveal himself as the Father is entirely inconsistent with the character of Jesus as he is shown in the poem up to this
point, subordinating everything he does, and anything he wishes, to the
will of the Father. Jesus lets himself be led into the wilderness, and into
the danger of starvation, with perfect confidence in the Father's will. By
surrendering himself to the radical otherness of the Father's will, he
brings the otherness deep inside him.

The otherness of the Father as something deeply interior to the self
emerges from the question of food, of survival. Jesus notes that for
forty days in the wilderness he felt no hunger. He claims no particular
virtue for his abstinence because he had no appetite for food: "if nature
need not, / Or God support nature without repast / Though needing,
what praise is it to endure?" (2.249–251). Jesus then says something I
should find it hard to agree with. He says that even if he *did* feel the
need for food, but God had removed the actual, physical need for food,
then in that case too Jesus would still deserve no praise for his endur-
ance of the agony of starvation. I can't see why not. But in any event
that is the circumstance he finds himself in now: he hungers.

> Now I feel I hunger, which declares
> Nature hath need of what she asks; yet God

> Can satisfy that need some other way,
> Though hunger still remain: so it remain
> Without this body's wasting, I content me,
> And from the sting of famine fear no harm.
> ᷒ *Paradise Regained* 2.252–257

The Father can sustain Jesus' body without food, even while Jesus hungers as if he really did need food to survive. Yet Jesus makes a condition: so long as his body does not actually waste with starvation but is sustained by the Father in "some other way" than eating, he is content to suffer the agony he would suffer if his body really were wasting away. More important, he knows no fear, no uncertainty, as to whether the Father is indeed sustaining his body. It is an astonishing confidence which no one else, maddened by the pangs of starvation, could sustain. Nor will Jesus even mind those pangs, he says, in one of the most arresting verses of the poem, because he is preoccupied with "better thoughts that feed / Me, hung'ring more to do my Father's will" (2.258–259).

If, however, we take the meaning of Jesus' utterance "Tempt not the Lord thy God" to be centered not in the psychological subject but in the linguistic object, that is, in the very words that are spoken, then we may conceive of a temporal sequence in which the meaning as psychologically intended gives way to a new and larger meaning that suddenly, dramatically appears in the words—to Jesus' surprise as well as to Satan's amazement. After the entire course of the temptations as recounted in *Paradise Regained*, how could those words, "Tempt not the Lord thy God," *not* refer to the one whom Satan has been tempting in the poem up to this moment? Satan has been tempting God by tempting God's son, Jesus. But at this moment the words Jesus utters show the Father and the Son brought together: by tempting Jesus, Satan is tempting God. Let me repeat that Jesus' intention is merely to quote scripture, and perhaps to say, "In tempting me you *also* tempt the Father, since he sent me here." But as Jesus utters his quotation, he has an experience of self-recognition not unlike what he has earlier reported experiencing when reading the scriptures, after his mother told him of the events at his birth:

> This having heard, straight I again revolved
> The Law and prophets, searching what was writ

> Concerning the Messiah, to our scribes
> Known partly, and soon found of whom they spake
> I am.
>
> ᔓ *Paradise Regained 1.259–263*

I said before that we can hardly doubt that the phrase "I am," placed for strong emphasis at the beginning of a line after an enjambment, is intended to recall the voice of God speaking from the burning bush in Exodus 3:14: "I am that I am." It might also recall Milton's earlier use of the phrase, in *Paradise Lost*, when the Father says, "Boundless the deep because *I am* who fill / Infinitude" (7.168–169, my emphasis). Even this early in the poem, notwithstanding his subordinationism, Milton is at least toying with the notion of metaphysical identity subsisting between the Father and the Son. At the revelation on the pinnacle, Jesus' will has become so completely united with the will of the Father that Satan might just as well be tempting the Father, since the Father's glory and, more to the point, the Father's wrath are "substantially expressed" in the Son. The presence, here, of the Father in the Son is not a metaphysical identity. That presence is a moment of delirious identity when the Son is at once acknowledging the transcendence of the Father in heaven and affirming the immanence of the Father in the Son.

ᔓ To be "substantially expressed," conferring the authority of presence on another, is more in the nature of a *political* than a *metaphysical* event. We first encounter the notion of substantial expression in book three of *Paradise Lost*:

> Beyond compare the Son of God was seen
> Most glorious. In Him all His Father shone
> Substantially expressed and in His face
> Divine compassion visibly appeared:
> Love without end and without measure grace.
>
> ᔓ *Paradise Lost 3.138–142*

Here it is divine compassion that visibly appears, rather than wrath, which will be "full expressed" in the Son ("he all his Father full expressed" [6.720]) when the rebel angels are defeated in heaven. The entangling of political and metaphysical presence is more evident when

the Father is conferring on the Son his authority and power to defeat
the rebel angels in war. The Father can speak metaphysically of the Son
as the "Effulgence" of his glory (6.680). But when the Son accepts his
commission and with it the Father's "Sceptre and power," he does so
with a humility that inevitably marks a difference between him and the
Father, a humility that flows from the complexity of the political situation when the office and power of one agent are legally conferred on
another. Yet the Son concludes with an expression of functional identity when he says that he is the full expression of the Father's hate and
of the Father's terror:

> This I my glory account, . . .
> That Thou in Me well pleased declar'st thy will
> Fulfilled which to fulfill is all my bliss.
> Sceptre and pow'r, thy giving, I assume
> And gladlier shall resign when in the end
> Thou shalt be all in all and I in Thee
> For ever, and in Me all whom Thou lov'st.
> But whom Thou hat'st I hate and can put on
> Thy terrors as I put thy mildness on,
> Image of Thee in all things.
>   ⌁ *Paradise Lost* 6.726–736

Unlike the metaphysical expression of an identity, as in orthodox
Trinitarianism, the political situation where regal presence is conferred
on another involves a *temporal* movement from the initial self-subordi-
nation of the agent as a servant (the motto of the Prince of Wales is
"Ich dien") to a later performance by the agent of the very presence before which that agent was originally humbled. Moreover, the possibility of assuming the mantle of presence depends on the original subordination, the humble marking of a difference between master and
servant. But as the distance grows between master and servant, the division between them actually and, as it seems, paradoxically closes. The
presence of the master streams forth from him to the servant with increasing power as the distance between them widens: "My overshadowing Spirit and might with Thee / I send along: ride forth, and bid
the deep / Within appointed bounds be Heav'n and Earth!" (7.165–
167). That is what the Father says when the Son is in his presence and

the Father is commanding him to create the world. But as the Son passes through the gates of heaven into chaos, "with radiance crowned / Of majesty divine," he is not merely accompanied by, or equipped with, his Father's "spirit and might." The Son becomes himself the kingly presence of his Father. It is the Father who is now acting in his "Word" and "Spirit" instrumentally, but he is nevertheless acting from within them and is therefore present in them:

> Heav'n opened wide
> Her ever-during gates, harmonious sound
> On golden hinges moving, to let forth
> The King of Glory in his powerful Word
> And Spirit coming to create new worlds.
> ∿ *Paradise Lost 7.205–209*

In *Paradise Regained*, the Father becomes a more interesting figure than he is in *Paradise Lost*, even as the distance between him and the Son is increased. He says something quite remarkable about the Son, remarkable because it removes entirely the mystical and metaphysical resonance of shared being. God wants the angels to discern now, as he wants humans to discern later, "From what consummate virtue I have chose / This perfect man, by merit called my Son, / To earn salvation for the sons of men" (*PR* 1.165–167). Here the question of identity is transferred to the ground of the human. Jesus seems to start out as wholly human, though perfect, and to have been merely "chosen," because of this perfection, to earn salvation for mankind. (There is a hint of arbitrariness to this "choosing," however, which is reminiscent of God's choosing the Hebrews.) Jesus has also *earned* (for that is surely the sense here of "merit") the title Son of God. He has earned it by having attained to moral perfection, rather than by having had the title from his birth, aristocratically, as an expression of his being. Milton is here promoting an idea of the Son as a human being without any metaphysical ground in the Father.

That too is what we are to hear when Jesus says, "Tempt not the Lord thy God." I spoke of it before as a dialectical, or delirious, identity between the Son and the Father. By that I meant that at this moment Jesus' words affirm an older religious vision from the deep past of European culture, one in which the Father is a metaphysical power in the heavens wielding the thunderbolt and spreading out the sky like a tent. At the same time, however, Jesus' words affirm that creative work is centered not in the building of nature from without but in the revolution of history from within.

⤳ MILTON MAY APPEAR TO withdraw from this moment of delirious insight when the choir of angels which rescues Jesus sings to him a chorus, instructing him further on the identity he has inadvertently discovered. But in truth Milton is gathering the entire Christian vision into this delirious insight. The angels tell Jesus that he is the "true image of the Father" and exists eternally in heaven "in the bosom of bliss," even when he is incarnate in "fleshly tabernacle, and human form"; that he has defeated Satan before, in heaven; that his recent victory symbolizes the "fairer paradise" he is to raise in the wilderness, "for Adam and his chosen sons"; and, most important, that his victory over temptation is a victory over the original cause of the Fall, reversing the direction of history from sinful collapse to moral ascent (4.596–635). The inaugural power of this revolution in history has become creative action in the world, replacing the original Creation.

Paradise Regained gives us a vision of history which is centered in this revolutionary moment. The vision begins in chaos and hell and recounts the Creation of the world, the placing of humanity in its initial, paradisal state, and the expulsion of humanity from paradise into a new kind of existence—a historical existence. The vision moves onward through the recurring miseries of captivity and exile, briefly relieved by episodes of human penitence awakening divine mercy, only to descend again, and to descend further, into the savagery of war and the abjectness of worshipping false gods, including the false gods of commerce, with their commodifying idols. The vision then turns into the eye of the historical whirlwind, where Jesus, as a man and not a god, stands balanced on the pinnacle of the temple. The temptation in the wilderness is an exercise and an initiation of Jesus into his ministry, which will begin when he returns from the desert, after the conclusion of the poem. Since that ministry will effect a revolution in the world, and a revolution not only within history but of history, there is in the concluding lines of the poem a fine effect of understatement not unlike the conclusion to *Paradise Lost*, where an intimate human action—"hand in hand, with wandering steps and slow"—has the weight of something vast before it and something vast behind it. In *Paradise Lost* that something vast to come is the impending weight of history. In *Paradise Regained* it is the overturning of that weight by revolution: "he unobserved / Home to his mother's house private returned."

What kind of revolution is it? What Jesus says with the phrase "Tempt not the Lord thy God" is a prophecy. It may be paraphrased as follows: "To try to destroy me, since I represent the nobility of the human, is as evil as any of the crimes formerly committed in defiance of God the Father. Henceforth, crimes against humanity are crimes against God." With that, Milton's hero reenters the whirlwind of history by entering his ministry. The purpose of that ministry is to show humanity that Jesus' exemplary act, taking into himself a divinity formerly reserved for a transcendent God, or invested in idols, is the only way to salvation. This is not the serpent's promise, that we shall be "as gods" (Genesis 3:5), a promise that one will be able to rejoice in oneself as an idol and be served by those who are not. The lesson of taking divinity into oneself is not a lesson that will lead to anything that would be easy to rejoice in, since it entails the negation of a transcendent, caring Lord. Its initial spiritual effects have been largely disillusionment and terror. Rather than a promise of power, the lesson that divinity is to be re-created in the self is a call to take up responsibilities that were formerly entrusted to God, such as the care of Creation and of nature. Everything is up to us. The angels who save Jesus are therefore the last of the oracles to cease. It is to a human being that they speak their last prophecy, "now enter, and begin to save mankind" (4.635), because they know there is nothing left for angels to do.

ᕽᕽ 9

Samson and the Heap of the Dead

*I*F THE CONFRONTATION between Satan and Jesus on the pinnacle of the temple is the strangest moment in Milton's poetry, *Samson Agonistes* is Milton's strangest work. In *Paradise Regained*, historical and metaphysical certainties are held in the balance of a single, ironic exchange from which they emerge transformed and triumphant. In *Samson Agonistes* these certainties give way to an irony that is sustained through every encounter and event in the play. This irony is not in the service of truth understood as correctness of assertion with respect to an order beyond it. Instead, the irony of *Samson Agonistes* is in the service of a truthfulness that renders everything uncertain, everything that was once taken for true. Milton's poetic career, a career that had been more assertive than any other except perhaps Dante's, ends in the mode of the question.[1]

Consider the most obvious question. Is Samson's death a historical triumph, the achievement of national liberation, or is it only a moment—one the reader of the Bible has visited before and will visit again—in the absurd cycle of liberation and captivity from which the nation of Israel will never be freed? We may suppose that Milton, the justifier of the ways of God to men, intends us to look beyond the time frame of the action of the play to the time of the new covenant, when Israel, and not only Israel, will be freed from the bondage of history and even from the bondage of the Law. That is the point of *Paradise Re-*

gained, which is expressed in the song that the angels address at the end
to the Son. The Son is told who he is, what he has accomplished in the
past, what he will accomplish in the future, at the end of time, and what
he has accomplished just now (*PR* 4.596–635). Similarly, in *Paradise
Lost*, in the passage to which this one corresponds, Adam, like a good
pupil, repeats the lesson he has received:

> Henceforth I learn that to obey is best,
> And love with fear the only God, to walk
> As in His presence, ever to observe
> His providence and on Him sole depend . . .
>   that suffering for Truth's sake
> Is fortitude to highest victory
> And to the faithful death the gate of life.
>   ·⌒ *Paradise Lost 12.561–571*

Lest there be any doubt in our minds of the general applicability of that
lesson, the angel confirms it: "This having learned, thou hast attained
the sum / Of wisdom" (12.575–576). At the conclusion of both of Milton's epics, the principal character is fully instructed in the meaning of
what has occurred. Milton did not regard ambiguity as a poetic virtue.

That metaphysical promise of certainty, however, is not delivered by
the text of *Samson Agonistes*. It is delivered by a dubious typological
reading of the play which the poet has anticipated and teasingly dared
us to attempt. Do you dare to interpret Samson's death, which he
courts, as he says in his prayer to the Father, "that I may be at once
avenged of the Philistines for my two eyes" (Judges 16:28), as a type of
the sacrifice of Christ, whose last prayer was "Father, forgive them, for
they know not what they do" (Luke 24:34)? To read the figure of Samson typologically as a prefiguration of Christ or even, more modestly,
as a prefiguration of the new, more direct relationship between God
and Man is to risk seeming naïve.

Some justification for taking the risk might be found in Hebrews
11:32–34, where Samson is named together with other heroes of the
Book of Judges—Gideon, Barak, and Jephtha—as one of the witnesses
of faith, "*who out of weakness were made strong,*" as it says in verse 34:
"And what more shall I say? for the time would fail me to tell of
Gedeon, and of Barak, and of Samson, and of Jephthae; of David also,

and Samuel, and of the prophets. Who through faith subdued kingdoms, wrought righteousness, obtained promises, stopped the mouths of lions, quenched the violence of fire, escaped the edge of the sword, out of weakness were made strong, waxed valiant in fight, turned to flight the armies of the aliens." That phrase, a variant of 2 Corinthians 12:9, was adopted by Milton as his motto when he was blind: "I am made perfect in weakness."[2] Also relevant is 2 Corinthians 13:4, "For though he was crucified through weakness, yet he liveth by the power of God. For we also are weak in him, but we shall live with him by the power of God." That the phrase appears in Hebrews is another and, I think, a rather striking reason for supposing that the poet saw a personal connection between himself and Samson. But the burden of the chapter of Hebrews in which this mention of Samson occurs is to contrast, not to identify, the relationships between God and Man in the old and new covenants. Indeed, the addition of Samuel, David, and the prophets to the list of heroes in Judges is meant to suggest the entire Old Testament: "And these all, having obtained a good report through faith, received not the promise: God having provided some better thing for us, that they without us should not be made perfect" (Hebrews 11:39–40). This passage from Hebrews serves less as an incentive to interpret Samson typologically, or teleologically, than as a warning not to.

Yet there is no safety in holding back from a typological or a teleological reading of some kind, insisting that the play is an archaeological representation, in an isolated temporal frame, of the circumstances of Israel in the period between the conquest and the kingdom. The very last phrase of the chapter in Hebrews ("hina mē chōris hēmōn teleiōthōsi") suggests a teleological connection between Old Testament figures and "us," who perfect them, as it were, retrospectively. "Apart from us" ("chōris hēmōn"), their readers, these Old Testament figures mean nothing. With "us," that is, out of our decision to read the Old Testament figures as witnesses of faith, they have meaning. But this meaning depends on our decision, not on anything historically present in the Old Testament figures. From this perspective, Milton's asceticism in *Samson Agonistes* is necessary to his purpose, which is to leave the freedom, and the responsibility, of decision to us. To congratulate oneself, therefore, on one's tough-mindedness in refusing to be drawn into a symbolic reading of *Samson Agonistes* is to fall into an error that is just as credulous as facile typologizing: the error of supposing that a correct answer is there to be discerned in the text. It will not be completed without us.

∽ IT MAY BE THAT, out of an ironic delight in the contrast between the majesty of what is signified and the contemptibleness of what signifies, the poet intended to evoke a connection between Christ and Samson, between the omniscience of the one and the ignorance of the other, or between the majesty of redemption through faith in Jesus and the grim satisfaction of temporary deliverance by means of revenge. To refuse to consider as possible such an intention, and such a reading, is to run as great a risk of seeming naïve as one does in promoting such a reading without acknowledging the opposite risk. The irony of *Samson Agonistes* is so pervasive, and so uncontrollable, that it reaches out of the text to seize us, ironizing the process of reading itself. As a result, reading is shown to be not just an act of decipherment but one of decision. We cannot avoid deciding for ourselves, on the basis of who we are and what we want, what the poem means and whether it means.

The final speech of Manoa, Samson's father, is as good an example as any of the impossibility of the truth in *Samson Agonistes* being something we can decipher in the text and positively assert:

> Samson hath quit himself
> Like Samson, and heroicly hath finished
> A life heroic, on his enemies
> Fully revenged, hath left them years of mourning,
> And lamentation to the sons of Caphtor
> Through all Philistian bounds.
>
> ∽ *Samson Agonistes 1709–14*

One could comment on Milton's fine evocation in these lines, and on more than one level, of the heroic world of the *Iliad*, from the epithet "sons of Caphtor," which not only sounds Homeric but also, as John Carey observes in his note on the line, connects the Philistines with Greeks of the Homeric period, to the peculiar austerity with which glory is bound up with death; for in these lines, as in the *Iliad*, as Pietro Pucci has said of the latter, "the song of glory coincides with the fu-

neral *threnos.*"³ To what extent are we to share in the mood of the heroic ethos, and to what extent are we to cast on it a cold, ironical eye?
The logical aberrancy of this question lies in its suggestion of a compromise between exclusive terms. To find the correct interpretation is
not at all a question of determining an *extent* to which either alternative
should be taken seriously, as if a third or middle term could be found.
There is no intermediate place to stand where heroic and Christian
values can exist together in a reasonable mixture. In interpreting
Manoa's words, we must choose one way or the other, the heroic or the
ironic; and whichever way we choose will be done according to a principle that the *other* way (the other wrong one) defines. The interpretive
crux here is isomorphic with the crux, famously analyzed by Paul de
Man, concerning the final verse of Yeats's "Among School Children":
"How can we know the dancer from the dance?" The verse has usually
been read as a purely rhetorical question, affirming the mystical, organic state in which dancer and dance become one. But the question
can also be read as a real question: Knowing them to be different, as we
do, how *can* we tell the dancer from the dance? To read the question as
a real question, however, is to overturn the traditional interpretation of
the poem as a whole. As de Man puts it:

> Two entirely coherent but entirely incompatible readings can be
> made to hinge on one line, whose grammatical structure is devoid
> of ambiguity, but whose rhetorical mode turns the mood as well as
> the mode of the entire poem upside down. Neither can we say . . .
> that the poem simply has two meanings that exist side by side. The
> two readings have to engage each other in direct confrontation,
> for the one reading is precisely the error denounced by the other
> and has to be undone by it. Nor can we in any way make a valid
> decision as to which of the readings can be given priority over the
> other; none can exist in the other's absence.⁴

How can we tell Manoa's heroic perspective from the larger enigma in
which it is wrapped? How can we tell character from narrative when
each is convertible into the other? How can we tell the dancer from the
dance?

We can see the irony of this larger enigma at its most concentrated,
and at its most opaque, in the apparently heroic auto-referential simile

"Samson hath quit himself / Like Samson." The irony turns (and turns again) around whether that comparison is to be understood as favorable or not. Everything every character says in *Samson Agonistes* is easily intelligible with respect to that character's intentions; yet almost nothing any character says is unambiguously intelligible to us: their statements are non-mysteries wrapped in an enigma. We could say that this comes about, speaking technically, because the context of every statement in the play is a tangle of contrasting codes. The lugubrious, yet brilliant, retrospective glory of the Homeric code is superimposed on the "great code" of the Bible, which is homely by comparison, forward-looking, and eschatological. The code of Greek tragedy, its irony brooding over its concentration on necessity and doom, is superimposed on the code of historical narrative, which is open-ended and inclined to an economy of progress. The noise created by the interaction of these heterogeneous systems would be nothing other than that, noise, or aesthetic confusion, were it not for our sense that the poet's active, shaping mind is present everywhere in the discord we hear. But what that mind shapes is neither justification of the ways of the Father, as in *Paradise Lost*, nor praise of the hidden deeds of the Son, as in *Paradise Regained*. It may be wrong to speak of that mind as shaping anything at all, active as it is. For its activity is everywhere to set irony free as a profoundly disarticulating force.

I have said that this irony is in the service not of the truth as correctness of assertion but of the truthfulness of questioning at length, a truthfulness that disarticulates—that is, tears "joint by joint"—every seductive form presented to it as objectively true. The phrase I have just quoted, "joint by joint," which is what *disarticulation* literally means, is from Samson's warning reply to Delilah's request to touch him: "Not for thy life, lest fierce remembrance wake / My sudden rage to tear thee joint by joint" (*SA* 952–953). In these lines in the play, which are not the least memorable, or the least shocking, a new kind of truthfulness emerges: the truthfulness of disclosure or unveiling. Beneath that pervasive irony, which takes away the certainty of our certainties, metaphysical and historical, is the only truth with which the poet keeps faith to the end: the power of vehement, disarticulating wrath. How does one make a monumental artifact, a *poiema*, of the unveiled truth of wrath? By composing "that sort of dramatic poem which is called tragedy" (preface to *SA*). Milton's tragedy will erect the only monument that he can regard as more satisfying than the achievement of Paradise Lost: a gigantic heap of the dead.

⚜ THERE ARE FOUR TRADITIONAL problems faced by criticism of *Samson Agonistes:* the date, the extent to which the poem is autobiographical, the extent to which the poem is dramatic, and the question whether Milton's poetic telling of the Old Testament story must be interpreted in the frame of a total vision of history that also encompasses the New Testament. None of these problems is wholly independent of the others. The earlier date would entail the work's being less autobiographical, more dramatic, and less concerned with a total vision of history than with the revolutionary demands of the moment. The later date would reverse all these statements. The question whether *Samson* belongs to the 1640s or to the 1660s will perhaps never be decisively settled, that is, with external, documentary evidence. But internal evidence, in particular the strongly autobiographical tone to Samson's lamentation over his blindness, has discouraged proponents of the earlier date, and a consensus has emerged that *Samson* is Milton's last major work. A further matter of dating should be mentioned. Because *Paradise Regained* and *Samson Agonistes* were published together, it is not certain whether *Samson,* assuming it belongs to the 1660s, was composed before or after *Paradise Regained.* While it is conceivable that *Samson* could have been written between *Paradise Lost* and *Paradise Regained,* it strikes me as psychologically improbable. In any event, Thomas Ellwood's account of Milton's showing him *Paradise Lost* and *Paradise Regained* in such close succession, and as works just completed, suggests that nothing major was written between them.

Yet even if we regard the problem as settled, the question of dating returns in a subtler form to affect the other three questions: autobiography, genre, and interpretive framing. To what extent is Milton in the 1660s, in *Samson Agonistes,* returning to the activist stance of the 1640s? To what extent is Milton seeking, despite his statement that *Samson Agonistes* was never intended for the stage, to awaken the mood of an earlier, if imaginary, revolutionary theater, doing so in polemical opposition to the hedonistic theater of the Restoration? Last, and most important, to what extent is Milton in *Samson Agonistes* continuing the creative project begun in *Paradise Lost,* a total poetic vision of history, and to what extent is he returning to the mood of the 1640s when, in considering Old Testament subjects for tragedy, he meant not to antici-pate the events of the New Testament but to give political examples for the revolutionary present?

It was in the 1640s, the period of his most violent rhetoric against those of whom he disapproved or with whom he disagreed, that Milton compiled his list of biblical subjects for tragedies. The notion of theat-rical performances showing the confounding of the wicked, who had not yet been sufficiently confounded on the field of battle, must have been great. And the picture Milton paints of London in *Areopagitica* shows an ideal place for a revolutionary theater: a city under siege, bravely withstanding every kind of threat from without while within men reason openly and freely in pursuit of the truth, undismayed by uncongenial or heterodox views. What kind of plays would such a com-munity wish to see? Even for the theater of a community as committed as the one Milton describes, it would be somewhat crude to stage such a scene as is imagined in the conclusion to *Of Reformation*, where the bishops are trampled and ravingly abused by all the other damned in hell. As we see in Brecht, the subject matter of even the most revolu-tionary theater is not directly topical but allusive, employing stories from the past that will resonate powerfully with what is happening now. Milton drew such stories from the Old Testament, in particular from the historical books, for the satisfying vehemence they held in re-serve.

The revolutionary mood, and the aesthetic questions that are raised by it, is rekindled in *Samson Agonistes*. When we set aside the strictly philological question of the date of *Samson Agonistes*, the critical impli-cations of the question continue to resonate, now in more complicated ways. As to autobiography, we must ask to what extent *Samson Agonistes* reflects not only the pain of an embittered man but also the reawak-ened passions of a young revolutionary. As to interpretation, we must also ask to what extent is the play about Samson as a symbol of faith and to what extent is it about Samson as the servant of a political cause, the liberation of Israel from Philistine oppression? I have left the question of genre for last. We still have to come to terms with *Samson Agonistes* as a work that, while continuing the creative project begun in *Paradise Lost*, reinvigorates the aesthetic and political concerns of Milton's revo-lutionary period by showing them dramatically.[5] It is a dramatic poem rather than a play pure and simple, but it retains more of the direct, incendiary purpose of revolutionary drama than it does of the argumentative or deliberative purpose of *Paradise Lost* and *Paradise Regained.* The play does not intend to justify the ways of God to men; it intends to wring commitment from their hearts. After the masterly restraint, the quiet intensity, of *Paradise Regained*, there is in *Samson Agonistes* a rekindling of older, angrier fires. With them is rekindled a poetic vehemence that may remind us of the sonnets—"Avenge, O Lord, thy slaughtered saints."

⮞ AN EXTREME ACT OF poetic vehemence is to imagine one's enemies leveled in heaps. I have mentioned the conclusion to *Of Reformation*, where the bishops in hell are at the bottom of the heap of the damned. The scene is re-created, with more maturity, in *Paradise Lost*, when the devils are prostrate on the burning lake of hell and when the same devils, during the war in heaven, are crushed in heaps under the mountains that are thrown on them. In *Samson Agonistes* we hear of two heaps of the dead, one made by the hero at Ramoth-Lechi, before the play opens, and one made at the end of the play, offstage. The latter is made known to us first by the noise of destruction and then by the messenger's report how Samson pulled down the temple of Dagon on himself and on the thousands inside it. In reflecting on the image of the heap of the dead, I shall have to range widely, beyond the immediate critical concerns of Milton's *Samson Agonistes*, because the image is to some extent an archetypal one, even a biblical one: the Book of Revelation overwhelms us with heaps of the dead. But if in confronting the image of the heap of the dead we are dealing with something larger than *Samson Agonistes*, this does not in the least diminish the importance of Milton's poem. On the contrary, it is an indication of the power of Milton's final masterpiece to evoke structures vastly larger than itself and to raise problems of human psychology that are more profound than the poet himself would have known. In this work, and particularly in the image of the heap of the dead, gigantic forces are not, as I said they are in *Paradise Regained*, held in the balance of a single, ironic exchange, for the forces are not in the poet's control. As in all great tragic literature, *Samson Agonistes* is not so much a self-contained aesthetic object as it is a conduit for exchanges between two extremes of mystery: the nausea and horror of defilement, *miasma*, and the narcosis of spiritual transcendence, *catharsis*. It is with the former that I concern myself here. But we shall see that the latter depends on it. There is no vision of God without a vision of a heap of the dead.

᪐ LET ME REVIEW the biblical tale on which Milton based *Samson Agonistes*. The story of Samson, the most famous of the military heroes, or "judges" in the book of that name, is punctuated with heaps of the dead. When the bride of Timna betrays Samson's riddle to the men whom he had challenged in a wager to solve it, Samson kills and strips thirty men of Ashkelon to pay the debt. Irritated when the bride's father, under the assumption that Samson has deserted her, gives her to another, Samson sets fire to three hundred foxes and releases them in the Philistine fields, destroying the crops. Holding father and daughter responsible for this loss, the Philistines burn them both, whereupon Samson "smites them with a great slaughter" and then retires to a high rock. The Philistines take up arms, and when the men of Judah are told why they are being attacked, they send three thousand men to bind Samson and surrender him to the Philistines (Judges 15: 89). Samson agrees to be bound. But when brought to be delivered, he is visited by the power of the Lord, breaks the cords as if they were "flax that was burnt with fire," takes up the jawbone of an ass, and kills one thousand Philistines. After this he composes the song by which his deed is remembered: "with the jawbone of an ass, heaps upon heaps, with the jaw of an ass have I slain a thousand men," the punning sense of which is something like, "with a heap have I heaped them in heaps" (Judges 15:16).

This is the first heap that is regarded as a military achievement and a trophy. The second is Samson's last and best heap, which is said to be larger than the total number Samson had already killed in his entire life (Judges 16:30). Briefly, the story in Judges is as follows. Having eluded capture in Gaza and carried its gateposts to the hill above Hebron, Samson takes up another Philistine woman, Delilah. She is visited by all five Philistine kings, each of whom promises to give her eleven hundred pieces of silver if she will trick Samson into revealing the secret of his strength. He makes a fool of her three times, tempting her first to tie him up in new bowstrings, then to tie him up in new ropes, and then telling her he will lose his strength if she weaves his seven locks of hair on a loom, which she does, with no better success. By persistent nagging, however, she gets the truth out of him and, while he sleeps, has his seven locks shorn. He is then easily captured, blinded, and imprisoned in Gaza, where he grinds at the mill, and where his hair starts growing again. It is then that he is brought into the temple of Dagon to entertain at the festival celebrating his capture. The five kings are present, together with thousands of men and women inside the temple, including all the Philistine lords, with three thousand more observers on the roof. All are slain when Samson pulls the temple down on them and on himself, his last words being "let me die with the Philistines" (16: 30).

The hero's body is involved with those of his victims; he is as physically entangled with them as he is entangled, in the chorus's words, "in the fold / Of dire necessity" (*SA* 1665–66). While this latter entanglement is expressed in the somewhat abstract language of Greek tragedy, the former, the hero's entanglement with his victims, is more physically intimate, more suffocating, more resonant with horror. Samson can no more evade this entanglement with dead Philistine bodies than he can his tragic fate of dying in the Philistine temple.

There is something about this entanglement in the heap of the dead that is more extreme than what we find in the emotional range of Greek tragedy, notwithstanding the references in Greek tragedy to cannibalism, matricide, dismemberment, and the like. It is open to question whether Hebraic subject matter can ever be contained within the Hellenic form of tragedy, which always, as Nietzsche said, draws a veil of beautiful forms over the truth. The veil is consciousness itself, individuated consciousness. Tragedy is about a lone, individuated consciousness that is superior to the circumstances in which it is caught, the superiority being felt precisely in this consciousness's achievement of reflective distance from its own fate. Tragic entanglement in the fold of necessity—that is, Greek tragic entanglement—is centered in consciousness, and is thus an *existential* event. In contrast to this, physical entanglement in the heap of the dead is a purely *corporeal* event, one that requires for its undoing the extrication, ritual cleansing, and monumental entombment of Samson's dead body.

It is not so simple, however, for us, the readers of Milton's tragic poem. The vision of the heap of the dead, wherein the hero is entangled with his victims, is a traumatic event from which the mind cannot gain relief in catharsis because the event lies beneath the emotions of pity and terror. The event is indeed the exposed source of the emotions of pity and terror, as it is the source of any artistic process that arouses and purges those emotions. The experience over which tragedy draws a veil is not the knowledge that life is unbearably painful. It is not any knowledge at all. It is simply the vision of the heap of the dead, which indeed rouses the emotions of pity and terror but also, more shamefully, the exultation of the survivor. We are cleansed by the tragedy simply because we survive.

The vision is represented for us in the speech of the messenger, who describes himself as attempting to flee what he has seen:

> O whither shall I run, or which way fly
> The sight of this so horrid spectacle
> Which erst my eyes beheld and yet behold;
> For dire imagination still pursues me.
>
> ᛞ *Samson Agonistes 1541–44*

The sight clings to his eyes, after it is no longer before him, so that he can't shake it free. He says that he has been guided in his blindness to where Manoa and the Hebrew chorus stand by providence, by instinct, or by reason—"though disturbed and scarce consulted" (*SA* 1546). The sight blinds him to everything except what he has seen in the past so that others may see what he says he continues to see. We are meant to see it, accordingly, with terrible clarity, *enargeia*. Yet we feel that the messenger's horror is a horror the full force of which we have been spared, since it is mediated to us by him. We have not been blinded, as he has, by the sight of the heap of the dead. Yet we know we have shared in his horror when we find that the sight—or the idea of that sight—sticks to our eyes as we read. I do not mean only that it sticks to our eyes as we read from this point to the end of the play. I mean it sticks to our eyes, or rather lingers before them like a transparent image through which we see everything in the play when we reread it, from the very opening lines: "A little onward lend thy guiding hand / To these dark steps, a little further on." Lead me out of the heap of these bodies.

I would not confine this lingering presence of the sight of the heap of the dead to the experience of reading. There is also, in the memory, the lingering presence of the vision of the heap of the dead as seen in the black and white films taken in the German death camps, shortly after their liberation by Allied troops. One of the most arresting things about these heaps of the dead is the way the bodies are confusingly entangled. As bulldozers roll the bodies into pits, the limbs flail in a way that separates them from their particular bodies. The arms and legs become the panicky, waving, gesturing limbs of the single body of the heap. The child who sees the film of the rolling heap of the dead looks on in fascination as much as in horror. A similar, fascinated horror is in the background when we read *Samson Agonistes*. The play is experienced as a kind of veil through which we occasionally catch sight of what is perhaps the one truth—the moving heap of the dead—into which it moves.

࿓ THE PLAY HAS TRADITIONALLY been read as motivating a double perspective that is structurally akin to tragic irony, different as the contents of that perspective must be. The material events represented in the play occur in the context of the Old Testament, under the dispensation of the Law. Events therefore unfold, and are understood by those who take part in them, according to the flesh. But these same events are secretly guided according to a dispensation that belongs to the future, specifically to the period of the New Testament, and under the dispensation of Grace. Events therefore unfold, as *we* can understand them but as the represented characters cannot, according to the spirit. Dramatic irony is just this difference of knowledge between those who are inside a situation, and can see it only in part, and those who are outside it—who *comprehend* it—and can see it whole.

It is then a fairly inevitable reading of *Samson Agonistes* which says that the poet adds another level of irony to what is experienced in Greek tragedy. In Greek tragedy some characters know more than others, enjoying the ironic pleasure of that knowledge; and we, the audience, know the most concerning what will happen to the characters in the play. There is Greek irony in Delilah's exulting over the fame she will win for her heroic deed, for it is her infamy that will be imparted to the ages, since her story is to be told by Hebrews, not by Philistines. But in *Samson Agonistes* there is the much more sustained irony of our being able to see the events in the play as symbolic of what is to come, Samson being a *martyr*, or "witness," as we are told in the epistle to the Hebrews, pointing to an entirely new relationship between Man and God. It is not Samson's death but the faith that leads him to that death that is a *sacramentum futuri*.

It is along these lines that the opening words of the play, "A little onward lend thy guiding hand / To these dark steps," which are Samson's request to be led to a place where he may rest from his labor at the mill, are seen as an ironic reference to the mysterious guidance he receives from the Father throughout. But when we know where this guidance will lead him, having heard the messenger's report, we see him led not toward something that lies in his future but toward something that lies in his past, at Ramoth-Lechi. He is led back not to his God, not to the Law, not to his nation, not even to himself, seated on that bank where his mind is tormented with remorse as soon as his body can rest. He is being guided toward the scene that sticks to our eyes: his physical entanglement with the bodies of those he has slain. We are ourselves involved in what I would call the aesthetics of the heap of the dead, the psychological impact of the sight of dead bodies heaped up and entangled with one another, so that it is nearly impossible to see any one body as a whole. Every body we see there has parts which, when examined more closely, actually belong to another. We are challenged to understand *Samson Agonistes* through that disturbing experience. But at this radical level our understanding cannot stand apart from the entangling, for our understanding is as entangled and confused as the bodies we see. We feel almost as if we should have to lie down there among the bodies in order to know, to feel, what a whole body is, where its boundaries are, and what parts belong to it and not to others.

To strive to understand *Samson Agonistes* through the aesthetic experience of gazing on the heap of the dead is to allow oneself to become entangled with more than the critical problems associated with this dramatic poem. We cannot place limits on what we choose to know any more than the teachings of Christ can be limited to a moral doctrine we can state apart from our involvement in the teacher and his method of teaching. I mention this example because Milton spoke of Christ's teaching as not so much a teaching as an entangling. What you know when you have passed through such instruction is not a body of information you merely possess. What you know is what you have been forced to become. The most radical enquiry leads us down to a level of fundamental questioning where we are entangled in apparent contradictions in the subject matter, contradictions which reflect our own entanglement in what we try to keep apart from ourselves as a thing we can possessively know while remaining, in ourselves, essentially unchanged. To strive to understand Milton's tragic poem *Samson Agonistes* on the most radical level means becoming entangled with more than the play. It means becoming entangled with more even than the totality of Milton's creative project, which begins with a heap of the slain (if we may call them that): the devils rolling on the flaming lake of hell. We are entangled with the concept of the heap of the dead as a thing made, as a work of art, and not just as any work of art but as the vision of the desire out of which works of art arise.

This horrifying, fascinating vision is as fundamental for Milton, and that means for poetry in general, as is the vision of God: "Dark with excessive bright thy skirts appear" (*PL* 3.380). By "fundamental" I mean it has the same deeply contradictory structure from which an organized system is raised. From the root vision of God as "dark with excessive bright," Milton raises the structure of the world. From the root vision of the heap of the dead, Milton raises the structure of history.

৵ AESTHETICS IS FROM the Greek *aisthesis*, which means "perception." The earliest work on aesthetics was concerned not just with the beautiful but with perception in general, and perception in art. When I speak of an aesthetics of the heap of the dead, I refer to a perceptual experience created for an artistic effect, which in this instance is not so much beauty as it is fascination and shock—though we shall see that beauty is not so far removed from these things as we might suppose. The aesthetics of the heap of the dead is concerned with the problem of a realism that represents what we have never before seen. The problem may be isolated in the word *represent*. How can we *re*present the unprecedented? The realistic vision becomes, by the shock of this unprecedentedness, a hallucination that sticks to our eyes, capturing our visual field and temporarily blinding us to what is in front of us. We hear first of the heap in the surreal phrase "A thousand foreskins fell, the flower of Palestine, / At Ramoth-Lechi, famous to this day" (144–145). Literally, these verses say that the army of the *arelim*, of those provided with foreskins, were killed at the place, now famous for that reason, called Ramoth-Lechi. But we shall see that this reading of the literal sense, and in particular of the metonymy "foreskin," is not literal enough. Or, to put this more cautiously, the very notion of "the literal" is exposed as an attempt to reduce textuality to determinate perception. When we reflect on the psycho-political event of contemplating dead bodies, and parts of dead bodies, we do so in terms of what may be called the phenomenology of the heap.

To *look* at a heap of the dead is to recognize that the status of the thing contemplated oscillates between unity and plurality, between that of a thing and that of many separate things tangled together. The indeterminacy is so radical that it uncovers the deep articulation of phenomenology to ethics, making us collude in the slaughter if we imagine the bodies in the heap as anything less than irreducible units called *persons*, and yet also making us collude in what we see if we ignore the negation of bodily integrity in the indifferent unity of the heap. Both states are represented in *Samson Agonistes*, the first on the field at Ramoth-Lechi, with its pile of foreskins, the second at the collapsed temple, where Samson's body is to be extricated from those of the slaughtered Philistines, cleansed, and lovingly buried alone.

This structure of phenomenal indeterminacy in the contemplation of heaps of dead bodies—in particular the unexcluded middle between unity and plurality—lies behind the rhetorical complexity of the verse we are examining, with its metaphorical flower and its metonymical foreskins, and the dubious figurality of those foreskins, which calls up two heaps in our minds. The semantic instability suggests the sort of disarticulation we get in the syntax of Latin—"a thousand, of Palestine, foreskins, the flower, fell"—while by a more radical drift in the sense, the plural of "foreskins" contaminates the "flower" (O rose thou art sick) so that we no longer see one blossom crushed into foreskins but a cascade of blossoms, all in the flower of youth, withering and yellowing as they fall in a heap at the place of the leaving of the jaw. Notwithstanding what is said of its hero in the epistle to the Hebrews, *Samson Agonistes* is a poem of psychologically explosive political desire, a desire not at all different from that of the prophet Jeremiah, who imagines God exulting over an earth filled with corpses. We see it more locally in Manoa, who has the pleasure of imagining Samson walking over heaps of slaughtered Philistines. Just as the temple in Jerusalem is the image of the political self, so the heap of the dead is what he wants to make of the political other, leveling and compressing it, even as far as stamping it down, "insulting on the slaughtered foe." We see the pleasure at its uncensored height in the *reprehensio* concluding *Of Reformation*, which is the best gloss we have not only on the heaping of Philistines in *Samson Agonistes* but also on the heaping of angels in *Paradise Lost*:

But they contrary that by the impairing and diminution of the true *Faith*, the distresses and servitude of their *Countrey* aspire to high

Dignity, *Rule* and *Promotion* here, after a shameful end in this Life (which *God* grant them) shall be thrown downe eternally into the *darkest* and *deepest Gulfe* of HELL, where under the *dispightfull controule*, the trample and spurne of all the other *Damned*, that in the anguish of their *Torture* shall have no other ease than to exercise a *Raving* and *Bestiall Tyranny* over them as their *Slaves* and *Negros*, they shall remaine in that plight for ever, the *basest*, the *lowermost*, the *most dejected*, most *underfoot* and *downe-trodden Vassals* of *Perdition*.

What is here represented as ease for the damned is in fact the secret eschatological joy of the elect: to trample the damned underfoot. This is the true marriage of heaven and hell.

꒛ Now WE CAN TALK about foreskins. It must of course be stated that the word is a Hebraism, *arelim*, literally "the foreskinned ones," the usual substantive, "the uncircumcised," being in one sense a less accurate rendering, though in another sense a more accurate one because it captures negation in its grammar. Gentiles are not those who *lack* circumcision but those who are provided with the foreskins lacked by Hebrews, though to be so provided turns out to be a cultural lack, thus rendering the foreskin unclean. The foreskin is not just a metonymical part of the other, like a scalp or an ear: it is that which by its uncleanness constitutes the political other as such. We may even find it appropriate to remark the power of this figure—and of figures of contiguity generally—to concentrate our hatred of the corporeal other by fastening on one site of the body, as do expressions like "thick-lips," "redskins," "chinks," "cunts," and "towelheads."

The last of these epithets, which denotes a person wearing a turban, refers to a cultural mark applied to the body. But such marks cannot be as rigorously distinguished from what we might incautiously refer to as "natural" or "racial" differences, since these, to do any ideological work, must themselves undergo a practice as artificial as circumcision or the wearing of a turban. This is evident in the semiotics of Negritude, which begins in the social constitution of the self as black in opposition to white, whatever one's exact shade, in order to extend the body into the realm of the political as diacritically "unwhite." Circumcision has a similar logical structure, and its constructedness appears in one of the antiprelatical tracts in which to be "uncircumcised" means to be ignorant of Hebrew, which is what Milton is accusing the lightly educated prelates of being.

As soon as circumcision is established as a necessary practice in a collectivity, it becomes the political statement of what is normal, even natural, in a penis, while the absence of circumcision in the "uncircumcised"—four negatives bring us around to the start, with the penis intact—becomes a positive mark, like Cain's, of those who are other, the *arelim*, the "foreskinned ones," or, as the Philistines are indifferently referred to in the Septuagint, "those other troops" *(allophuloi)*, those whom one would like to reduce to a heap. What we may call the politics of the heap is played out in *Samson Agonistes* through the relations articulated between the image of an army as a highly ordered structure representing the nation ("the flower of Palestine"), the image of that army as a heap of foreskins, and the sudden, violent act of crushing by which one is reduced to the other.

I said that the figurality of Milton's "foreskins" is uncertain. One reason for this is that the practice of removing the foreskins of the slain is not unfamiliar in war, as evidenced in 1 Samuel 18:24, when David, commanded by Saul to obtain one hundred foreskins, brings the king, in an excess of zeal, two hundred. Emphasis is laid in the story on the care with which these were publicly counted out to support David's worthiness to be the king's son-in-law. It seems likely that this—and not something more arduous like castration—is the unspeakable act reported in the first part of *Henry IV* to have been committed on a slain English army. Circumcision perhaps originated as an act of defensive psychological warfare, making it impossible for the enemy to exult over the foreskins of those he has killed, as the chorus exults over that less transportable heap at the end of *Samson Agonistes*. A pile of foreskins is a portable heap.

We have been told recently—after the first Iraq war, which gave us the suffocating heap, the heap of men buried in sand—that an accurate body count is unrecorded in the annals of war. But it is something men have gone to some lengths to obtain by collecting, assembling, and heaping up physical tokens taken from the enemies' bodies. One thinks of scalps among the North Americans, the pyramids of severed heads that Tartar kings placed before their thrones, the substitution, during the Enlightenment, and as an accommodation to desert conditions, of ears for heads by the Turkish general Mohammed Ali, the English display of Irish heads on spikes, and of course the collection of ears in Vietnam (a bucket of them in an office is observed by Michael Herr as something he initially took for dried fruit). Since a body has two ears, this was an appropriate trophy in a war in which "body counts" had to substitute for the pleasure of seeing one's enemies reduced to a heap. Statistics are American heaps. Accordingly, Robert Lowell multiplies Milton's by a factor of ten: "when that kingdom hit the crash: / a million foreskins stacked like trash."[6]

The two images silently evoked by Elias Canetti's great book *Crowds and Power*, images that capture both sides of the temporal structure of the heap, are the Nazi rallies filmed in Leni Riefenstahl's *Triumph of the Will* and, from the liberated death camps, the heaps of bodies being bulldozed into the earth. These things are not spoken of in the book— and in this alone it is a masterpiece of what the rhetoricians call the "scheme of silence"—but every sentence in it is a reference to them. The first of these crowds, the Nazi rally, is characterized by the massive and meticulous order through which it represents the nation as an army and the army as an organism the parts of which have discharged their individuality onto one greater man, "himself an army," as we are told also of Samson. The parts are made to stand out by torches, or by arms raised in salute, so that the crowd has an articulate, military order within, like combed as opposed to tangled hair. We recall that Samson's new hair, replacing what was cut off and gathered in a heap, is compared to a troop of soldiers. The other crowd, the heap of the dead at the camp, is filmed in the light of day, though because it is tangled, like Samson's cut hair, we have much more trouble distinguishing its parts. It is an utterly disordered collectivity of the dead, during the viewing of which our eyes strain to see individual bodies instead of what the film makes us see: an indifferent, quivering mass being crushed into the earth. Since this is the heap of us—the heap from which we have somehow escaped—and not the heap of our enemies, it allows us only secretly to exult over our escape from this death, even as it justifies the incinerated heaps we created in the enemy's firebombed cities. For those heaps have behind them the image of an army rising up from under the heap of its dead, a heap bodily resurrected after Versailles as the giant of the thousand-year Reich. Every heap carries this menace of resurrection, a kind of bad eschatology, in which the heap rouses itself

like a strong man after sleep. This is perhaps why we hear in heroic poetry a certain satisfaction in the thought of enemies being eaten by
birds. A heap is not just disorder; it is the violent negation of an order,
an army, a flower, that is nevertheless preserved in and by this negation.

    ᔓ IT HAS OFTEN BEEN remarked that *Samson Agonistes* is set
in an Old Testament context that prevents any explicit recourse to
Christian imagery, Christian hope, and Christian comfort, and that this
shows a kind of bitter ascesis. I conclude by observing that this is not
entirely true, because the poem indulges one strong appetite of Milton's that from a Christian perspective would appear somewhat indeco-
rous: the pleasure of trampling on heaps of the slain. If this Old Testament pleasure is fulfilled in the New, in the winepress of the Passion,
we can still admit that there are some things the Old Testament gives
which the New has taken away—at least until Revelation, when the
Son "treadeth the winepress of the fierceness and wrath of Almighty
God" (19:15). We shall doubtless never know whether Milton came to
see this as a troubling place for the Bible to end, and a bad one for politics to begin.
    When we think of the trajectory of Milton's poetic career, inscribed
as it is in the Christian structure of history, *Samson Agonistes* does make
a curious end. This impression has been behind most criticism of the
poem, not to mention the doubts raised as to its date. When, however,
we read *Samson Agonistes* through the dyseschatology, which is to say
the politics of the heap, we can see Milton making a powerful final
statement about his task as one who transmits the Word of God. This is
not the Johannine Word, but the Word of Revelation, which invites the
birds to devour the heap that that same Word has made in the person of
the rider with the sword in his mouth (Rev. 19:17–18, 11–13). He is, as
I would call him, the Slaughtering Word, and is recognized as such by
Satan at the climax of *Paradise Regained*. His emergence in the Bible is
gradual, anticipated in the Old Testament in figures like Samson and
Jehu, resolved into the Christ of the gospels, who drowns a herd of
swine, theorized historically in the epistles, and disclosed in Revelation
as the supreme maker of heaps. Samson is one of his earliest, most
clownish and brutal avatars—a curious end indeed, unless Milton in
Samson Agonistes is moving backwards in an archaeological quest for
the birth of the Slaughtering Word in the primitive and enduring psy-

chology of war. The impact of the heap, which touches the extremes of horror and exultation, begins in the spectacle of the other as phenomenologically uncertain, which in the realm of texts means *having no literal sense*. This is also true of poetry at its most fundamental level, that of metaphor, which is not so much a figure of transport, of "carrying across," as it is of uncertainty and drift, of ungroundedness, like black milk (even if it is blackened by ash), or like a grave in the clouds, which is how Paul Celan, in "Todesfuge" ("Deathfugue"), describes the airborne heap of the incinerated dead. Delirium is metaphor. Like all delirium in art, it seems to communicate spirit from afar—yet without, as I said, having a literal sense on which any positive, doctrinal assertion can be grounded. In approaching the heap and uncovering its mystery, Milton draws near to the origin of the beautiful things he made. How do we approach it ourselves? Not by gazing upon it, for the sight blinds us to everything else, as it does the messenger in *Samson Agonistes*. We might approach the mystery by listening first and then making a sound like Celan's entangling fugue. As Celan says in another poem, "Die Posaunenstelle" ("The Trumpet Part"), "hör dich ein / mit dem Mund": "hear yourself in / with your mouth."

Notes
Index

Notes

1. Artificial Paradises

1. Regina Schwartz, *Remembering and Repeating: On Milton's Theology and Poetics*, 2nd ed. (Chicago: University of Chicago Press, 1993).

2. Rainer Maria Rilke, *Briefe aus Muzot, 1921–1926* (Leipzig: Insel-verlag, 1935), pp. 100–101.

3. Northrop Frye, *Creation and Recreation* (Toronto: University of Toronto Press, 1980).

4. Ibid., p. 6.

5. Ibid., p. 5.

6. Rem Koolhaas, *Delirious New York: A Retrospective Manifesto for Manhattan* (1978; rpt. New York: Monacelli Press, 1994), p. 82. Psychoanalytic delirium generates hallucinations that are adjusted to the authority of the words of an interior God, causing a displacement of the usual conception of the relation of the subject to speech. Jacques Lacan, *Le Séminaire*, vol. 3, *Les Psychoses, 1955–56* (Paris: Seuil, 1981).

7. Koolhaas, *Delirious New York*, p. 87.

8. *The Marriage of Heaven and Hell*, plate 6.22, in *William Blake's Writings*, ed. G. E. Bentley, Jr., vol. 1 (Oxford: Oxford University Press, 1978), p. 80.

2. Milton's Halo

1. *The Genealogy of Morals*, 3.6.

2. Giorgio Vasari, *Le Vite de' più eccellenti architetti, pittori, et scultori italiani, da Cimabue, insino a' tempi nostri*, 1st ed., vol. 2 (Florence, 1550), 914. In the circle of the Florentine Neoplatonists, the idea that man, as an artificer, most resembles the great artificer, God, was commonplace. In his commentary on Dante, Cristoforo Landino remarks that the poet is a creator like God because the verb used for "cre-

ation" in the Greek Septuagint translation of the Bible, *epoiesen*, "created," is from the same root as "poet," *poietes*. Marsilio Ficino says that man has a divine mind because he is an *artifex* like God. Similar thoughts are expressed, not surprisingly, by Leone Battista Alberti and Leonardo da Vinci. See E. N. Tigerstedt, "The Poet as Creator: Origins of a Metaphor," *Comparative Literature Studies* 5 (1968): 455–488. Tigerstedt follows the development of the idea into the sixteenth century in Italy, in J. C. Scaliger ("the poet establishes/founds/creates like another God," "velut alter deus condere") and Torquato Tasso ("God and the poet alone merit the name *creator*"), to the sixteenth century in England, in George Puttenham, who says, cautiously ("by manner of speech"), that poets are "creating gods." Donne invokes the idea in sermon 26; John Dryden speaks of Shakespeare's Caliban as a "creation"; Sir William Temple describes gardening and building as "a sort of creation"; the earl of Shaftesbury speaks of the poet as being like Prometheus, a "second maker" under Jove, who imitates the Creator; Addison, in *Spectator* 419 and 421, speaks of poetry as "a new creation" and as being "like Creation"; and Joseph Warton speaks of Shakespeare's "creative power." For the development of the idea in eighteenth-century England to its seminal presence in German romanticism, see Logan Pearsall-Smith, *Four Words: "Romantic," "Originality," "Creative," "Genius,"* Society for Pure English tract 17 (Oxford: Oxford University Press, 1924); and M. H. Abrams, *The Mirror and the Lamp: Romantic Theory and the Critical Tradition* (New York: Oxford University Press, 1953), pp. 272–285, who remarks that by the earlier nineteenth century, *create* had become a routine, technical term (p. 282).

3. Charles Baudelaire, "Perte d'auréole," no. 46 in *Petits poèmes en prose (Le Spleen de Paris)*. Baudelaire worked on this collection after the publication of *Les Fleurs du mal* (1857), and it was still unpublished at his death in 1867.

4. Walter Benjamin, "Das Kunstwerk im Zeitalter seiner technischen Reproduzierbarkeit" (1936), from *Illuminationen*, in *Ausgewälte Schriften*, vol. 1 (Frankfurt am Main: Suhrkamp, 1977), pp. 141 and 146. In English, "The Work of Art in the Age of Its Technical Reproducibility," in *Selected Writings*, vol. 3, *1935–1938*, trans. Edmund Jephcott, Howard Eiland et al. (Cambridge, Mass.: Harvard University Press, 2002), pp. 103–4 and 106. For "the threat to the aura posed by the experience of shock," see Benjamin, *The Arcades Project*, trans. Howard Eiland and Kevin McLaughlin (Cambridge, Mass.: Harvard University Press, 1999), p. 375. Benjamin speaks there of the final part of the poem, in which Baudelaire laughs at the thought of other poets picking up his aura and wearing it, as showing that in modernity the "exhibition of the aura" is "an affair of fifth-rate poets." "Perte d'auréole" is discussed by Benjamin in "On Some Motifs in Baudelaire" (1939), in *Illuminations*, pp. 192–194; *Ausgewählte Schriften*, 1:227–229.

5. Benjamin, "Das Kunstwerk," p. 158; English trans., p. 233.

6. Guy Davenport, *The Geography of the Imagination: Forty Essays* (San Francisco: North Point Press, 1981), pp. 20 and 28.

7. See Baudelaire's discussion of modernity in his essay on Constantin Guys in *Le Peintre de la vie moderne*.

8. Paul Bénichou, *Essai sur l'avènement d'un pouvoir spirituel laïque dans la France moderne*, vol. 1, *Le Sacre de l'écrivain (1750–1830)* (1973; rpt. Paris: Gallimard, 1996).

9. Angus Fletcher, "Complexity and the Spenserian Myth of Mutability," *Literary Imagination* 6.1 (2004): 1.

10. See Ignace Gelb, *A Study of Writing*, cited in Jacques Derrida, *De la Grammatologie* (Paris: Minuit, 1967), p. 13. Edmund Spenser, *The Faerie Queene* (1590), 3.12.47, from the last of the stanzas canceled in 1596.

11. Stanley Fish, *How Milton Works* (Cambridge, Mass.: Belknap Press of Harvard University Press, 2001); Arthur Barker, *Milton and the Puritan Dilemma* (Toronto: University of Toronto Press, 1942).

12. Vasari, *Vite*, 2:895.

13. Wallace Stevens, "Final Soliloquy of the Interior Paramour," in *Collected Poems* (New York: Knopf, 1954), p. 524.

14. See Calum M. Carmichael, *The Story of Creation* (Ithaca: Cornell University Press, 1996), p. 16.

15. Samuel Johnson, *Lives of the English Poets*, ed. George Birbeck-Hill, vol. 1 (Oxford: Oxford University Press, 1905), 185.

16. Arthur Rimbaud to Paul Demeny, May 15, 1871.

17. Friedrich Hölderlin, "Bread and Wine," stanza 6.

18. Cited in Logan Pearsall-Smith, "The History of Four Words," *Society for Pure English* (1924): 15 and 29 n.

19. Ibid., p. 15. Hugo calls Mme. de Staël "cette femme de génie" in the preface to *Odes et Ballades* when observing that she was the first to pronounce the phrase "littérature romantique" in France. Mme. de Staël, "De la littératue allemande," chap. 17 in *De la littérature considérée dans ses rapports avec les institutions sociales* (1800), and "De la poésie," chap. 10 in *De l'Allemagne* (1813).

20. Mme. de Staël, *De l'Allemagne*, vol. 1 (Paris: Garnier-Flammarion, 1968), pp. 207 and 209.

21. Victor Hugo, "Ibo" (1853), in *Les Contemplations*.

22. Edward Young, *Conjectures on Original Composition* (London, 1759); cited in Pearsall-Smith, "History of Four Words," p. 27.

23. William Collins, "Ode on the Poetical Character," final stanza.

24. Victor Hugo, *Cromwell* (Paris: Garnier-Flammarion, 1968), ll. 2484–90 and 2496–2509, pp. 262–263. In Hugo's preface, see especially p. 91: "Ainsi le but de l'art est presque divin: ressusciter, s'il fait de l'histoire; créer, s'il fait de la poésie" (The end of art is almost divine: to resuscitate, if it is concerned with history; to create, if it is concerned with poetry).

25. *Miscellaneous Sonnets*, 2.3.

26. *The Prelude* (1850), 3.170–173.

27. Thomas Newton, quoted in the Todd edition of *Poetical Works* (London, 1826), 3:7.

28. Michael Lieb, *Milton and the Culture of Violence* (Ithaca, N.Y.: Cornell University Press, 1994).

3. Milton and Modernity

1. Roland Barthes, *S/Z* (Paris: Éditions du Seuil, 1970), p. 10.

2. William Kerrigan, *The Sacred Complex: On the Psychogenesis of "Paradise Lost"* (Cambridge, Mass.: Harvard University Press, 1983), p. 2.

3. David Kolb, *The Critique of Pure Modernity: Hegel, Heidegger, and After* (Chicago: University of Chicago Press, 1986), pp. 2–4.

4. Christopher Kendrick, *Milton: A Study in Ideology and Form* (New York: Methuen, 1986), p. 2.

5. Herman Rapaport, *Milton and the Postmodern* (Lincoln: University of Nebraska Press, 1983), p. 1.

6. Kerrigan, *Sacred Complex*, p. 96, my emphasis.

7. Francis MacDonald Cornford, *Plato's Cosmology: The Timaeus of Plato* (London: Routledge and Kegan Paul, 1937), pp. 177–188; Jacques Derrida, "Comment ne pas parler: Dénégations," in *Psyché: Inventions de l'autre* (Paris: Galilée, 1987), pp. 566–568.

8. Martin Heidegger, "Der Ursprung des Kunstwerkes," in *Holzwege* (Frankfurt am Main: Klostermann, 1950), pp. 49–50. In English, "The Origin of the Work of Art," in *Poetry, Language, Thought*, trans. Albert Hofstadter (New York: Harper and Row, 1971), pp. 63–64.

9. Kerrigan, *Sacred Complex*, p. 2, my emphasis.

10. Heidegger, "Ursprung," p. 65; "Origin," p. 79.

11. "Kreuzweise Durchstreichung." See Martin Heidegger, *The Question of Being (Zur Seinsfrage)*, ed. and trans. William Kluback and Jean T. Wilde (New York: Twayne, 1958), p. 80.

12. Derrida, "Comment ne pas parler," pp. 588–589.

4. Why, This Is Chaos, Nor Am I Out of It

1. *Theogony*, l. 116. Later, at line 700, Hesiod appears to suggest that Chaos is the space between heaven and earth when Zeus throws his thunderbolts at the Titans and "divine burning seized Chaos."

2. Ovid, *Metamorphoses* 1.5–9.

3. "Periechein hapanta kai panta kubernan," Aristotle, *Physics* 203b6. See Indra Kagis McEwen, *Socrates' Answer: An Essay on Architectural Beginnings* (Cambridge, Mass.: MIT Press, 1997), p. 136 n. 13. I am more indebted to this book for its discussion of Anaximander and of Greek science than this one citation implies.

4. A. R. Ammons, *Garbage* (New York: W. W. Norton, 1993), p. 8.

5. Jorie Graham, "Even Horizon," in *Materialism* (Hopewell, N.J.: Ecco Press, 1993), p. 53.

6. *De Doctrina Christiana* 7.15.23. See John Rogers, *The Matter of Revolution: Science, Poetry, and Politics in the Age of Milton* (Ithaca, N.Y.: Cornell University Press, 1996), p. 113. For background, see Stephen M. Fallon, *Milton among the Philosophers: Poetry and Materialism in Seventeenth-Century England* (Ithaca, N.Y.: Cornell University Press, 1991).

7. Regina Schwartz, "Milton's Hostile Chaos: 'And the Sea was No More,'" *English Literary History* 52 (1985): 337–394, the basis of the chapter "'And the Sea was no More': Chaos vs. Creation," in *Remembering and Repeating: On Milton's Theology and Poetics*, 2nd ed. (1988; rpt. Chicago: University of Chicago Press, 1993), pp. 8–39.

8. Schwartz, *Remembering and Repeating*, pp. 22 and 26.

9. Ibid., p. 31.

10. Rogers, *Matter of Revolution*, pp. 129 and 133.

11. Ibid., p. 123.

12. *De rerum natura* 5.259. Robert Martin Adams, "A Little Look into Chaos," in *Illustrious Evidence: Approaches to English Literature of the Early Seventeenth Cen-*

tury, ed. Earl Miner (Berkeley: University of California Press, 1975); rpt. in *Paradise Lost*, ed. Scott Elledge, 2nd ed. (New York: W. W. Norton, 1993), p. 619n.

13. "Caedebant pariter pariterque ruebant / victores victique" (alike they slew and alike they fell, victors and vanquished). *Aeneid* 10.756.

14. *De bello civili* 1.25.5.

15. Moya Cannon, *Oar* (Loughcrew Oldcastle, County Meath, Ireland: Gallery Press, 2000), p. 20.

5. God's Body

1. A. S. P. Woodhouse, *The Heavenly Muse* (Toronto: University of Toronto Press, 1972), pp. 154, 156, and 360 n. 50.

2. Arthur Barker, *Milton and the Puritan Dilemma* (Toronto: University Of Toronto Press, 1942), pp. 318–319: "Dualism was unpalatable to one whose highest delight was the integration of form and substance in poetry. Man must therefore be regarded as an indivisible unit. . . . It is ultimately to this conviction of the unity of soul and body that one must trace the monism which issued in the several heresies of *De Doctrina Christiana*. It was because he could not accept any doctrine which involved a dualistic view of man or his world that Milton refused to believe that the universe 'was formed from nothing,' and insisted that 'the original matter' was intrinsically good, and the chief productive stock of every subsequent good,' since it was 'of God and in God.'" Citing *De Doctrina Christiana*, Col. 15, ll. 17–27.

3. *De Doctrina Christiana*, Col. 15, ll. 39–41.

4. *Jerusalem*, plate 69, l. 25.

5. *Enquiry Concerning Human Understanding* 12.3. See A. J. Ayer, *Language, Truth, and Logic* (London: V. Gollancz, 1936).

6. Woodhouse, *Heavenly Muse*, p. 157.

7. Ibid., p. 148.

8. Gordon Campbell, Thomas N. Corns, John K. Hale, David I. Holmes, and Fiona J. Tweedie, "The Provenace of *De Doctrina Christiana*," *Milton Quarterly* 31.3 (1997): 67–117. Stanley Fish, *How Milton Works* (Cambridge, Mass.: Harvard University Press, 2001), pp. 15–19.

6. A Bleeding Rib

1. "On Shakespeare and Milton," in *Complete Works of William Hazlitt*, vol. 5, ed. P. P. Howe (London: Dent, 1930), p. 58.

7. Milton's Choice of Subject

1. *Of the Laws of Ecclesiastical Polity*, final sentence of book one.

2. *History of the Life of Thomas Ellwood*, cited in *The Life Records of John Milton*, ed. J. Milton French, vol. 4 (New Brunswick, N.J.: Rutgers University Press, 1949–1958), pp. 419–420; cf. p. 417.

3. F. T. Prince, *The Italian Element in Milton's Verse* (Oxford: Clarendon, 1954), p. 48. The standard studies are Bernard Weinberg, *A History of Literary Criticism in the Italian Renaissance*, vol. 2 (Chicago: University of Chicago Press, 1961), esp. pp. 954–1073; and Baxter Hathaway, *The Age of Criticism: The Late Renaissance*

in Italy (Ithaca, N.Y.: Cornell University Press, 1962), and *Marvels and Common-places: Renaissance Literary Criticism* (New York: Random House, 1968). See also Daniel Javitch, *Proclaiming a Classic: The Canonization of the "Orlando Furioso"* (Princeton: Princeton University Press, 1991). I believe that Irene Samuel, "Paradise Lost as Mimesis," in *Approaches to "Paradise Lost": The York Tercentenary Lectures,* ed. C. A. Patrides (London: Edward Arnold, 1968), pp. 15–19, was the first to discuss the importance of the connection between Italian Renaissance poetics and Milton's choice of subject. For a brilliant discussion of Milton's very free use of Aristotle and his Italian commentators, see Mary Ann Radzinowicz, *Toward "Samson Agonistes": The Growth of Milton's Mind* (Princeton: Princeton University Press, 1978), pp. 8–14.

4. "Quella famosa questione sopra la Gerusalemme di Torquato Tasso." The phrase is from Manso's dedication of a 1628 tract to Luigi Carrafa, a descendant of Marcantonio Carrafa, to whom the incendiary dialogue by Camillo Pellegrino, "Il Caraffa, o vera della epica poesia," was dedicated at the height of that debate, in 1584. See Angelo Solerti, *Vita di Torquato Tasso,* vol. 1 (Turin and Rome, 1895), p. 414 n. 2. For Pellegrino's treatise, see Bernard Weinberg, ed., *Trattati di poetica e retorica del cinquecento,* vol. 3 (Bari: Laterza, 1972), pp. 307–344. Manso had been Tasso's patron in the poet's last years. For estimates of his influence on Milton's epic plans, see David Masson, *The Life of John Milton,* vol. 1 (London: Macmillan, 1859), p. 756; and John Arthos, *Milton and the Italian Cities* (New York: Barnes and Noble, 1968), p. 92.

5. Torquato Tasso, *Discourses on the Heroic Poem,* trans. Mariella Cavalchini and Irene Samuel (Oxford: Clarendon, 1973), pp. 5 and 56.

6. "*L'Idea,* o Rittrato della poesia heroica, practicata con gli esempi di tutti i poeti eroici," in "Discorso intorno ai contrasti, che si fanno sopra la Gerusalemme Liberata di Torquato Tasso, del Signior Orazio Lombardelli, Senese Academico Umoroso," in *Apologia del S. Torquato Tasso, in difesa della sua Gerusalemme liberata, a gli Accademici della Crusca* (Florence, 1586), p. 19. See also p. 58 for Lombardelli's reference to subject matter as "mere history" ("mere istoria") not yet shaped by the poet into the formal structure of a plotted tale, a *favola.* Lombardi's title refers to the "contrasts" made between Ariosto and Tasso by the della Cruscan academy's Bastiano de' Rossi, in "Difesa dell' 'Orlando Furioso' dell' Ariosto contro 'l dialogo dell' epica poesia di Camillo Pellegrino," which was very much in Ariosto's favor, Pellegrino's "Il Caraffa" being in Tasso's.

7. For *metaphor* and *metonymy,* their association with relations of similarity and contiguity respectively, and their larger significance for poetic analysis, see Roman Jakobson, "Two Aspects of Language and Two Types of Aphasic Disturbances," in *Selected Writings,* vol. 2 (The Hague: Mouton, 1971), pp. 239–259.

8. *Orlando Innamorato* 1.1.3–4 (see note in the Charles Stanley Ross edition). See Peter V. Marinelli, *Ariosto and Boiardo: The Origins of Orlando Furioso* (Columbia: University of Missouri Press, 1987), pp. 5–6.

9. See *The Poems of Robert Henryson,* ed. Denton Fox (New York: Oxford University Press, 1981), lxxxii. For Dictys and Dares, see Douglas Bush, *Mythology and the Renaissance Tradition in English Poetry,* rev. ed. (New York: W. W. Norton, 1963), pp. 3–5.

10. Torquato Tasso, *Gerusalemme Liberata* (Ferrara, 1581).

11. See *Poetics* 1450b–1451a; Pierre de Ronsard, *Oeuvres complètes,* ed. Gustave

Cohen, vol. 2 (1950), p. 1009; Bernard Weinberg, *Critical Prefaces of the French Renaissance* (New York: AMS Press, 1959), p. 219; Torquato Tasso, *Prose*, ed. Ettore Mazzali, La Letteratura Italiana 22 (Milan: Ricciale, 1959), pp. 1145–46, cited in Margaret W. Ferguson, *Trials of Desire: Renaissance Defenses of Poetry* (New Haven: Yale University Press, 1983), p. 208 n. 2. See also Ralf Coplestone Williams, "The Theory of the Heroic Poem in Italian Criticism of the Sixteenth Century" (Ph.D diss., Johns Hopkins University, 1917), pp. 8–10.

12. For organic unity based on allegorical interpretation, see Simone Fornari, *La spositione sopra l'Orlando Furioso* (Florence, 1549–50).

13. Cyril of Jerusalem, cited in C. A. Patrides, *Milton and the Christian Tradition* (Oxford: Clarendon, 1966), p. 263.

14. Abraham Cowley, *The Civil War*, ed. Allan Pritchard (Toronto: University of Toronto Press, 1973), p. 22.

15. See the concluding lines of Giovanni Giorgio Trissino, *L'Italia Liberata da Gotthi*, vol. 3, 3 vols. (Rome and Venice, 1547–48).

16. Luiz Vaz de Camoëns, *The Lusiads*, trans. William C. Atkinson (1952; rpt. Harmondsworth: Penguin, 1980), p. 20; see also *Os Lusiadas*, ed. Frank Pierce (Oxford: Clarendon Press, 1973), canto 10, stanza 156, and note. Milton knew this poem in Sir Richard Fanshawe's great translation of 1655, *The Lusiad, or, Portugals Historicall Poem*. See *The Poems and Translations of Sir Richard Fanshawe*, ed. Peter Davidson, vol. 2 (Oxford: Clarendon Press, 1999).

17. Balachandra Rajan, *The Lofty Rhyme: A Study of Milton's Major Poetry* (London: Routledge, 1970), pp. 94–95.

18. See Peter Brown, *Lionardo Salviati: A Critical Biography* (New York: Oxford University Press, 1974), p. 180, and, for the furor over Tasso and Ariosto, p. 206.

19. Trissino, *Italia Liberata da Gotthi*, vol. 1, sig. *iii.

20. Ludovico Castelvetro, *Poetica di Aristotele Vulgarizzata, et Sposta* (Vienna, 1570), pp. 16 and 281. See also Page DuBois, *History, Rhetorical Description, and the Epic from Homer to Spenser* (Cambridge: D. S. Brewer, 1982), p. 1, who speaks of the epic as a "model of the course of the world."

21. Orazio Lombardelli, "Discorso intorno ai contrasti," in *Apologia*, p. 58; see also pp. 80–81.

22. Tasso, *Discourses*, p. 54.

23. For example, "Salomon Gynaecocratomenus . . . aut Thysiazusae," Col. 18:237. See G. K. Hunter, *Paradise Lost* (Boston: Allen and Unwin, 1980), pp. 17–19.

24. Herman Melville, *Moby-Dick*, chap. 104, "The Fossil Whale."

25. "Les mythes pensent à travers les hommes, et à leur insu." Claude Lévi-Strauss, *Le cru et le cuit* (Paris: Plon, 1964), p. 20.

8. Revolution in Paradise Regained

1. See, e.g., the remarkable essays in Balachandra Rajan, ed., *The Prison and the Pinnacle* (London: Routledge, 1973); and Barbara Kiefer Lewalski, *Milton's Brief Epic* (Providence: Brown University Press, 1966), p. 510.

2. Cf. Vulgate: "Vade, Satana"; Luther: "Weg mit dir, Satan."

3. Barbara Kiefer Lewalski, *The Life of John Milton: A Critical Biography* (Malden, Mass.: Blackwell, 2000), p. 514.

4. Northrop Frye, *The Return of Eden: Five Essays on Milton's Epics* (Toronto: University of Toronto Press, 1965), p. 136.

5. See *Complete Shorter Poems*, pp. 418–419, for principal discussants, among whom especially Hugh MacCallum, *Milton and the Sons of God: The Divine Image in Milton's Epic Poetry* (Toronto: University of Toronto Press, 1986), pp. 255–262.

6. Ibid., 4.549n.

7. Josephus, *Antiquities* 15.11.5.

8. A. S. P. Woodhouse, "Theme and Pattern in *Paradise Regained*," *University of Toronto Quarterly* 25 (January 1956): 181. See also Woodhouse, *The Heavenly Muse: A Preface to Milton*, ed. Hugh MacCallum (Toronto: University of Toronto Press, 1972), p. 343.

9. Samson and the Heap of the Dead

1. "As interpreters, we are never stronger than we are as the play opens . . . [A]s foreknown events unfold, they are not clarified, but shrouded increasingly in mystery." Stanley Fish, *How Milton Works* (Cambridge, Mass.: Harvard University Press, 2001), p. 472. See also Fish, "Question and Answer in *Samson Agonistes*," *Critical Quarterly* 11.3 (1969): 251–252.

2. "En astheneia teleioumai." J. M. French, ed., *Life Records of John Milton*, vol. 4 (New Brunswick, N.J.: Rutgers University Press, 1949–1958), pp. 118–119, literally, "Through my very weakness will I complete myself." See William Riley Parker, *Milton: A Biography*, 2nd ed., ed. Gordon Campbell, vol. 2 (Oxford: Clarendon, 1996), p. 479n.

3. Pietro Pucci, *The Song of the Sirens: Essays on Homer* (Lanham, Md.: Rowman and Littlefield, 1998), xi.

4. Paul de Man, "Semiology and Rhetoric," in *Allegories of Reading: Figural Language in Rousseau, Nietzsche, Rilke, and Proust* (New Haven: Yale University Press, 1979), p. 12.

5. Mary Ann Radzinowicz, *Toward Samson Agonistes: The Growth of Milton's Mind* (Princeton: Princeton University Press, 1978), pp. 356–359.

6. Robert Lowell, "Waking Early Sunday Morning," in *Near the Ocean* (New York: Farrar, Straus and Giroux, 1967), p. 20. I am grateful to Paul Sawyer for drawing my attention to these lines.

Index